Brands of Faith

In a society overrun by commercial clutter, religion has become yet another product sold in the consumer marketplace. Faiths of all kinds must compete not only with each other, but with a myriad of more entertaining and more convenient leisure activities. *Brands of Faith* argues that in order to compete effectively faiths have had to become brands – easily recognizable symbols and spokespeople with whom religious prospects can make immediate connections.

Mara Einstein shows how religious branding has expanded over the past twenty years to create a blended world of commerce and faith where the sacred becomes secular and the secular sacred. In a series of fascinating case studies of faith brands, she explores the significance of branded church courses, such as Alpha and 40 Days of Purpose, the growth of mega-churches, and the popularity of televangelists like Joel Osteen and their counterpart television talk-show host Oprah Winfrey, as well as the rise of Kabbalah. She asks what the consequences of this religious marketing will be, and outlines the possible results of religious commercialism – good and bad. Repackaging religion – updating music, creating teen-targeted bibles – is justifiable and necessary. However, when the content becomes obscured, religion may lose its unique selling proposition – the very ability to raise us above the market.

Mara Einstein is Associate Professor of Media Studies at Queens College as well as a professor at the business school at New York University. Prior to teaching, she worked as a marketing executive at NBC and MTV Networks as well as at a number of major advertising agencies.

Religion, Media and Culture series
Edited by Stewart M. Hoover, Jolyon Mitchell and David Morgan

Religion, Media and Culture is an exciting series which analyses the role of media in the history of contemporary practice of religious belief. Books in this series explore the importance of a variety of media in religious practice and highlight the significance of the culture, social and religious setting of such media.

Brands of Faith

Marketing religion in a commercial age

Mara Einstein

Routledge
Taylor & Francis Group

LONDON AND NEW YORK

First published 2008
by Routledge
2 Park Square, Milton Park, Abingdon, Oxon OX14 4RN

Simultaneously published in the USA and Canada
by Routledge
270 Madison Ave, New York, NY 10016

Routledge is an imprint of the Taylor & Francis Group, an informa business

© 2008 Mara Einstein

Typeset in Sabon by
HWA Text and Data Management, Tunbridge Wells
Printed and bound in Great Britain by
Antony Rowe Ltd, Chippenham, Wiltshire

British Library Cataloguing in Publication Data
A catalogue record for this book is available from the British
Library

Library of Congress Cataloging-in-Publication Data
Einstein, Mara.
Brands of faith : marketing religion in a commercial age /
Mara Einstein.
    p. cm. – (Religion, media, and culture)
Includes bibliographical references and index.
1. Church marketing. 2. Religious institutions–Marketing. I. Title.
BV652.23.E56 2007
306.6–dc22   2007012061

ISBN10: 0–415–40976–4 (hbk)
ISBN10: 0–415–40977–2 (pbk)
ISBN10: 0–203–93887–9 (ebk)

ISBN13: 978–0–415–40976–6 (hbk)
ISBN13: 978–0–415–40977–3 (pbk)
ISBN13: 978–0–203–93887–4 (ebk)

To my daughter, Cayla,
in whom daily I see the wonders of the Universe

Contents

Series editors' preface

Media, Religion and Culture is a series of interdisciplinary volumes which analyze the role of media in the history and contemporary practice of religious belief. Books in this series scrutinize the importance of a variety of media in religious practice: from lithographs and film to television and the internet. Studies from all over the world highlight the significance of the cultural, social and religious setting of such media.

Rather than thinking of media purely as instruments for information delivery, volumes in this series contribute in various ways to a new paradigm of understanding media as an integral part of lived religion. Employing a variety of methods, authors investigate how practices of belief take shape in the production, distribution, and reception of mediated communication.

Stewart M. Hoover, University of Colorado
Jolyon Mitchell, University of Edinburgh
David Morgan, Valparaiso University

Preface

The line in front of the Kabbalah Centre that cold winter day snaked far down the block and around the corner. People stood two and three deep trying to get to the registration tables, which were adorned with stands of blue and white balloons and oversized heaters—a futile attempt to ward off the bitter cold. Dozens of volunteers assisted people in filling out registration cards for the free open house. "Come, come, come," they said, madly waving their hands in an attempt to move the lines along more quickly. Someone handed me a card that asked how I had learned about the event (should I say Madonna sent me?) and, more importantly, how I could be contacted in the future. (Naively, I thought the e-mail address was the key piece of information they were looking for. I would soon learn, however, that it was my phone number that would provide a source of never-ending sales opportunities.) Once the registration card was completed, a bright yellow band was attached to my wrist and I proceeded to walk through the Centre's doors, which were guarded by two seriously oversized men—de rigueur post-September 11 New York City.

Inside I was greeted by another volunteer who explained where the lectures would take place. However, before reaching the lecture halls, I had to pass through the bookstore—a marketing gauntlet filled with the latest tomes written by the Centre's teachers. Hundreds of books, representing dozens of titles, were prominently displayed on three center tables. Along the periphery of the room was an array of ancillary products connected with Kabbalah. These included the ever-pervasive red string—now worn by the aforementioned Madonna, as well as Ashton Kutcher and even one of the *Queer Eye* guys—which, when tied onto the left wrist by a member of the Centre who says the appropriate blessing, is a means to ward off the evil eye. This string is available with an accompanying book for $26 or with a CD for $36. There were also candles, cards, mezuzahs, and even Kabbalah Water, claimed to be so charged with positive energy that it even changed the molecular structure of the water at Chernobyl, thus reducing the level of nuclear damage. I don't know if this is true, but that's what I was told again and again. This water could be mine for a mere $2 a bottle.

Making my way up the two flights of stairs and into the lectures, I found the rooms filled to overflowing with people of all ages and all levels of understanding. Some people were at the Centre for the first time, trying to figure out what this Kabbalah thing was all about. Others came because they wanted the teachings but didn't want to pay the steep prices for them. (The introductory course, a prerequisite for all subsequent classes, is the most expensive at $270 for a ten-week course or one all-day event.) Still others came because they thought there would be free food. "Last year, they had a nice buffet. This is very disappointing," explained an elderly woman next to me.

The lectures themselves, while informative, were only slightly veiled sales pitches for enrolling people in the spring catalog of classes. Beyond the basic coursework of Kabbalah 101 and 102, classes included Fears, Phobias & Anxiety, 12 Steps to Lasting Love, and Mastering Negativity. Each lecture began with a gushing introduction by a Centre member who described the lecturer/teacher's qualifications, followed by an explanation of the subject to be discussed. Each session concluded with additional praise for the lecturer and an imperative to the audience to sign up right away, because a 15 percent discount was available "today only." Volunteers (again!) waited patiently at tables throughout the Centre, eager to get you started on your path of kabbalistic learning, and equally eager to accept your cash, check, or MasterCard.

As people waited to sign up for classes, I heard one woman say in a tentative voice barely above a whisper, "I'm not Jewish…is that okay?" The volunteer responded, "Sure. I'm not Jewish either."

From enlightenment to enterprise

How did we get here? How did a once esoteric, Jewish tradition become a religious commodity? How did Kabbalah get to be a pop culture phenomenon instead of a serious religious practice? How did it turn into a product for enterprise and entertainment instead of enlightenment?

It was these types of questions that led me to pursue a study of the interrelationship between religion and marketing. As a lifelong religious shopper and 20-year marketing professional who has worked on campaigns for everything from Miller Beer to MTV, I thought, who better to explore this topic than me?

I began to think about this issue in the mid-1990s when I was working as a marketing executive at NBC in New York. As an arbiter of all things pop culture, it was my job to stay on top of trends in everything from music to minivans. One day I was surprised to find within the piles of research on my desk a packet of articles about trends in religion—baby boomers going back to church, the advent of megachurches, religious institutions exploring the online space, and so on. I began to question if there was a corollary between my personal religious search, which was scattershot and expensive, and broader trends within our mass-marketed culture. I considered these questions at the same time as I was pursuing a PhD in media, so analyzing and overanalyzing the situation made perfect sense to me, both as an intellectual pursuit and as a means to better understand my own search. Why was religious shopping an expanding trend? Why were megachurches so popular? How did marketing play a part in this, and why was religious marketing proliferating now? Why not in the 1960s, when religious pluralism and religious experimentation first came into vogue? And what, if any, would be the consequences of mass-marketed religion?

As I explored these questions and many more, I came to realize that religious products (and by that I mean institutions, not simply crosses and tchotchkes) have become branded in much the same way that consumer products have been branded. Religious organizations have taken on names, logos or personalities, and slogans that allow them to be heard in a cluttered, increasingly competitive marketplace. Purpose Churches (those associated with *The Purpose Driven Life* phenomenon), Alpha Churches, Joel Osteen, Kabbalah—these, and others, are what I am calling faith brands. Faith brands, like their secular counterparts, exist to aid consumers in making and maintaining a personal connection to a commodity product. Introducing, sustaining, and perpetuating the brand across product lines allow these faith brands to be "top of mind" in an overcrowded commercial environment. It seems inevitable that branding would occur since these institutions are competing not only among themselves, but also with the popular culture.

But with all products—and one of the key ideas I intend to convey in this book is that religion *is* a product—when you introduce marketing into a category, you change the category and the products that compete in it. First, in the case of religion, when you market spirituality, you introduce people to the idea that they can shop for it, and so they will, or at least are more likely to. Second, as people are increasingly prone to shop, religions will not only have to increase the level of marketing and promotion in order to be heard among so many competing forces, but they will also be increasingly prone to creating a product that religious consumers will buy. They will change the product to suit the market. Now, this is not to say that religions have never changed with the times. Of course they have. What is different now, however, is the rate at which change occurs.

Finally, adding marketing to the mix creates a new goal for religious institutions—growth. The need to megasize has led to the phenomenon of megachurches, oversized houses of worship that by definition cater to more than 2,000 parishioners, but in several cases serve upwards of 20,000 or more. These bigger churches demand more attention than the neighborhood church down the block serving fewer than 200 people. These bigger churches are overwhelmingly evangelical and blatantly conservative. And these churches demand to be heard in the political process. Thus, marketing religion is not without its consequences.

Brands of Faith is divided into three sections. The first section of the book explores why religious marketing has been proliferating over the past 20 years and particularly over the past decade. It puts religious marketing into context within the broader commercial culture in which we live.

Chapter 1 lays the groundwork for understanding how religious marketing and commercial culture have becoming inextricably linked and why religious marketing is so in evidence now. From popular culture, like *The Passion of the Christ* and the *Left Behind* book series, to spiritual jewelry and clothing to religious services themselves, religion and spirituality are popular products that have led to a proliferation of promotion. Chapter 2 deals specifically with social trends that have affected the level of religious marketing. Little or no social stigma attached to not attending church, the commodity aspects of the religious product, and a cacophonous media environment have all contributed to ratcheting up the need (and the noise) of religious marketing. Chapter 3 focuses on the consolidation of producers of religious products, particularly books, and how multinational media corporations' infiltration into the category has increased the sophistication of the marketing used. Chapter 4 explains branding and why it is so necessary for religions to be branded in order to be heard in our saturated media environment. We will look at the similarities between religion and marketing/branding and its implications for identity creation. Included here are the models of brand communities and brand cults and the introduction of a concept I call faith brands.

The middle section will be case studies of several faith brands. One main focus here is to understand the selling of faith brands from the point of view of the marketers. Through interviews with various people responsible for the marketing of these brands, we gain critical insight into how they view their work. In addition, these chapters include in-depth content analyses of the marketing materials used by various groups. Since I have also acted as a participant/observer at a number of religious courses and church services, and I have interviewed course participants and church goers, I was able to see first-hand if the marketing messages delivered on the product for the end user. Sometimes they did and sometimes they didn't. All of the interviews, observations, and analyses have been developed into faith brand case studies, providing historical and current data about the respective institutions and people as well as putting them into a broader social context.

Chapter 5 looks at church courses like 40 Days of Purpose and the Alpha Course as well as at Willow Creek, which is not specifically targeted to consumers but is the granddaddy of church teachers. I present these brands and the marketing tools they have used to become so successful. There is also a focus on religious personalities who are themselves faith brands. Chapter 6 evaluates two of today's most influential televangelists: Joel Osteen, pastor of the Lakewood Church, the largest megachurch in the United States; and Oprah Winfrey, the queen of daytime talk. The two are parallel examples of secularization—Joel Osteen is the sacred becoming more secular while Oprah is the secular becoming more sacred. The final faith brand case study, in Chapter 7, is Kabbalah. Through a combined strategy of persistence and catering to celebrities, this little known Jewish mystical tradition has become a household name.

The last part of *Brands of Faith* examines the consequences of religious marketing. It should be noted that this will not be the traditional tirade about how horrible marketing is for religion, as I believe that approach is too flip and too limited in scope. Chapter 8 examines the impact of faith brands on the current political climate. As faith brands become larger, they exert more and more power on the political process. Moreover, they are able to influence the direction of policy, and this affects their ability to do business as well as to block policy that goes against their conservative religious beliefs. Through a combination of research into the finances of various religious organizations and conversations with the White House Office of Faith-Based Initiatives, as well as secondary source material, I explain how some faith brands, particularly evangelical megachurches, influence our political process. Chapter 9, the concluding chapter, offers an answer to the question of what we can expect from long-term marketing of religion. There have been changes in religion due to marketing—there is no doubt about that —and we will consider these changes through the experience of the New Age movement, a bellwether for faith brands. New Age products, and the New Age generally, have been aggressively and successfully marketed longer than other faith practices. Today, however, the New Age is in disarray. We will see how marketing has contributed to its decline, and how this could happen to larger, more established religious institutions as they become more marketing-oriented.

In researching and writing this book, I have had the great fortune of being assisted by dozens of colleagues, friends, and family. First, there are my series editors—Stewart Hoover, David Morgan, and Jolyon Mitchell—who have helped shape this book from concept to completion. Thank you for sticking with me. I am especially grateful to Stewart for being an unending source of support and mentorship since Nashville in 1995. Thanks to Lesley Riddle at Routledge, who believed in the value of this book and Gemma Dunn, who helped pull it through the production process.

I was supported by grants from PSC-CUNY, which afforded me the opportunity to travel around the country to study religious marketing in its many facets. These grants also afforded me the opportunity to replace my computer when it crashed—an invaluable help at a critical time.

To my colleagues at Queens College, most notably Rick Maxwell, Susan Macmillan, Heather Hendershot, and Roopali Mukherjee, many thanks for your support. The debates, the sharing of information, and the comraderie were more helpful than you probably know. Here, I must in particular acknowledge Rick Maxwell, who believed in me even when I wasn't so sure—you can't ask for more in a mentor.

From the very beginning of my switch to academia, I have been encouraged to pursue my interest in media and religion by both junior and senior scholars. Wade Clark Roof graciously and enthusiastically welcomed a new scholar, and I am indebted to him for his kindness and wisdom. Lynn Schofield Clark, Hilary Warren, and Eric Gormly were wonderful colleagues to travel with on the journey of our early careers, much to my luck and heartfelt gratitude.

I want to thank all of the interviewees, scholars, and professionals who so generously gave of their time so that I could better understand the interplay between religion and marketing. In particular, I want to thank Michelle Rapkin, who assisted in multiple ways and whose depth of knowledge and breadth of spirit is something to aspire to. Thanks to Jonathan Mahler for providing his insights on megachurches, and to Henri Gooren, Barry Lowenthal, and Gail Joseph for reading drafts of this work. Then there is Scott Saufer, my transcriber and teaching assistant, with whom I couldn't have written this book (nor could I ever have done what he did).

As for friends and family—the most important of life's blessings—I would be remiss if I did not include my sisters, biological and otherwise. Thanks to Dari Bookamer, Jan Dannenberg, Karyn Slutsky, and Ellen Matson for your patient ears and for indulging my endless talk about this project. Lastly, I want to thank my mom, Barbara Schwartz, who as a teacher instilled in me the value of an education and the importance of social justice. More importantly, her love and support during the difficult writing of this book are gifts I can never repay. Because of you all, I am so very, very lucky.

In conclusion, this book is about why religious marketing is proliferating today. It is about how religious groups have become more sophisticated in their marketing, and how that is changing the way in which faith is practiced. It is about how religious marketing, in contributing to the super-sizing of religious institutions, is having a fundamental impact on the American political climate, nudging it ever more toward conservatism, ever more to the right. This work has been enlightening for me, causing me to question some long-held beliefs while at the same time reaffirming others. If you have ever shopped for religion, contemplated shopping for religion, or truly don't understand why anyone would bother to shop for a religion (either because you are devoted to your faith or because you don't have one and don't ever want one), then this book is for you.

My profound hope is that this book is the beginning of an important conversation about the interplay among religion, marketing, and the political process. Many of us are taught that these topics are not to be discussed openly and questioningly in civilized company, but given the state of the world today, I believe we can no longer afford to be so polite.

Mara Einstein
May 2007

Chapter 1

Introduction

Mel Gibson's *The Passion of the Christ* was the surprise box office hit of 2004. Generating in its first year more than $370 million in domestic revenue, the movie went on to garner more than $600 million from theater attendance revenues and another $400 million in DVD sales. Who could have guessed that a movie about the horribly torturous final 12 hours of the life of Jesus, told in Aramaic and Latin, would become one of the top ten box office hits of all time? Evidently Mel Gibson knew because he was willing to risk $30 million of his own money to fund this picture when no one else would touch it.

Was it simply the brilliance of this cinematic masterpiece that fueled attendance and the subsequent purchasing of *Passion* products? Was it the driving hunger of the majority of Americans to see the last hours of their savior portrayed so vividly on the screen?

Actually it was neither of these things. What got moviegoers into the theaters was, quite simply, marketing. Advertising, sales promotion, and ubiquitous publicity are what got people off their couches on a Friday night and into the local multiplex. But unlike other mediocre Hollywood films, *The Passion* had several elements that enhanced its box office potential: an A-list movie star as director and spokesperson, a story with a built-in audience, and a topic—religion—that readily lends itself to controversy.

At first the controversy revolved around whether *The Passion* was anti-Semitic. That controversy was initiated and then exacerbated by the film's producers for months before the film's release. Leading up to the movie's opening on Ash Wednesday (a brilliant marketing idea—getting people to see a movie about Jesus on a day when they are most likely to be thinking about him anyway), news outlets ran stories about rabbis going to see the movie, priests going to see the movie, and pastors going to see the movie, and after having viewed the film, their providing commentary on who thought what parts of it were anti-Semitic. Of course this "debate" fueled desire to see the film on the part of ordinary citizens, so that they, too, could make an assessment of the film. Also, by framing the controversy as anti-Semitic, the producers opened up the film to a new market—Jews—an audience that would likely have otherwise avoided the film altogether.

As this controversy began to die down, a new one appeared. This latter controversy became a question as to whether Mel Gibson himself was anti-Semitic. Mr. Gibson's personal religious beliefs are based in strict pre-Vatican II Catholicism and are therefore ultraconservative. The extent of his conservatism and possible anti-Semitism was fueled by stories about Gibson's father, who was widely reported as being anti-Semitic (he claimed that the Holocaust was mostly fiction) and was believed to have passed those beliefs down to his son. This, too, got considerable airtime leading up to the movie's release, particularly from conservative television and radio hosts like Bill O'Reilly and Sean Hannity.

Of course this was not the only publicity associated with the film. There were stories about Mel Gibson funding the movie himself. There were stories about how true to the Gospels the movie was. There were the typical stories about the making of the film. In sum, the publicity machine was humming in full force right up to the opening day.[1]

This free publicity, which was valued in the millions of dollars, was supplemented by other traditional film marketing elements. For example, there were e-mails from Amazon.com promoting the movie to anyone who had purchased religious or spiritual books, there were appearances by Mr. Gibson on a number of television talk shows and newsmagazines, and there were the typical commercials on television and ads in local newspapers.

However it was the marketing that most people did not see that drove the ultimate success of *The Passion*. Grassroots marketing, led by Gibson himself, was developed in conjunction with local churches throughout the country. Evangelicals, charismatics, and Roman Catholics were the target markets for this film. Thirty invitation-only screenings were held for high-level church leaders and the heads of prominent evangelical organizations. The first of these occurred in Colorado Springs, Colorado, home of many of these institutions, including the ultraconservative Focus on the Family run by James C. Dobson. The leaders of these organizations, and many others, were encouraged to purchase blocks of tickets for their institutions and to suggest that the local churches do the same. More than $3 million in advanced tickets sales were generated through this campaign.

After these private screenings, marketing materials were presented to churches through Outreach, Inc., a California-based organization that specializes in Christian marketing. Audience members were offered "door hangers, invitation cards, church bulletin inserts, Bible excerpts and study guides. In addition, in keeping with the latest trends in technology, over 250,000 DVD's about the film were mailed to minister's nationwide" (Caldwell, 2004, quoted in Maresco, 2004). There were also millions of witness cards promoting the film on one side and providing an evangelical message on the other that were distributed and used by thousands of churches and religious organizations (Howard, 2004).

These church promotions began in December 2003—a full two months before the movie opened. The "Pastors' Action Kit" provided churches with information via the Internet (www.passionmaterials.com) on how to tie into *The Passion*. Promotional ideas included showing trailers of the film at church, putting up banners, inviting parishioners to attend a screening, and, of course, buying out an entire theater screening and taking the congregation. Sermon suggestions corresponded with the Christian calendar, and information about what aspects of the movie to discuss in relationship to these sermons was provided.[2] There were also special materials targeted to the teen audience via church youth groups; Teen Mania sponsored a site that provided a DVD set to aid youth workers in running "a four-week curriculum leading up to the movie, a guide to the outreach itself, and a two-week post-outreach curriculum" (Sheahen, 2004a).

Churches were also given commercials that they could customize to tie the movie into their local church. Specifically what this meant was that a commercial was created with the first 20 seconds being footage from the movie while the last 10 seconds were left blank to be used to promote the local church. Someone seeing the commercial on television would see 20 seconds of trailer for *The Passion* and be pulled in thinking they are watching a commercial for the movie, and in the last 10 seconds they would be presented with information about attending the local church. From a marketing perspective it was a win–win—more exposure for the movie (paid for by the local church), and the local church gets to be connected with a major Hollywood hit.

Just as with secular films, ancillary products were created in conjunction with the movie's release. These products included book tie-ins and coffee mugs like other Hollywood fare, but they also included crosses and—one of the most popular items—small and large pewter nail pendants on a leather string, which retailed for between $12.99 and $16.99. As with most major motion pictures, a soundtrack was created. *The Passion* soundtrack sold 50,000 units the day it was released, making it the third highest selling first-day soundtrack. Initially this product, as with others associated with the film, was distributed primarily through traditional Christian bookstores. However, products were distributed more widely as the success of the film translated beyond the initial narrowly targeted groups.

From movie tickets to books to jewelry, all things *Passion* flew off store shelves. The repercussions of this marketing miracle continue to be felt in the religious publishing and products industry years later. This is true not just for *Passion* products, but also for all categories of religious products and services. More spiritual books of all types were sold. Crosses, spikes, even Jesus refrigerator magnets grew in popularity in response to this cultural phenomenon.

Why was *The Passion* important?

The Passion of the Christ showed in the most blatant of ways that religion is a product, no different from any other commodity sold in the consumer marketplace. *The Passion* started with a defined target audience, created secondary targets through promotion and publicity, and perpetuated the product's relevance through creating ancillary businesses. And while initially the objective was to sell a film, we can see from the sustaining campaigns and comments made by the director that the ultimate objective was to promote religion itself.

Another reason why *The Passion* was important is that it furthered the notion that while religious practice is very much privatized, religious presentation and promotion has become widely acceptable within our culture. Many forms of religion are being advertised and promoted in a way never seen before. Churches advertise on billboards and in print media. Books sell us all types of religious and spiritual wisdom. Television has become overrun with religious content with no fewer than eight channels presenting sermons and faith-based programming 24 hours a day, not to mention religious content in broadcast prime time and as regular content for nightly newsmagazines.

While the intensity of religious messages is new, marketing religion is not (Finke and Iannaccone, 1993; Moore, 1994). It has been going on for centuries. When Gutenberg invented the printing press in the fifteenth century, for example, much of the early advertising was to sell Bibles. In America the need for religious marketing stemmed from the First Amendment right to freedom of religion, something the Founding Fathers believed was fundamental to the establishment of the democracy. Choosing one's religion was as important a right as freedom of speech or the right to petition the government against grievances. Establishing no state religion meant that people would be free to choose how to worship, or not to worship. With no state-mandated religion, religions had to compete for parishioners and oftentimes that meant using marketing techniques, from simple print advertising to door-to-door salesmen, as evidenced by the Jehovah's Witnesses.[3]

However, competing in the religious marketplace was simple in simpler times. For centuries new Americans brought religion with them from their home countries and passed that religion down from generation to generation. If Mom and Dad went to the Baptist church around the corner, so did you. Not only were religions carried across the sea, but also traditions. Weekly church attendance, Sunday dinners with the family, and singing in the church choir were all part and parcel of a simple religious life. Houses of worship carried significance in the communities where they served because they were a place *for* community as well as a place for worship. Going to church was not only about God, but also about making social connections. Churches were able to maintain their value and their numbers because social agents—

family, work, and even the congregation itself—supported remaining in a single faith throughout one's lifetime.

This began to change as American society moved from agrarian to industrial. First, the opportunities to connect with other people presented themselves as part of daily life, particularly through one's place of business, thus usurping the church's monopoly on community building. Second, as the baby boom generation came of age in the 1960s, children rebelled against the older generation in myriad ways including rejecting the faith of their parents. The flexibility to choose one's faith combined with reduced social stigma attached to not attending services meant that churches were no longer ensured a congregation. Finally, increasingly more sophisticated communications technologies—first the radio and then television and the Internet—provided alternative forms of communication that could be used for connecting with others as well as a means for distributing religious content. The church was no longer the only source of religious information—and in fact has become the least convenient one—and thus continued to erode in value.

This is not to say that religion or spirituality has diminished in acceptance. America is one of the most religious countries in the world, certainly the most religious industrialized country. Poll after poll touts the fact that 90 percent or more of Americans believe in some form of higher power, whether it is God, Jesus, Moses, Mohammed, Buddha, Krishna, or some other lesser known entity (though almost 75 percent claim to be Christian according to Simmons Marketing Research [2004, p. 124]). A 2003 Harris Interactive poll "found that 79% of Americans believe there is a God, and that 66% are *absolutely certain* this is true" (Harris Interactive, 2003). In the same survey, researchers learned that 9 percent of Americans do not believe in God and 12 percent aren't sure.

Not only are Americans religious, or spiritual as some prefer to call it, but we readily buy products and services that relate to our faith. We do this because, as mentioned earlier, traditional religious institutions are not the primary source of spiritual sustenance for most people anymore. While nearly eight out of ten Americans claim belief in a higher power, only one out of three attends religious services on a regular basis. Specifically, only 36 percent of Americans go to church or synagogue regularly—that is, at least once a month—even though close to 80 percent believe in God. Doing the math, that means more than 60 percent of Americans get their faith from something other than a religious institution. People attend movies, read books, and participate in religious chat rooms, all of which are diminishing religious bodies' direct influence on religious consumers. Instead of going to church, we wear T-shirts with WWJD (What would Jesus do?) or Jewcy emblazoned on our chests. We buy Christian rock albums and New Age crystals. In fact we spend more on religious/spiritual/ self-help books than any other country, which makes total sense given the size of the target market (79 percent of Americans), our faith beliefs, and our consumerist culture.

All of this is to say that religion as practiced in the United States is an autonomous, self-oriented religion. This individualized religious practice, famously noted by Bellah and his colleagues in the mid-1980s, was called "Sheilahism," named after a nurse who created her own form of religious practice (Bellah et al., 1985). Since that time other scholars have seen this pastiche of religious practice as a continuing trend (Cimino and Lattin, 1998; Roof, 1993b, 1999). More recently this "cafeteria religion" is believed to be increasingly fueled by a commodity culture (Carrette and King, 2005; Miller, 2004).

In 2003, research estimates put the market for religious publishing and products at $6.8 billion and growing at a rate of nearly 5 percent annually. This market is subdivided into three categories: books (the largest segment, with $3.5 billion in sales and a 7 percent growth rate); stationary/giftware/merchandise (sales at $1.4 billion and a 4.5 percent growth rate); and audio/video/software ($1.4 billion in sales and flat). Given the current interest in religious products which continues to be fueled by *The Passion*, experts estimate that the market will grow at almost a 5 percent annual rate for at least the next three years, reaching $8.64 billion in sales (Seybert, 2004, p. 50).

But even this tells only part of the story. Unlike other product categories, there is no standardized means for collecting data on religious products and services. Therefore these numbers are misleading and in fact significantly underreport the money consumers spend on these products and services. In the book segment, for example, there is little uniformity in what constitutes religious or spiritual content. Some religious-oriented titles can be categorized as fiction or even science fiction in one store, as in the case of the *Left Behind* series, a fictional series based on the End Times, for example, and as religion in another. In terms of other media, these numbers do not include theatrical films like *The Passion of the Christ*, which in and of itself would add 14 percent to the total spending in the category. Nor does it include religious television, which is a viewer-supported, several billion dollar industry and growing as evidenced by the recent introductions of numerous digital channels dedicated to religious programming. These numbers do not reflect the money spent on religious seminars, lectures, or spiritual adventure travel. So from a consumer product and service perspective what is being tracked is just the tip of the iceberg.[4]

A good indication of where religious marketing is heading is evidenced by the fact that Wal-Mart, the behemoth of all retailers, has jumped on the religious retail bandwagon. In 2003 the company sold more than $1 billion in Christian book and music titles, and they are quoted as saying that they are "looking at this as a huge opportunity for the future" (Seybert, 2004,

p. 13). With the introduction of religious content into big box stores, the commoditization of religion is virtually complete.

But let's stop for a minute. Many of these things, after all, have been going on for decades. Religion more generally has *always* had to sell itself in the marketplace of ideas. The questions that need to be asked are: Why has religious marketing become so pervasive *now*? Why now do religious institutions feel compelled to employ consultants, focus groups, and surveys to fill their pews? Why now are sales of religious items growing at exponential rates? Why now are religions and religious products branded, marketed, and promoted at a level never before seen in history?

Why religious marketing has proliferated

There are two main reasons why religious marketing has permeated our culture. First, millions of Americans have been set free to choose their religion. The ability to choose has created the *real* open market for religion. Yes, when the Founding Fathers chose not to force a particular religion on the country, they were promoting the proliferation of religious choices. However choice is no choice if the rest of society (and particularly your mother) makes you go to a specific religious institution. In addition to the elimination of familial pressure to attend religious services, there is no longer a social stigma attached to not attending church. Given the aforementioned statistics, you are more likely to see your neighbor in the local mall on Sunday than in your local church.

Second, in the last 20 years the level of media saturation in general has reached a height never imagined. In addition to cable television, we now have digital cable, with the average home having the ability to receive more than 130 channels, not to mention direct broadcast satellite with its capacity to deliver several hundred channels to the home of anyone willing to pay for them. The Internet has become a household item for many people and where this is not the case, people readily access cyberspace in their workplace or at their neighborhood library. The media beast needs to be fed with content— all types of content. The simple fact that there is more media means that there is more *religious* media.

Tied into the proliferation of media is the ubiquitous advertising that goes with it. And while I will address in some detail in this and in subsequent chapters the influence of marketing and advertising on our culture, let me briefly say here that our interactions with advertising have led us to expect certain things from marketers, specifically convenience and entertainment. These expectations have migrated to the realm of spiritual practice. Religion is no longer tied to time and place; it can be practiced any time of the day or night via the media without going to a sacred space. So traditional religious institutions have to compete not only with brick and mortar churches, but also with religion presented in other forms. Religion is increasingly moving from pew to pixel. The Internet presents information about all aspects of religious products and activities, from Beliefnet, a comprehensive site about all things religious, to opportunities to worship through online churches—everything from the Vatican to the Church of the Blind Chihuahua. A 2004 study called Faith Online, by the Pew Research Center, found that almost two-thirds of Internet users had used the computer for religious or spiritual purposes (Hoover *et al.*, 2004).

Television presents religious programming through 24-hour cable channels, including the Inspiration Network and the Prayer Channel, and Sunday morning religious infomercials too numerous to mention. Thus seekers can receive the word of God in their homes 24 hours a day. This is not to say that the physical church or synagogue or mosque will disappear. Just as the VCR did not eliminate the local movie theater, the computer or plasma screen will not destroy the local place of worship. People like to experience events—religious or otherwise—in physical community. It does suggest, however, that traditional and nontraditional institutions have to compete with more entertaining forms of religious practice. In the same way that elementary schools have been forced to compete with *Sesame Street* over the past 30 years, religious institutions now have to compete against online churches, 24-hour religious networks, and even a recently announced 24-hour gospel music channel. If one does choose to go to church, consumers have a heightened expectation of being entertained, which is usually met with music and dramatic presentations. Moreover believers expect an experiential practice, that is, a more personal connection to God wherein they experience His presence. Sermons from on high just won't cut it for the majority of today's religious consumers.

One of the most successful segments of religious media is the book publishing industry, which in the last few decades has become big business and getting bigger. Look at *The New York Times* bestseller list on any given week and you'll see multiple religious or spiritual titles on it. For example, books by popular pastors, such as *The Purpose Driven Life* by Rick Warren and Joel Osteen's *Your Best Life Now*, have become perennials on this list. In the 1990s, large multinational book publishers began purchasing smaller, independent religious book publishers (e.g., HarperCollins's acquisition of Zondervan) or creating faith-based divisions within their larger book divisions (Warner Faith in Time Warner books). This created considerable consolidation within the industry. This consolidation has meant not necessarily more competition, but bigger competition—and not only bigger competition, but competition with considerable marketing expertise in multiple media outlets. In response to this, religious institutions have had to become savvier in their use of sophisticated marketing tools.

In sum, the severe declines in church attendance, due to everything from changing social codes to the pedophile priest scandals of the Catholic

Church, demonstrate why marketing has become necessary. While earlier polls suggested that religious attendance was closer to 40 to 45 percent, now the number is closer to 35 percent and church leaders must have seen this decline long before it appeared in any research numbers. As theologian Tom Beaudoin has said, "I think we are well past the day when the majority of American Christians have their religious identity formed in church" (Religion Surges, 2004, p. 9).

I would add that non-Christians are also finding their religious identity outside of established institutions.[5] Attendance numbers at most traditional religious houses of worship have been declining due to increased pressure from two key sources—individuals' freedom from religious affiliation, which means competition from other religious institutions, and significant competition from external media sources, which provide similar if not identical content as the religious institutions. People are free to find their faith whenever and wherever they choose, which may or may not be in the confines of a religious institution. We shouldn't be surprised then that religion—whether in the form of a film or a church—is being marketed in the current commercialized culture. In order to be heard above the noise of the rest of society, religion, too, must participate in order to survive.

Religion and the modern-day consumer

While being able to choose one's faith was a major change, there have also been changes in people's beliefs about money and childrearing. The generations that grew up after World War II are simply different from those that came before. Baby boomers, Gen Xers, and Gen Yers (or Echo Boom, or the Millennials, as they are also called) have all grown up in a society in which prosperity reigned. Previous generations faced economic depression and uncertainty. They believed that money should be saved for a rainy day because you never knew what was going to happen. More recent generations' money philosophies are ones of spend, spend, spend, because there will always be more tomorrow.

In addition to a life of prosperity, post-war generations have been involved in purchase decisions almost from the time they were able to talk. Starting in the 1940s and the introduction of Dr. Spock, children were consulted about how they felt and what they wanted, from what cereal to eat to where to go on family vacations. This inclusive, and more permissive, parental style became the vogue and drove these generations to have input into virtually every aspect of their lives. Today this translates into children influencing 72 percent of food and beverage decisions and teenagers being the most highly prized target by marketers in part because they spend $172 billion annually and influence the spending of billions of dollars more.[6] Compare this to earlier generations who were told what to wear, where to go to school, what profession they should have, and even who to marry. The post-war generations are made up of individuals who have been catered to since birth. They expect products how and when they want them.

This consumer-focused environment is what Cheryl Russell, a former editor of *American Demographics* magazine, calls "the personalized economy." She explains that while the industrial economy was based on mass production, the personalized economy is based on "customized products for individualistic consumers" (Russell, 1993, p. 56). We see this in multiple consumer segments, from media to packaged goods. Cable channels exist for everyone—from decorating enthusiasts to the avid golfer, with channels for specific demographic groups from women to children to gays and lesbians. *Sports Illustrated* is no longer just *Sports Illustrated*. It's *SI Women* and *SI Kids*. The proliferation of brands in the supermarket is an area where this customization is strikingly evident; the typical store now carries more than 30,000 items (Adamy, 2005). In the orange juice section of your local supermarket you can find products with or without pulp, calcium fortified, low carb, and half the calories. Toothpaste is made with a whitening agent, tartar control, and/or baking soda and is available in gel or paste form. Even jeans can be customized to your individual specifications. Levi's will take your measurements and create an individualized pair of jeans in 24 hours for just $15 more than an off-the-rack pair plus shipping. Products from telephones to television, from water to weight-loss products, are created with personal preferences in mind.

To support this expanding line of products and to be heard above the noise of all the other competing products, merchandisers have to find multiple and various ways to promote their products. Advertising has become so pervasive that even going to the stall in a public bathroom has become a place of promotion. According to James Twitchell, author of *Adcult*, the only way to avoid advertising is to go to sleep. This, however, is not a realistic option. Since we choose to stay awake, we are almost continually bombarded with marketing messages.

People, on average, will see close to 200 advertisements a day, but may see upwards of 3,000 marketing messages in the same time period through branded products, T-shirts, and product placement; that's almost 11 million branded messages per year. The level of assault by marketers has reached an all-time high. Let's take television as an example. During prime time television on the broadcast networks, there are between 14 and 16 minutes of "non-program" content, that is, commercials. This number has been steadily increasing over the past several years and is expected to continue to climb. Don't look for respite from the cable networks. They're not any better, though—thankfully—so far they are no worse.

But it's not just the commercials between shows; now the shows themselves are essentially commercials. The success of *Sex and the City* is proof of this. A shoe is not a shoe; it's a Manolo Blahnik. *Queer Eye for the Straight Guy* is one hour of wall-to-wall product placement disguised as a makeover show, with designers showing clueless straight men the right brands to wear and the right gel to use in their hair. There is now even a Web site (www.StarStyle. com) that enables viewers to buy products they see on television shows, thus facilitating the commercial effectiveness of these programs. *American Idol* is a Coke and AT&T commercial dressed up as a talent competition, and *The Apprentice*, a reality series that pits one team against another in improving a brand's awareness, is discussed in college courses to demonstrate effective advertising practices. But whether it is in the program or in between it, the underlying messages of these shows are the same: You are great, but you could be better. You are smart, but you could be smarter. The bottom line is that you are not okay just the way you are, but if you buy this product you can be.

These commercial messages are being delivered by a ubiquitous media. The average American household watches more than seven hours of television a day, the average adult four hours per day. The only thing we do more than watch television is work and sleep. Internet use is at an all-time high, with many Americans spending more than five hours a day online. In a study published in *The International Digital Media and Arts Association Journal*, researchers found that historic media usage statistics may in fact be *under*reported. In this study, called the Middletown Media Studies, researchers asked people to track their media usage in a diary. Simultaneously the researchers observed people's media usage. What they found was that "people spend more than double (129.7 percent) the time with the media than they recall—an average of 11.7 hours of media in total" (Papper *et al.*, 2004, p. 24). That translates into almost 12 hours—or half of every day—spent interacting with media.

This proliferation of advertising and marketing has changed the way we see the world. We live in a never-ending onslaught of fearful messages—you're too fat, you're face/body/teeth aren't perfect, you drive the wrong car, terrorists could kill us all tomorrow. The list is endless. The solution to these problems, of course, is to buy something that will alleviate the fear. Buy insurance and you can protect your family. Purchase the right mutual fund and you can relax in your retirement. Use the right deodorant, mouthwash, and shampoo and you'll get the girl or the guy.

Advertising and marketing have taken hold of the American psyche and co-opted the American Dream—the embodiment of the rugged individualist—so as to distort individuality into a perversion. Individualism is no longer about making the world a better place or making your mark on the world; it's about how much you can buy and create your identity through those purchases. Advertising is narcissism. It has taught us that we are the most important thing in the world. Advertising has taught us that we should be happy, and if we are not, that we can transform our lives and that somehow, somewhere, there is a product or service that will enable us to do just that. Take the diet industry as an example. At any given time almost half of all American women are on a diet. We know from statistics that 90 percent of dieters fail. Yet year after year millions of people buy into the latest diet craze, whether it is low-carb, South Beach, or Dr. Phil's *Ultimate Weight Loss Challenge*. What is propelling this obsession (not necessarily for the morbidly obese, but for women who think they need to lose 10 to 20 pounds) is the impact of pervasive pictures of perfectly beautiful and painfully thin women. They would not influence us, according to Jean Kilbourne (1999), "if we did not live in a culture that encourages us to believe we can and should remake our bodies into perfect commodities. These images play into the American belief of transformation and ever-new possibilities, no longer *via hard work but via the purchase of the right products*" (p. 132; italics added).

If this is true about our bodies, how much more so would we crave it for our very souls? If we can buy a new body, we should be able to buy salvation and inner peace, and we should see immediate results from our purchase. Now more than ever, religious and spiritual products are trying to convince us of just that. The personalized economy has taught us to expect immediate gratification and customized products to suit our every need and that expectation has been transferred to our religious practices.

Within this environment of being able to select your religion, or religions, combined with unfettered access to information, religion must present itself as a valuable commodity, an activity that is worthwhile in an era of over-crowded schedules. To do this, religion needs to be packaged and promoted. It needs to be new and relevant. It needs to break through the clutter, and for that to happen, it needs to establish a brand identity.

Branding to compete in a material world

Brands are commodity products that have been given a name, an identifying icon or logo, and usually a tagline as a means to differentiate them from other products in their category. Branding also occurs through the creation of stories or myths surrounding a product or service. These stories are conveyed through the use of advertising and marketing and are meant to position a product in the mind of the consumer. For example, Wal-Mart is a friendly (note the smiley face logo) discount store (dropping prices) where you can find anything you need for the whole family (notice the range of ages in their commercials); Target is a hip (rock music in their advertising), trendy (they sell Isaac Mizrahi), variety store (multiple product lines in advertising) for the budget conscious consumer. Two low-cost stores; two different ways that consumers perceive them. That's branding.

Another aspect of branding is that over time consumers don't have to intentionally think about a product's attributes. The name or the logo appears and everything that is associated with that brand comes to mind. Think of the Nike swoosh. In and of itself, it doesn't mean anything. It's a curved line. But if you know it's the Nike swoosh, for you it may symbolize the best in athleticism, "Just do it," or it might even evoke images of women slaving at poverty wages to produce an overpriced sneaker, depending on your point of view. These almost unconscious ideas about a product allow for split-second information to be transmitted in a cluttered media environment.

Brands also assist in creating personal identities. This idea has been popular in the beer segment for decades and is known as "brands as badges." For example, when you see someone in a bar carrying a can of Budweiser, you might automatically drum up images of this same guy sitting at home with his beer belly sticking out watching football on a Sunday afternoon. Put a bottle of Heineken in the same guy's hand and suddenly he is sophisticated, probably middle to upper-middle class, and at least middle management. The same idea translates to cars and clothes and cosmetics, and thus we communicate to other people who we are by the brands we buy and the products we use. We use brands for identity creation.

That religious products would turn to branding makes perfect sense in the current cultural environment. To remain relevant in our commercial culture means at a minimum being heard among the multitude of competing messages. Branding faith becomes shorthand for reaching the new religious consumer.

Branding faiths is also necessary because religion is a commodity product. The majority of religions offer the same end benefit for the consumer (salvation, peace of mind, etc.). Though packaged differently, fundamentally they are the same product, no different than buying one shampoo versus another. For a marketer, this makes things very difficult. The only way to differentiate one religion from another, or any product for that matter, is through the services provided (the added value) and the symbols that designate it. What we are talking about here is branding.

Traditionally, religious brands have been denominations. Episcopalians are the blue bloods, Catholics were the poor and immigrant class, and so on. Denominations were the identifiers for how to think about the people who attended these institutions. As well as identifying the members of the congregation to those outside the congregation, it also gave the members an identity. If you were Episcopalian, then you ran the Ivy League, the major cultural institutions, and Wall Street. You just knew that.

Today the branding of religion has changed. Churches have increasingly become nondenominational. Churches prefer the flexibility of being able to run their churches in the way they see fit, and many of them are very successful in doing so. A look at the numbers here is enlightening. According to James Twitchell (2004) in his book *Branded Nation*, "half of all churchgoing Americans are attending only 12 percent of the nation's four hundred thousand churches. To look at it another way: half of American Protestant churches have fewer than seventy-five congregants" (p. 81). This means that a limited number of *very* large churches are providing services to the majority of religious consumers. These churches are the so-called seeker churches, or megachurches. They were the first institutions to discover the use of marketing on a broad scale for religious institutions. What they have done is create brands that religious shoppers identify and that readily become part of their consideration set when selecting a religious institution.

But megachurches are not the only religious groups to indulge in marketing. One of the most successful religious marketing endeavors to date is Kabbalah, the centuries-old Jewish mystical tradition that has been transformed into a pop culture phenomenon. Televangelists are also making a comeback. After the scandals of the 1980s televangelism took a hit, seeing declines in contributions and viewership. Thanks to the proliferation of cable television outlets, these televised prophets have returned to the airwaves in full force and they are doing it with a combination of on-air charisma and off-air commerce. All of these—megachurches, Kabbalah, televangelists— are what I call faith brands, religious products and services that are part of a comprehensive, cohesive marketing plan to create a product that resonates with today's consumer-conscious religious shopper.

Religion and marketing: two worlds not really at war

While "culture war" is the term that has been used to describe the battle between religion and popular culture, the interaction between religion and marketing seems to be less of a war than a negotiation. Religion and marketing are not, in fact, at war. Nor are they mutually exclusive. Rather, there is a symbiotic relationship between religion and marketing. Religion and marketing are both forms of meaning making. Religion and marketing are both part of identity creation. Religion and marketing share a similar process of acceptance by their users. In all, these institutions are much more alike than they are different.

The focus of this book is not to bemoan religious marketing, as is usually done by religion scholars. This is not to say that the marketing of religion will not be criticized. As a former marketer of television and packaged goods who left that world for academia, I am readily qualified to take on the task of media criticism. Moreover, I have spent the last three years attending religious courses, interviewing attendees and marketers, going to church and synagogue, and watching hundreds of hours of religious television programming as well as reviewing church Web sites and other marketing materials. Through this analysis, it is safe to say that marketing religion likely has been a contributing factor in transforming religion into "religion lite," and yes, religion probably is being watered down, and, no, that may not necessarily be a good thing. But I will leave it to religion scholars to assess this impact. Rather, throughout this book I will present what I have seen so that you, the reader, can decide if you think it is a good or bad thing. Before we start, I will say that above all else, marketing religion is a balancing act— a delicate dance of how far one must go to remain relevant while at the same time remaining true to one's faith. This is no easy task.

Chapter 2

The changing religious marketplace

Religion is more widely practiced in the United States than in any other industrialized nation in the world. The most widely publicized statistics are that 40 to 45 percent of Americans attend a religious service on a weekly basis while more than 90 percent claim to believe in a higher power. Other statistics put weekly attendance figures at 26 percent, monthly attendance at only 11 percent, and annual attendance at 19 percent (Harris Interactive, 2003). But even at these reduced levels, the importance of religion in America cannot be underestimated.

The vast majority (84 percent) of Americans consider themselves to be Christian, with 57 percent claiming to be of a Protestant denomination (Barna Group, 2006, pp. 8, 10). Increasingly one faith is not enough for many Americans as 19 percent claim that their faith practice is influenced by more than one religion (Gallagher, 1996). Moreover, "seven out of ten Americans strongly assert that their religious faith is very important in their life" (Barna Group, 2006, p. 20). Perhaps not surprisingly, this number is correlated with age. As we get older it seems that faith is more important to us. While researchers have found this to be true across all faiths, we can see it strongly in the number of Americans who consider themselves to be "born again." The average age of the nearly 101 million adults who say they have been reborn is 50 (p. 29). Nearly half of Americans say they read the Bible weekly and an astounding 84 percent claim to have prayed to God in the last seven days (p. 40). All of this is to say that while people may not be attending church or synagogue, they do interact with their form of a higher power on a very consistent basis.

Compare this with other so-called first world countries. According to the Pew Global Attitudes Project (2002), there is no other country in the industrialized world where religion plays such an important part in people's lives. The percentage of people who said that religion is very important to them was 33 percent in Great Britain, followed by Italy, Germany, and France at 27 percent, 21 percent, and 11 percent respectively. This is compared to 59 percent in the United States. Eastern Europe was similar to Western Europe, with numbers ranging between 11 percent and

36 percent. In Japan, religion is very important to only 12 percent of the population.

In "less advanced" cultures, religious practice is much more prevalent. According to the same Pew study, in predominantly Catholic Latin America the percentages are the same as the United States or higher, with only Argentina coming in lower at 39 percent.[1] In Africa all countries had percentages higher than 80 percent, with the highest (Senegal) at 97 percent. In Asia the percentages are in the 80s and 90s, except for Korea (25 percent),Vietnam (24 percent), and the previously mentioned Japan.

So why does the United States look more like a less developed nation than the industrial superpower it is when it comes to its attachment to religion? Why have Americans not tossed religion aside like their European counterparts? According to the prevailing sociological theory of religion—the new paradigm—the underlying reason has a lot to do with marketing.

Religious institutions

Secularization theory

Before discussing the new paradigm, we need to set the stage with the old one—the secularization theory. This is the idea that as societies become more industrialized they will become less religious.[2] The advent of science and technology and the ability to analyze the world from an empirical perspective would eliminate over time the need for organized religion and its seemingly irrational worldview. Thus as religious institutions exert less influence in society, the need to attend church similarly decreases, creating an unending cycle of decline. Adults attend less church, and in turn their children have less religious exposure. This pattern progresses from one generation to the next until religion has little impact on the lives of individuals and then the broader culture.

However secularization is not only this. Secularization describes *both* the declining relevance of religion in society as well as how religion itself becomes more secular. In order not to lose out to the broader culture, organized religion changes to accommodate the culture within which it exists, taking on the trappings of secular institutions out of fear of becoming marginalized for not having done so. In doing this, it is believed that the faith will be simplified, syncretized, or in some other way diminished.

While that may be true, secularization is not a one-way street. Rather, secularization is a mutual process—the sacred becoming more secular and the secular becoming more sacred. Current day music is played in church, for example, but at the same time religious lyrics appear in popular rock music. The secularization theory interprets this give and take between the sacred and profane as negative because it threatens organized religion. Secular institutions will overtake religious ones, thus contributing to their increasing loss in authority. But while that has happened, religion has not disappeared. Instead the secular and the sacred have continued to blur, each taking on aspects of the other (Ostwalt, 2003).

What we are really talking about, then, is the decline of *organized* religion and not the elimination of the human impulse to appreciate the sacred. In his bestselling book *The End of Faith*, Sam Harris (2005, p. 40) bemoans Americans' tenacious hold on religion. Yet even this harsh critic of religion admits that:

> [T]he range of possible human experience far exceeds the ordinary limits of our subjectivity. Clearly, some experiences can utterly transform a person's vision of the world. Every spiritual tradition rests on the insight that how we use our attention, from moment to moment, largely determines the quality of our lives. Many of the results of spiritual practice are genuinely desirable, and we owe it to ourselves to seek them out.

By this, Harris gives support to the point—organized religion may lose its appeal but that does not mean a person cannot advocate for his or her spiritual experience. Thus it was the limited definition of religion—religion as organized religion—that was a sticking point in the secularization thesis. People want to have faith. They want to believe in something. But the religious impulse is increasingly being satisfied someplace other than in a traditional religious setting, as evidenced by the statistics at the beginning of this chapter.

While the give and take between the secular and the sacred remains an important element of the secularization theory, the declining practice of religion has not borne out, at least not in the United States. Because of this, secularization theory declined in acceptance and scholars began to look elsewhere for answers. In the early 1990s a new paradigm—one based on economic theory—emerged for understanding what was happening in the world of religious practice.

Supply-side religion

The "new paradigm"—the supply-side theory of religion—claims that changes in religion stem from changes in the production side (the supply side) of religion rather than from the societal (or demand) side. R. Stephen Warner (1993), in his groundbreaking article, "Work in Progress Toward a New Paradigm for the Sociological Study of Religion in the United States," provides a history of this economic point of view. Warner explains that "supply-side" terminology was introduced by Terry Bilhartz in 1986 and expanded by Nathan Hatch, who wrote about a "religious marketplace" among "spiritual entrepreneurs." Hatch stressed that the important point is not that there is so much diversity of supply, but that suppliers must serve the needs of their consumers—setting the stage for marketing religion. Warner further outlines the anthropologists, sociologists, and economists, including Rodney Stark, William Bainbridge, Roger Finke, and Laurence Iannaccone, who have added to the theory. Their contributions include the ideas of free enterprise—religion operating in an unregulated market open to a variety of producers; and rational choice theory—people will select religion based on what best serves their individual needs or goals.

In "Supply-side Explanations for Religious Change," Finke and Iannaccone (1993) explain that preceding theories "share the unexamined assumption that religious change usually occurs in response to the shifting desires and needs of religious consumers...[however] the most significant changes in American religion derive from shifting supply, not shifting demand" (p. 28). In a free-market environment such as the United States then, as supply increases or decreases, the market for religion should change accordingly. In *The Churching of America* (1992, p. 21) Stark and Finke demonstrate support for this theory. These researchers found that:

> where many faiths function within a religious economy, a high degree of specialization as well as competition occurs. From this it follows that many independent religious bodies will together be able to attract a much larger proportion of a population than can be the case when only one or very few firms have free access.

Thus a robust market for religion exists when religion does not act as a monopoly. Further, there is a diversity of options for practitioners and more of these practitioners should be able to find a faith that suits their needs.

Many supply-side developments have occurred historically in response to changes in government regulation. Finke and Iannaccone list these as being: the parish system in colonial America, which allowed clergy to maintain a monopoly in the area where they served; "sustaining time," an FCC regulation that required broadcasters to provide airtime to preachers in the early days of television;[3] and the change in immigrant regulations in the 1960s, which allowed increased numbers of Asians into the United States, radically altering the face of religious products.[4] As regulations were enacted or eliminated, the types of religious products offered increased, allowing for more religious practice than the secularization theory would have suggested.

Viewing religion as a product, rather than as a social mandate, brings considerable insight into understanding not only why religion has flourished in the United States, but also why it has been marketed historically as well as today.

The market model views churches and their clergy as religious producers who choose the characteristics of their product and the means of marketing it. Consumers in turn choose what religion, if any, they will accept and how extensively they will participate in it. In a competitive environment, a particular religious firm will flourish only if it provides a product at least as attractive as its competitors'.

(Finke and Iannaccone, 1993, p. 29)

Under this theory, religion is a product subject to the whims and changes of the market.

Breaking this down further, we can examine religion based on its attributes and benefits, which is how marketers look at a product. Religion's attributes are written texts, a place to go on Saturday or Sunday, a source of information from a leader, and other tangible elements found in most organized religions. Its benefits are fellowship, interaction with likeminded people, a better sense of well-being, and, perhaps, salvation. At its base, then, one religion is not much different from another. The differences lie in the packaging—the music, the type of texts used, and what additional services are available beyond the prayer service (a food court? a large singles community? childcare? types of recovery groups?). Based on the options, consumers will make a rational choice about what compendium of services best fits their desires for a religious practice.[5]

In an unregulated market where the benefits for suppliers are high and barriers to entry are low, there will be considerable competition for these religious consumers. What this has meant in recent years is that clergy have taken on a more active marketing stance, promoting their product and changing its packaging to appeal to those who are seeking religion. This creates an unending cycle of competition because in markets where there is more than one player, competition increases consumption simply because more people will be able to find a product they like.[6]

However, you cannot create demand where it does not already exist, and this is where I differ in my thinking from supply-siders.[7] Rodney Stark, a major proponent of this theory, has said, "The potential demand for religion has to be activated....The more members of the clergy that are out there working to expand their congregations the more people will go to church" (Porter, 2004, p. 14). True, the more people hear about different religious options the more likely they are to find something that fits their basket of attributes and benefits sought, and this, in turn, should increase religious practice overall. However you cannot drive demand for a product that people do not want. You can't activate demand for religion anymore than you can activate it for a snow blower in the desert. Trying to artificially create demand for religion is one of the fundamental differences between religion and other marketed products and services.

In summary, then, religion operates in a free market in the United States with the number of suppliers driving the level of religious practice as much as, if not more than, religious demand. Because there is no religious mandate, each form of religion must compete with others (as well as with other discretionary time activities). An important way of remaining competitive is through marketing and promotion. Increased marketing means increased competition, which in turn generates more marketing.

Religious practice

The religious switch—after the 1960s everything changed

Historically religion has been an element of personal identity in the United States. A person's denomination was as much a determinant of who he or she was as language or social class (Warner, 1997). It is a factor that sociologists considered to be ascribed rather than achieved. That is, it was a factor determined by birth, rather than something you worked for. "This tendency to treat religion as an ascribed aspect of individual identity existed for the simple reason that it had roots in reality; a Gallup Poll taken in 1955 found that only 4 percent of Americans—one in twenty-five—did not adhere to the religion of their childhood" (Wolfe, 2003, p. 41). Thus, in the beginning of the last century, you were the religion that you were born into. Leaving the faith of your birth would have been a serious, well-considered action because it fundamentally changed who you were. Religious switching became widely acceptable, however, after the societal upheaval of the 1960s, the decade of the baby boom generation.[8]

Wade Clark Roof, first in his book *A Generation of Seekers* (1993a) and later in *Spiritual Marketplace* (1999), outlines how religious practice changed for baby boomers. While the baby boom cohort is not irreligious, they do not practice in the way that previous generations did. One-third stayed with their faith of origin, but two-thirds—66 percent—dropped away from religion when they were young, which is a huge number when you consider that only 4 percent of the general population switched only a decade before. While 40 percent of those who dropped their faith returned to some type of faith practice, the majority of those who dropped out did not have an ongoing connection with a religious institution (Roof, 1993b, p. 164). Rather, this generation moves freely from one faith practice to another. As Roof (1993a, p. 5) explains:

> Many within this generation who dropped out of churches and synagogues years ago are now shopping around for a congregation. They move freely in and out, across religious boundaries; many combine elements from various traditions to create their own personal,

tailor-made meaning systems. Choice, so much a part of life for this generation, now expresses itself in dynamic and fluid religious styles.

Religion for baby boomers, then, is something they select through purchase and creation.

A number of factors have contributed to this marketing mentality. First, religion became voluntary (Roof and McKinney, 1987). This was due, in part, to the elimination of a stigma attached to not attending church. Second, the religion of a person's parents was no longer mandatory. Renouncing the faith of their birth was one of the many ways that boomers rebelled against authority. Finally, the influx of other faiths into the United States led to increased experimentation in religious practice. Many scholars have noted the changing landscape of American faith in the wake of changing immigration laws in the 1960s. However it is not just Asian immigrants, but also Latin Americans and other Hispanics who were affecting change. New immigrants added to the switching, or questing, phenomenon by providing additional, readily available alternatives.

In his book *The Transformation of American Religion*, Alan Wolfe (2003) notes that by the 1980s the number of Americans who left the faith in which they were raised was one in three (p. 41). Wolfe, like Roof, attributes this to the introduction of Eastern faiths, but he also includes the increases in intermarriage and in social and geographic mobility as part of his analysis.

Of note is the kind of switching that occurred. Seekers were switching from liberal denominations to more conservative ones. While Wolfe does not specify the cohort he is examining, it may well be that this switching is occurring in Generation X, the baby boomlet. In *The New Faithful*, Colleen Carroll (2002, p. 91) says:

> Reared in a media culture that relentlessly lobbies for their attention and panders to their whims, many young adults find it refreshing when religious leaders demand sacrifice, service, and renunciation of consumerism. They feel strangely liberated by orthodoxy's demands of obedience and objective morality, which belie their culture's tendency toward individualism and moral relativism.

Generations subsequent to the baby boom seem to have achieved a level of decision burnout. Having been asked their opinion about everything since birth, they now want someone else to make decisions for them.

The other trend Wolfe discusses is the tendency for switching to occur within faiths. That is, Protestants remained Protestants but chose a different denomination. Economics may help to explain this. Using human capital theory, Iannaccone (1990) found that "people switch denominations in ways that preserve the value of their religious human capital" (p. 313), that capital being the time and energy spent learning a religion's rituals, doctrine, and so forth. So, for example, it takes a lot more effort to convert to Judaism from Christianity than it does to move within Christian traditions, or even to combine one faith with another. Unlike Roof, Wolfe is conservative in his views. He is less tolerant of switching and sees religious shoppers as uncommitted to doctrine and unaware of the differences between denominations. However, he, too, sees that switching "is much better understood as a byproduct of...meeting individual needs" (p. 45).

Amanda Porterfield also pegs a free religious marketplace to social changes that affected the baby boom starting in the 1960s. In addition to the elimination of Asian immigration barriers in the United States, she examines the rise of feminism, the rise of religion studies as an academic area on college campuses, and the overall disillusionment with established institutions. First, she finds an important correlation between feminist and religious studies.

> People interested in analyzing gender roles kept running into religion, as did people who wanted to change those roles. And people involved in studying or advancing religion kept running into gender. Beginning in the 1970s, it became increasingly apparent that religion played a major part in defining and sanctioning gender roles. It also became apparent that religion was subject to deconstruction as part of the analysis of gender in any given society. Advocates of changing, loosening, or expanding gender roles saw the deconstruction and reformulation of religion as a means to their goal.
>
> (Porterfield, 2001, pp. 164–5)

Religion became open for analysis within the academy on two fronts— feminist scholarship and religious studies. In order to break feminine stereotypes, religion and its effect on the patriarchal social structure had to be thoughtfully analyzed. Breaking down these roles meant breaking down fundamental religious ideas.

Second, religious studies introduced new forms of practice to America's college students, who took it as an opportunity to experiment with rituals and beliefs previously unknown to them. Instructors delineated between practice and the study of religion, which Porterfield claims contributed to the personalized practices, the pluralism, we see today (p. 203).

> By involving many young Americans in studying a variety of different religious traditions and at the same time relieving them of the requirement of loyalty to any particular tradition, religious studies contributed to the rise of eclectic forms of spirituality characteristic of American culture since the sixties, to a lowering of barriers between religious groups, and to a tendency to tailor religious beliefs and practices to meet personal needs.

Finally, disillusionment with society and particularly the Vietnam War led many boomers to experiment with alternative religious practices. For some this included meditation and Asian traditions. For others it meant experimenting with the drug culture.

While the 1960s was a turbulent time in America, it was also a turbulent time for the practice of faith. Switching from one belief practice to another became increasingly casual and commonplace. This ability to switch also allowed for increased experimentation. Practitioners might switch multiple times or they might incorporate aspects of previously unknown faiths into their existing practice. From the provider's point of view, the religious institution was no longer guaranteed an audience. As religious switching, including switching to no practice, became increasingly acceptable, the need to use marketing to fill the pews also increased. As we will see, this did not come into full bloom until the 1980s and the church growth movement.

What do religious consumers want (how do they practice their faith)?

While it is difficult to describe what "religion" is in America today, it is possible to make some comments about trends in the way faith is practice. First, religion has become increasingly privatized. Second, religion is voluntary and when it is practiced, it is often a faith put together by the people who practice it—sometimes that means switching faiths, other times it means combining faiths. Third, there has been a reemergence of spirituality that has coincided with a desire for a more personalized relationship with God.

Scholars and practitioners would agree that religion has become increasingly privatized. As fewer and fewer people go to church, fewer and fewer people recognize others as those of faith. Just as the secularization theory proposed, fewer people attend services, and it perpetuates a cycle of decreasing church influence. However this does not mean that people don't go to church. One of the few days on which we are aware of others' religion is Ash Wednesday, when suddenly people are conspicuous in their faith. In of all places *Adweek*, an advertising industry trade publication, the following summation of our culture was described:

> The day [Ash Wednesday] serves as a reminder that religious faith remains a largely unseen phenomenon, even amid the religious revival now afoot in this country. That is, unless you're part of the churchgoing contingent yourself, it's easy to be oblivious to the role religion plays in the lives of people—including your own acquaintances. You know whether a colleague smokes, watches *Seinfeld*, eats sushi, can't stand Robin Williams, wears Dockers on Casual Friday. You're less likely to know whether he or she is religious. As the separation of church and

state has evolved into a separation of church and culture, the topic just doesn't come up.

(*Adweek*, 1998, p. 16)

Religion—so far anyway—has remained the last taboo. We can talk about sex, violence, drug use, and finances, but religion is still off limits. That may change in light of the increasing level of religious content in the media, but whether that leads to a more public religious practice is yet to be determined; it seems unlikely. Therefore, for now, religious practitioners are by and large not looking to flaunt their faith.

Second, religion is optional, but when it is chosen it is a personal construction. Instead of accepting the religion of their youth, many Americans have moved away from structure to a more amorphous personal set of beliefs. Starting in the 1960s, Peter Berger suggested that religious choice is like a supermarket; in the 1980s Reginal Bibby called it a "consumer item" that can be purchased "a la carte," and others see religion as a cafeteria—a place where you can pick and choose what you like and avoid what you don't. David Lyon (2000) has said that "religious activity is, increasingly, subject to personal choice, or voluntarism, and that, increasingly, for many in the advanced societies, religious identities are assembled to create a bricolage of beliefs and practices" (p. 76).

While most scholars are critical in their views about religious choice and merging religions, John Berthrong, in his book *The Divine Deli* (1999), makes a level-headed examination of the pluralistic religious practices in America today. While most theologians cry syncretism, Berthrong sees the combining of faiths as having been a part of religious practices throughout time. A good example he gives is the prayer bead: this staple of Christian practice was "stolen" from the Buddhists, though no one considers that inappropriate. Most critics pooh-pooh multiple religious participants, or MRPers as Berthrong calls them, but he does not see them as dilettantes or dabblers. They are not looking to replace religion but to "enrich and renew" it (p. 39). According to David Kinnaman, vice president of Barna Research Group:

Americans don't mind embracing contradictions, it's hyper-individualism....They're cutting and pasting religious views from a variety of different sources—television, movies and conversations with their friends. Rather than simply embracing one particular viewpoint, and then trying to follow all the specific precepts or teachings of that particular viewpoint, what Americans are saying is, "Listen, I can probably put together a philosophy of life for myself that is just as accurate, just as helpful as any particular faith might provide."

(Kang, 2003, p. A18)

Stewart Hoover (2006) relates this personalized, privatized religion to the expansion of mass media and the ability of seekers to access a diversity of religious information, an idea that will be explored more fully later in this chapter.

Third, since the 1980s an increasing number of people describe themselves as spiritual rather than religious. Not only is this move to spirituality about renouncing organized religion, but it is also about a more personalized religious experience, a more personal relationship with God.[9]

> Behind this shift [from religion to spirituality] is the search for an experiential faith, a religion of the heart not of the head. It's a religious expression that downplays doctrine and dogma, and revels in direct experience of the divine—whether it's called the "holy spirit" or "cosmic consciousness" or the "true self." It is practical and personal, more about stress reduction than salvation, more therapeutic than theological. It's about feeling good, not being good. It's as much about the body as the soul.
>
> (Cimino and Lattin, 1999, p. 62)

This focus on the personal and the therapeutic has its roots in psychology. Says Roof, "We might even go so far as to say that the psychological is the mode of the religious in middle-class American culture today" (1993b, p. 167). Religion has become less about salvation than about feeling good. Even in the halls of evangelicalism, the tone is less about helping the world and more about how you have already been saved. In a 2005 interview with Tom Brokaw, Ted Haggard, then pastor of the New Life Church in Colorado and the president of the National Association of Evangelicals (NAE), admitted that while they talk about sin in their church, it is not a main focus.[10]

> The emphasis in our church isn't how to get your sins removed, because that's pretty easy to do. Jesus did that on the cross. The emphasis in our church is on how to fulfill the destiny that God has called you to.... making it easier for them just like Jesus did, just like Moses did.
>
> (*Dateline*, NBC, 2005)

One of the places where this psychology arises is in the small group movement. These are no longer just 12-step meetings but any manner of group from Bible study to parenting meetings. These may happen in homes or within a church. In *Sharing the Journey*, for example, Robert Wuthnow (1994) examines the many small groups, or "moral communities," wherein people practice their faith.[11] A foremost sociologist of religion, Wuthnow claims that 40 percent of Americans attend these types of groups on a regular basis.[12] These groups are more private than church and they better reflect today's spiritual practice.

Religious groups that cater to one or all of these aspects of religious practice are the ones that are most likely to thrive. With the exception of evangelicalism, most faiths allow for private practice. Similarly while most conservative groups do not allow for syncretism, they do provide for a personal relationship with God. The religious consumer will be looking for one or more of these attributes—privacy, flexibility, personalization—depending on his or her wants and needs.

Thus far, then, we have examined how competition has contributed to a robust religious marketplace and an increased need for marketing. Adding on to that idea, we looked at how the freedom to choose your faith, and in turn switch from one faith to another, has further exacerbated competition because no congregant can be taken for granted. Finally, we examined how faith is practiced today and what "consumers'" expectations are. Now let's turn to how the ubiquitous nature of the mass media plays a part in changing the religious marketing landscape.

Getting out the message

Being able to choose your faith doesn't mean anything if you cannot find out about religious alternatives. That is where the media comes in. As far back as the days of old-time radio, people used media as a means to learn of and try out new faiths within the privacy of their own home (Hangen, 2002). Today television and the Internet provide the same types of opportunities but in a more elaborate setting and with a more intense marketing message attached to it. The explosive growth in the media industry in the last 20 years has contributed to more religious content on the airwaves and through the wires. If you doubt the importance of media in the lives of America's faith, know that "144 million Americans use some religious media—books, radio or television—at least once a month" (Winslow, 2005b, p. 28).[13]

A (very short) history of television in the United States

Television became a staple in American homes in the late 1950s. By the 1960s the three major broadcast networks—ABC, CBS, and NBC—garnered more than 90 percent of viewership during the prime-time hours. This was easy for them to do because there was very little competition in most markets. Only large urban areas had additional channels like PBS and possibly one or two independent stations, that is, stations unaffiliated with a broadcast network.

The 1980s saw the broad introduction of cable. Cable had actually started in the 1950s as a means to improve transmission to homes in remote areas. However it wasn't until the 1980s that the medium was more widely transformed into a means for disseminating original (and not so original) programming.[14] According to Nielsen Media Research, in 1980 there were 17.6 million basic cable customers, representing 22 percent of American television households. That number more than tripled to 63 million only 15 years later. With that increase, cable became available in more than 65 percent of American television homes (NCTA, 2006a). That percentage has remained consistently between 65 percent and 69 percent for the last decade.

Not only did the number of cable homes increase, but also the number of channels available to the home increased. By 2004 the average number of channels available in the home had risen to 132 from 41 only 10 years before. This growth in the number of channels has been fueled by the development of digital cable.

A little understanding of the technology here is helpful in explaining the sudden explosion in channel capacity. Limited shelf space—not being able to accommodate the number of different types of program networks available onto a cable system—had long been a bone of contention between cable operators (the company you pay your monthly bill to) and the program providers (networks like MTV, CNN, ESPN, etc.). When cable was first introduced, coaxial cable was used to transmit the television signal. These wires had limited capacity. Even before the introduction of digital, cable operators began to transfer their wiring from coaxial to fiber optic cable (some systems still use a combination of the two). With the introduction of fiber optics, channel capacity (or what we think of today as bandwidth) grew exponentially. In addition to increased capacity, digital technology allowed for the compression of the information being sent, which meant that less capacity was needed to send the same information. Thus:

more bandwidth + less needed space = room for more channels

This expansion relates to standard cable. In the late 1990s channel capacity expanded still further with the introduction of digital cable. As digital cable became more widely available, subscriber numbers increased markedly so that today 29.6 million homes, or nearly half of all U.S. cable households, subscribe to this program service. Direct Broadcast Satellite (DBS) technology improved in the 1990s and this service, too, increased in popularity. Non-cable video subscribers—for example, satellite users of all kinds—grew from a mere 2.3 million in 1992 to 28.3 million by the end of December 2005 (NCTA, 2006b). Cable and satellite services combined reach 92.6 million subscribers, or more than 91 percent of all U.S. homes. Therefore most U.S. homes now have three and four or more times the number of channels they did only a decade ago.

More channel capacity leads to more religious programming

As mentioned earlier, the average number of channels available in the American home is 132. If you have DBS it is many more than that—200 to 300 channels or more. According to the National Cable Television Association (NCTA), there are 390 *national* video programming services. Add regional and planned channels and that number almost doubles. When channel capacity increases, the amount of programming content increases in all genres—including religion.

A look through the NCTA database of programming networks is informative for this discussion. This database includes hundreds of channels of all types, from long-established networks to those in the planning stage. In terms of religious programming, in addition to large companies like Trinity Broadcast Network (TBN), EWTN, and The Word, there is a wealth of smaller and upcoming planned services. These include American David—"an American entertainment network with a fresh and unique Jewish flavor"— the Wisdom Channel, and the upcoming God TV, an import from England. Table 2.1 provides a sampling of some of the newer offerings in the religious television landscape.

Religious programming has become so important to the television industry that *Broadcasting & Cable*, the foremost trade publication for the television industry, puts out regular updates about this category of programming. In a special supplement for August 2006, the magazine promoted ten different religious or faith-based program channels including The Church Channel, Daystar, EWTN, INSP (The Inspiration Network), JCTV, Olympusat (a package of faith-based programming including some of the ones already mentioned), Smile of a Child, TBN, TBN Enlace USA, and The Word Network. This supplement was a promotional tool for these channels to receive increased distribution from cable and satellite operators. Each page contained the network's mission statement, the number of subscribers, programming highlights, demographic research, marketing support, and contact names and information for affiliate sales and marketing.

The channels are Christian in orientation, though one or two bow their hats to other religions. The category has even spawned subgenres. The Word Network specializes in "African-American ministries and gospel music." JCTV specifically targets 13 to 29 year olds and features music, sports, and reality programming, all with a faith-based undertone. We will likely be seeing more channels of this type. In an article entitled "Jesus Is My Homeboy," *Broadcasting & Cable* outlined the increasing importance of programming for kids and teens in this category (Downey, 2006, p. 18).

One of the fastest growing segments in television overall is Spanish-language programming, and that trend has extended into faith-oriented programs and networks. The value of this audience is reflected in the growth

Table 2.1 Sampling of religious television networks

Ecumenical Television Channel (Regional – Ohio)	ETC offers its viewers the best in local and national religious and inspirational programming and represents all denominations including Catholic, Jewish, Protestant and Orthodox.
Familyland Television Network (National)	Familyland® Television Network targets families looking for television programming in line with their values and beliefs, yet not strictly religious programming. It combines family values-centered entertainment and original Catholic programming, 24/7, offering exclusive spiritual talk shows with a family perspective, as well as movies and other entertainment programs without immodesty, foul language, excessive violence or disrespect for authority.
God TV	Dubbed by many as the "ESPN of Christian Broadcasting", God TV offers a younger, international dynamic mix of music, entertainment and ministry, catering to the 13–39-year-old audience, 24 hours a day.
Golden Eagle Broadcasting (National)	Golden Eagle broadcasting is America's licensed provider of Family Safe™ television. The network offers programming from a variety of categories including religion, education, sports and family. The network began service in 1998 from the campus of Oral Roberts University. GEB is proud to present a good mix of the most popular Charismatic based programs as well as an ever-growing number of ORU-GEB exclusive events.
Oasis TV On Demand (National)	Oasis TV is a global television programmer of cutting-edge body-mind-spirit news, inspiration and entertainment. Program topics include spirituality, metaphysics, visionary arts, earth changes and the environment, personal growth, world peace, natural health and healing, new sciences, love and sexuality.
Praise Television	Praise TV is a 24-hour, family entertainment network with an emphasis on music. Throughout the day, the top artists in adult contemporary Christian music are featured through music video programs.
Shalom TV (Planned service)	A premium digital cable television network celebrating Jewish culture, Shalom TV enlightens and enriches the lives of viewers through meaningful, educational and entertaining English-language telecasts touching upon issues of interest to Jewish people.

Source: National Cable & Telecommunications Association (www.ncta.com)

of this segment of the population and their increasing purchasing power, which is estimated to reach $1 trillion dollars by 2007 (Winslow, 2005b, p. 32). Several Christian broadcasters began Latin American operations in the 1980s and 1990s. As the Hispanic population in the United States increased, these companies launched channels to target it, among them EWTN Espanol, Family Christian Television, Maria Vision, and TBN Enlace USA.

Just a word here about Trinity Broadcasting Network (TBN), the world's largest Christian-themed television network. TBN is made up of four well-established networks: TBN, which is a lifestyle channel; The Church Channel, which is the worship channel; JCTV, which is a channel for young adults; and TBN Enlace USA, which is for Hispanic viewers. TBN's most recent addition, Smile of a Child, is a network for kids 2 to 12 years olds. It is "an enterprise lavishly supported by contributions from viewers around the world, where the 24-hour channel [TBN] is carried by 5,000 stations, 33 satellites, and cable systems" (Becker, 2005, p. 26). All of this is done without commercials. The company gets its support through donations and pledges, which explains why it is difficult to track the value of this market.

In addition to dedicated cable networks, religious content appears on secular networks. While prime-time series with religious content have their ups and downs on broadcast networks, religious content such as documentaries about Jesus and the holy land at Christmas time has been a staple for decades. In terms of continuing programming, the religious content is sometimes subtle, as in the case with the PBS children's show *Jay Jay the Jet Plane,* and sometimes it is quite blatant, as with *Touched by an Angel* and *Joan of Arcadia*, a prime-time broadcast network program wherein a teenage girl had weekly conversations with God. The difference in these shows versus some in the past is the separation of God from religion. On *Joan of Arcadia*, for example, Joan talks to God but God is not associated with a particular faith. Barbara Hall, the show's creator, wrote ten commandments for the show, one of which was, "God can never identify one religion as being right" (Poniewozik, 2003, p. 74). While for most of us that might be a problem, in the world of television it is required to draw in a larger audience. If God is Catholic, it turns off anyone who is not (an example is *Nothing Sacred*, ABC's short-lived series about a Catholic priest). One of the most successful shows on the former WB network was *7th Heaven*, the story of the tight-knit family of the local minister. Here, too, the faith was ambiguous. Over its history of more than a decade, it was the highest-rated show on the network (Chang, 2005, p. A1).

While *Touched by an Angel* and *Joan of Arcadia* are no longer on the air, religious practice and symbolism is still highly in evidence during network prime time even while God is not the specific focus of the program. In *Friday Night Lights*, a show about high school football in a Southern town, football players pray before games and after their star quarterback is severely injured. On *Cold Case*, a Philadelphia detective squad finds killers in unsolved murder cases. At the end of each episode, the murder victim appears in a ghost-like form before the lead detective to acknowledge the squad's good work in finding the person who sent him or her to the other side. Even *Desperate Housewives* makes much of the Catholic faith of one of the show's lead couples.

On the New Age side of the spectrum we have John Edward, a television psychic who has had three shows on three different networks over the last several years. While the psychic genre is not as successful as it used to be, it has done well on cable with programs such as *Psychic Detectives* on Court TV and *Psychic Pets* on Animal Planet, and in dramatized form on shows such as *Medium* on NBC and *Ghost Whisperer* on CBS. One of the few successful serialized programs of the 2006 season was *Heroes*, a sci-fi adventure in which different characters can fly, see into the future, or even stop time.

While networks traditionally shied away from specific representations of religion, more recently Jesus has appeared in a number of prime-time television programs. On *Rescue Me*, a show on cable channel FX, Denis Leary plays a New York City firefighter whose cousin died in the World Trade Towers on 9/11. This very troubled character regularly has conversations with Jesus. More blatant (and less successful) was NBC's *Daniel*, in which Jesus appears to talk to the main character, Reverend Daniel Webster, who is a substance-abusing minister (Lisotta, 2005, p. 2).

It is not just fictional programming where we see more religious content. Religion has also increasingly appeared in news broadcasts and documentaries. "Over the past 10 years, T.V. coverage of religious issues has been rising sharply, according to a study...by the Media Research Center. The major networks broadcast 303 stories on religion in the year ending March 1, 2004, compared with 121 in the same period last year." (Charles, 2004, p. 11). The popularity of *The Passion of the Christ* and *The Da Vinci Code* prompted network specials, such as ABC *News*'s "Jesus, Mary and Da Vinci." National Geographic Channel had its highest rated show ever with *Unlocking Da Vinci's Code*, a success that spawned comparable programming on other networks (Becker, 2005). The last few years have also seen significant time given to the death of Pope John Paul II and to the Terri Schiavo case,[15] and of course all the publicity surrounding *The Passion of the Christ*.

Religion has also received a lot of media coverage as it relates to politics. This issue presents itself in several ways. The religiosity of candidates has become a foreground issue because of George Bush's flagrant displays and comments in regard to his beliefs. This has forced competing candidates to profess their beliefs as well, which was seen in the presidential debates in 2004 and continues today in the lead-up to the 2008 election. Religion-as-strategy became a broader topic of discussion after that election when Democrats began to stress that they were not ceding the religious vote to the Republicans. Religion also arises in relationship to hot-button issues such as gay marriage, abortion, and stem-cell research. This came overwhelmingly to a head with the right-to-life debate and the Terri Schiavo case.[16]

Religious programming has proliferated because it produces ratings. This increased level of religious content increases audiences' exposure to different types of belief practices, whether it is through the platform of news, drama, or televised religious service.

Religion online

Much like television, the Internet became a staple in American homes in very short order. While created in the late 1950s as a tool for scientific researchers and the academic community, once Mosaic was introduced in the mid-1990s with its user-friendly, graphic interface the Internet became widely accepted among the broader population. Still, it would be almost a decade before the widespread availability of broadband delivery systems, which would allow for complex content beyond the static printed page.

In 2000 only about half of the United States (58 million homes) was wired for cable modem capability. By 2006 close to 120 million homes had access to cable broadband and more than 27 millions households selected this high speed option, based on information from Kagan Research. Cable modems were not the only means for increasing broadband capacity. DSLs (digital subscriber lines) have also made significant inroads into American homes. As of March 2006, according to the Pew Internet and American Life Project (2006), about 42 percent of Americans have broadband in the home, which enables them to access video content via the Internet.

So what does all of this expansion in technology mean in relationship to our discussion? First, people can interact with religious content continuously. Unlike television where the viewer has to wait for their favorite show to be programmed, the Internet is available 24 hours a day. Broadband allows for the transmission of video, which is widely in evidence on religious sites and makes them more appealing than the static sites of old. Sites associated with popular televangelists have streaming video available for viewing, for example. This is usually much-expanded content from what is available on television, so even though you can watch Joel Osteen's 30-minute program across the country on Sunday morning, you can view the full service (usually an hour or more) online any time of the day, any day of the week. (This will be covered more fully in subsequent chapters.) Second, there are thousands of sites to choose from. Many churches have an online presence, which allows parishioners (and nonmembers as well) to view information about their organizations. In 2001 Barna found that one in three churches had Web sites (Seybert, 2004, p. 18). By 2005 close to 60 percent of Protestant churches had a Web site, representing an increase of 68 percent (Barna Group, 2005). Third, like books and radio, the Internet enables people to test out new faiths—an abundance of new faiths—in private. In 2001 Barna projected "that within this decade as many as 50 million individuals may rely solely upon the Internet to provide all of their faith-based experiences" (Barna Group, 2001). This has not yet happened, but given practitioners propensity for private practice it may still come to pass. Finally, there are opportunities for community online that other forms of media cannot provide and that allow for additional means by which the Internet can provide privatized practice.

Even before the advent of widely available high-speed Internet connections, people were readily going online to retrieve spiritual and religious information. In 2004, Hoover *et al.* found that "64% of wired Americans have used the Internet for spiritual or religious purposes." These religious purposes included e-mail exchanges, reading news accounts about religion, finding out about religious services, and inquiring about holiday celebrations. These researchers also found that people did not use the Internet as their primary form of faith practice but to supplement their offline experiences. Elena Larsen (2004) noted that "more than 3 million people a day get religious or spiritual material" (p. 17) from the Internet. Most use the Internet for solitary purposes rather than interaction with others in this capacity. In light of our discussion, it is interesting to note that while 67 percent of "religious surfers"—Americans who use the Internet to find religious information—accessed information about their own faith, fully 50 percent accessed information about other faiths (p. 18). Perhaps not surprisingly, religious converts are active Internet users, as they use this technology to learn more about their new faith practice.

The Web is also a source for shopping for religious products. Both secular and religious marketers readily use the Internet. Amazon.com, for example, has a special section just for Christian products. As for religious content sites, there are of course thousands of them. Religious retailers sell everything from books to gifts to music to clothing. There are Web sites for all types of practitioners, from AllBibles.com to ChristianBook.com to Spreadtheword. com. More varied content can be found on iExalt.com, which provides chat rooms and movie and book reviews as well as a "Bible Question of the Day" newsletter; parable.com, which is an extensive religious product search engine; and iBelieve.com, which provides recipes in addition to links to Christian commerce sites (Seybert, 2004, p. 19).

While television has historically been the mass purveyor of information about religion, the Internet now adds to the dissemination of religious content. The Internet's key advantages over television include the wealth of information it provides, the 24-hour availability of user-selected content, and the ability it offers users to interact with others of faith either through chat rooms or e-mail. From a marketing perspective, it provides sales opportunities that are fast, customizable, and private.

Conclusion

The marketplace for religious practice has changed because people are free to choose their religion. You can stay with a single faith community for a week, a year, or a decade, or you can attend multiple faith communities simultaneously. Just as it is easier to leave a marriage now than it was 50 years ago, so, too, is it easier to leave your faith community—it's just not that big a deal. In addition, in our consumer culture we have been trained through years of advertising and marketing messages to think in terms of planned obsolescence. This has led to the prevailing belief that for every possession there is something to replace it that is "new and improved." There's always a better iPod, a better microwave, a better husband. Why shouldn't there be a better church, or one that better suits our needs at a particular point in time? Thus it is not just that we can choose our belief system, but that we have a propensity to leave it the minute it doesn't suit our needs.

It is not enough to be released to choose our faith. There also have to be mechanisms in place whereby people can readily and easily find out about possible alternatives. If I don't have to be Catholic but I can't find out about Buddhism, for example, or if I can find out about it but there's no way for me to put my faith into practice, then change is unlikely to occur. But with the introduction of electronic media into the home, information about different religions became available. Specifically, it was the advent of digital television and the Internet in the 1990s that made religious information ubiquitous and plentiful. This abundance of information created an environment in which people could readily create their understanding of truth with a capital T by selecting aspects of multiple faiths and combining them, or by switching from one faith to another to find what best suits their needs.

The ability to choose on the part of the seeker has made the religious marketplace more competitive. Monopoly practices no longer apply because churches cannot take their parishioners for granted. Marketing becomes the means to attract new parishioners as well as retain current ones.

In addition, churches are not competing with just other brick and mortar churches. They are competing with electronic and virtual churches. These "churches" more readily suit the marketing model because they enable seekers to decide not only where to practice, but also when to practice and how to practice, thus freeing religion from time and space. Easily accessible media with a plethora of alternative religious content allows people to practice their faith in the privacy of their own homes (and now with podcasts, anywhere they happen to be). While reading a Bible at home has been commonplace for centuries, it is only in the last decade that people can find almost any information about any belief practice they want 24 hours a day. Television is in 99 percent of American homes, with the majority of these having access to cable and/or satellite, which provide multiple outlets of religious programming. The Internet offers virtually unlimited content that users can access as they see fit. Users can tailor content choices to get "what I want, when I want it"—the goal of any consumer product or service provider.

Moreover, in recent years, religious content has also gotten qualitatively better. Today's televangelists are as well produced as any prime-time television production. Online content is unlimited and continuously available. We can pray, worship, exchange ideas, or take a class any time of the day or night. So, in order to compete with these consumer-oriented choices, churches have to cater to consumers more aggressively, since minimally they are asking religious practitioners to leave their homes to be part of their community. Religious institutions have to make the trip worthwhile.

In aggressively entering the market for leisure time activities (because that is really the category we're talking about), religious organizations find themselves having to take on more and more of the marketing elements used by the culture at large. How else to compete against television, video games, time with the family, sports, and everything else that occupies the lives and minds of Americans today? Beyond the issue of content, which will be discussed later, is the issue of giving up their expertise. Community, stability, and a foundational belief system are the elements of a religious organization's unique selling proposition—the things they have that no one else can offer. Most religious organizations have not found a way to capitalize on these assets. This is evidenced in that for most people (60 percent or more) religion is not experienced within community on a regular basis. Rather, worship as part of a group occurs a couple of times a year. The exception here is megachurches, which we will look at later in this book. These jumbo churches offer a multitude of activities, both religious and secular, that provide myriad opportunities for community, fellowship, and personal connection.

Chapter 3

The business of religion

Mary Baker Eddy, the founder of Christian Science, was arguably the most innovative promoter of religion of the nineteenth and early twentieth centuries. Long before the current explosion in religious publishing, she used a number of now-commonplace marketing techniques to publicize and sell her belief system. She distributed her book *Science and Health* in a secular bookstore; she aggressively used endorsements on the cover her book; and in a particularly innovative move, she designed *Science and Health* to look like a Bible, thus marrying the attributes and benefits associated with that best-selling tome to her own (Tickle, n.d.). In terms of distribution, Eddy again showed her ingenuity. She created Christian Science Reading Rooms, quiet spaces similar to public libraries where anyone could sit and read her books for free. Some have even called the Reading Rooms the first franchise, yet another marketing innovation.

A hundred years later, the religious book market has seen explosive growth beyond anything Mrs. Eddy could have imagined. Even so, she would readily recognize many of her methods being used to sell today's religious products and services, including distribution through secular outlets and packaging a new book to look like a previous best seller. These marketing techniques, as well as others developed in the wake of mass media, have turned the sales of religious products into big business. That growth has led to considerable consolidation among producers within the industry—religious marketers buying up other religious marketers—as well as inter-industry—secular institutions purchasing religious product companies. This is particularly true in book publishing where multinational media conglomerates have bought into this category and brought their significant marketing expertise with them. While we saw in the last chapter that sociological changes increased the prevalence of religious marketing, here we will examine the effect of economic changes on this category.

It is impossible in today's religious marketplace to separate out religion from religious products because they have become so intertwined. The Saddleback Church is the megachurch itself, *and* Rick Warren, *and* his book *The Purpose Driven Life*. These elements are often promoted together just so the success of one will drive the success of the others. For the purposes of understanding economic changes, however, we will look at the religious marketplace mostly in terms of religious products and the growth of religious consultancies, discussing the implications for religious institutions themselves when relevant.

The economics of the religious product market

The changing Christian marketplace

Changes in the religious product category, primarily books and movies, which are the largest and most visible manifestations, began in the mid-1990s. Most insiders trace these changes to the approaching millennium and its doomsday prophecies. Y2K was going to destroy our computers. ATM machines were going to randomly spit out money. An earthquake was going to devastate an entire continent. And on and on it went. Out of this madness rose a book that took the religion category by storm—*Left Behind*, published in 1996. This phenomenally successful book, and then series of books, was based on the "end times" and what would happen to nonbelievers in the event of the apocalypse: they would be "left behind" on a darkened earth while true believers would be brought to Jesus. The series was embraced by Christian consumers, many of whom already believed that the end times were near. While their secular brethren were not as immersed in the doomsday belief, they, too, readily accepted these books. According to a *Time* magazine cover story, evangelicals made up only about half of the series' readership (Gibbs, 2002). In this same article, a Time/CNN poll found the 59 percent of Americans believe in the events in *Revelation*, a widely debated and interpreted book of the New Testament upon which the *Left Behind* series is based. Driving these apocalyptic beliefs were heightened concerns about the fate of the world, particularly in light of the events of September 11 and the subsequent anthrax scares. Sales of the series "jumped 60% after Sept. 11. Book 9, published in October, was the best-selling novel of 2001" (p. 43).

Starting out as a single book, *Left Behind* grew to include 13 books and sold more than 60 million copies, with its final title, *The Rapture*, published in June 2006. In addition to the books, there have been two movies based on the series (they have grossed approximately $100 million), graphic novels, CDs, a separate series for children, and a board game. In late 2006 a computer game of the series was introduced that looks surprisingly like many secular violent and destructive games.[1] Called *Eternal Forces*, this game was made available for pre-sale to those who went to the *Left Behind* Web site. For $5, fans could reserve a copy of the game as well as receive a Sneak Peek Pack, which included key codes for the game, a DVD with the promotional trailer, and a bracelet.

The *Left Behind* series changed the publishing industry in a number of ways. First, the books crossed over from the traditional Christian market to the popular book market, opening up the series to a vastly wider audience. Second, *Left Behind* was the first Christian book to be sold in big box stores and demonstrated for these retailers the revenue that was possible from the Christian market. Today Wal-Mart and Costco regularly stock the top Christian titles. Third, the series showed the level of success that could be achieved with Christian fiction, a segment not previously known for sizable sales. According to Michelle Rapkin, former vice president and director of religion for Doubleday:

> The truth is that unless Christian books could get out of the ghetto of the Christian stores, very little of this could have happened [the explosion in Christian media]. The reason that *Left Behind* did so well was because Barnes & Noble stood up and took note of the fact that within the first few years, something like 50 million copies of *Left Behind* books were published just in America….So the price clubs like Costco started buying these books in massive numbers and they turned into very important outlets that reached people who did not typically go to bookstores…. They were everywhere in the country, and they were discounting them in huge numbers. Books in price clubs have quotas, and they will not be reordered and not placed on the tables unless they sell a very high number of books. And then the publisher kept adding books every other year so there was this appetite that was being fueled more and more so it became like an explosion, and now the booksellers [realized] they can make big sales and so the same thing happened with *The Prayer of Jabez*.
>
> (personal interview, 2006)

Published in 2000, *The Prayer of Jabez: Breaking Through to the Blessed Life*, is a small book—only 93 pages long—that espouses prosperity through devotion. According to the book, by saying a simple prayer every day and reading the entire book once a week, readers will have their prayers answered by God. *Jabez* sold more than eight million copies by the end of its first year and was *the* best-selling book (of all genres) of 2001 (Nawotka, 2006).

Jabez inspired a whole new category—prayer books. The appeal of these books from a sales and marketing perspective is obvious. First, they can be created in multiple formats, such as pocket and gift versions, which are less expensive to produce and are readily bought as impulse purchases. Second, these books can be developed to target specific audiences like women, parents, and children (there is a *Jabez* for women and one for teens, for example). And finally, religious Christians are not the only customers for these books, which is evidenced in the increase in sales of these books in general bookstores as well as via the Internet.

One other book, *The Purpose Driven Life*, built on the success of *Left Behind*, further demonstrating the broad appeal that could be derived from Christian texts in the secular market. *The Purpose Driven Life: What on Earth Am I Here For?* provides 40 days of "points to ponder," "verses to remember," and "questions to consider." Published in 2002, this book has sold more than 25 million copies and is the best-selling nonfiction hardcover book of all time (Saroyan, 2006). Like *Left Behind* and *Jabez*, *The Purpose Driven Life* was distributed through secular retailers including big box stores and major book chains. *The Purpose Driven Life* had one other channel of distribution that contributed significantly to its bottom line: churches. While most people have heard of the book, what they do not know is that the book is the text for a church course called 40 Days of Purpose. Churches that decide they want to become a Purpose Driven church receive copies of the book at a steep discount to distribute to all their church members. This is not to negate the success of this book—25 million copies is a lot of books—but rather to show an important means of distribution. What better endorsement for a product than the local church leader?

The success of these books at the beginning of the millennium put religious titles at the top of the best-selling fiction and nonfiction lists for the first time ever (Salamon, 2003). The combination of cultural phenomena that led to heightened spiritual interest (millennial fever, September 11) and expanded distribution resulted in heretofore unseen commercial success in this category. One last thing that drove the success of these books was the rise in evangelism, which has a tradition of passing books on to others. According to Michelle Rapkin:

> For devout Evangelical Christians, one of their purposes in life is to evangelize, and what better way to evangelize than to give books away. The Christian marketplace has a huge gift giving statistic....I did a book called *Travel Back to Heaven* a couple of years ago and it wasn't one of those major books but it did quite well and people would write in and say, "I read this book and I loved it and bought a dozen copies." And you don't think that happened with *Left Behind* and *Purpose Driven Life*? You can think of a whole church worth of people. So the numbers really explode in a way. I may love a new novel, but I am not going to buy you a copy no matter how much I like it.
>
> (personal interview, 2006)

While these three books are held up as the shining examples, they were not the only publishing successes in the religion category. The 1990s saw an overall expansion of religious and spiritual books, making it the fastest-growing adult book category. At the same time One Spirit, a spiritually oriented offshoot of Book-of-the-Month Club, became the "fastest-growing club in the company's history" (Harrison, 1997, p. 22). One book wholesaler reported a 249 percent increase in the category in the mid-1990s. Strong sales continued into the new millennium. While sales figures are heavily guarded by the industry, and there are mixed reports about the level of growth (one source says 50 percent, another 7 percent, another 4 percent), there is no disagreement that the category is growing. In 2004 there were more than 14,000 religious/spiritual books published, which makes it the fourth largest category only after fiction (28,010), juveniles (21,161), and sociology/economics (17,518) (Grabois, 2005). In 2004 religious books sold $1.9 billion, up from $1.5 billion only four years earlier, and there are estimates that the category will reach $2.5 billion by 2008 (Dooley *et al.*, 2006). While still small in terms of the overall category (total book sales in 2004 was more than $28 billion), the important thing to bear in mind is that the industry overall remains stagnant due to competition from alternative media sources; the religion/spirituality category is one of the few areas of steady growth in book publishing.

Religious book executives—sellers as well as industry analysts—peg this sustained interest in religion not to single book titles but to a number of cultural factors, both personal and global. According to Lynn Garrett of *Publishers Weekly*, "Religion is just so much a part of the cultural conversation these days, because of global terrorism and radical Islam. People want to understand those things. They're looking to go more deeply into the religious traditions" (Charles, 2004, p. 11). Phyllis Tickle, former religion editor of *Publishers Weekly* and author of numerous books on religion, attributes the industry's success to something more personal—people's reluctance to change their public selves. "We are especially slow to express aloud religious beliefs or visibly pursue religious patterns that are too divergent from those of our community. Books are private. Books don't tell, especially in matters of the spirit" (Harrison, 1997, p. 22). Others have attributed the success to the aging of the baby boomers. Lyn Cryderman, vice president and associate publisher at Zondervan, home of *The Purpose Driven Life*, has said, "They hit age 50 and they start asking, 'What significance do I have?' and 'What mark am I making?'" (Nelson and Garrett, 2004, p. S4). Michelle Rapkin summed up the zeitgeist perfectly:

By 2000 the baby boomers are just about fifty years old. So the biggest section of the entire population is beginning to learn about mortality. Their parents are really old, and they have to take care of them. They have to face up to their parents' mortality and their own mortality. And if that wasn't enough, the economy busts in 2000...and on top of that, 9/11 happened. So it is not just about age, it's about the fact that nobody knows what will happen. So now you have our whole country on high alert and everyone is thinking about that. And when you are getting older and you are watching your parents fail and die, and now a plane crashes into the World Trade Center and kills 3,000 Americans on our own soil, you start thinking about God.

Segmenting categories and audiences for maximum growth

Bibles remain the leading segment in the religious category, though most of them don't look anything like traditional, staid, black books of scripture. There are more than 50 different versions of the Bible, including the *King James Version* and *The New International Version* (NIV). There are numerous translations and specialized editions created for different audiences. One of the hottest demographics, for example, is the teen or young adult market. In terms of Bibles, products for this group have been some of the most successful—and the most controversial. *Refuel* and *Revolve* are Bibles that look like teen magazines and are targeted at guys and girls respectively. They feature tips on dating next to tips on how to live your faith. *Revolve* sold 150,000 copies in the first six months of its publication, making it the best-selling Bible in Christian bookstores (Boorstin, 2003).

Teens, of course, are not the only segment for Bibles. To appeal to more harried, older adults, publishers are creating religious texts that can be consumed in a minimal amount of time. *The 100-Minute Bible* gives readers the scripture in 64 pages, and *The HCSB Light Speed Bible* covers the key points of the Old and New Testaments in 24 hours. These books demonstrate a trend readily apparent in the secular market where producers cater to consumers' time constraints. For example, Stephen Hawking has recently published *A Briefer History of Time*, Shakespeare's plays are being produced in abridged versions that run less than two hours, and we're now seeing yoga classes that last for 30 minutes (Aucoin, 2005).

Christian Living is the second biggest segment in the religious book category and an area that has shown significant growth in the last decade. Because it is seen as the venue through which to increase sales, it is generating the most interest among publishers, both religious and nonreligious alike. Christian Living covers a broad spectrum of titles, but fundamentally it is about making Christianity widely accessible by relating religious and spiritual themes in a practical way to life and relationships. Included in this category are the *Left Behind* books, *The Purpose Driven Life*, *The Prayer of Jabez*, *God Chasers*, and *The Passion of Jesus Christ*, among many others.

Beyond the subject matter of the books themselves, much of the appeal of Christian Living titles come from the fact that they are nondenominational. *The Purpose Driven Life* and *Jabez* attract a large audience because they do not espouse a particular faith tradition. Thus Christian Living titles are purchased by practicing and nonpracticing Christians alike. This nondenominationalism and wider appeal are what allow for them to be sold through secular retail outlets, providing exposure to a large audience of Americans who would not ever enter a Christian bookstore. In addition, Christian publishers have become very savvy in how they market these books, making them indistinguishable from secular works.

> The books are implicitly, rather than explicitly, evangelical. The titles don't sound religious, the colophon (the publisher's logo printed on a book's spine) has no obvious religious significance, and the only clues to the author's Christian bona-fides, such as an affiliation with a church, are likely to be buried in the jacket copy, if they appear at all.
>
> (Nawotka, 2006, p. 2)

Because women are the primary purchasers of religious titles, Christian Living titles cater to their needs and interests, particularly in terms of family, relationships, and prayer. The importance of women to this market is evidenced by publishing house Thomas Nelson's Women of Faith division, which sponsors annual motivational conferences to further support this target audience. This group hosted close to 30 conferences attended by approximately 400,000 participants (Packaged Facts, 2004, p. 79).

A popular subgenre of Christian Living that developed in the 1990s was the "marketplace Christians" movement. According to an article in *Christianity Today*, "foremost in the minds of marketplace Christians is a vision for equipping evangelicals to be in decision-making positions of power in mainstream society" (Tapia and Stream, 1995, p. 103). This was a movement that began in the 1980s but did not start taking hold until the mid-1990s. Hundreds of book titles, including *Jesus CEO* and *The Heart Aroused: Poetry and the Preservation of Soul in Corporate America*, were published that address faith in the workplace. This mixture of faith and business was not limited to Christianity, however. In June 1995, *BusinessWeek* ran a story about spirituality in the workplace, outlining the increasing number of companies that were providing exposure to spiritual practices for their employees. This included a broad spectrum of institutions from such stalwarts as the World Bank and Boeing to more hippy establishments like Tom's of Maine (Galen and West, 1995). This subgenre has long-term sustainability as seen by new momentum in the early 2000s in the wake of the Enron scandal. With a focus on ethics as well as faith, Christian book publishers came out with a number of titles like *Life @ Work on Leadership: Enduring Insights for Men and Women of Faith* and *Running with the Giants: What Old Testament Heroes Want You to Know About Life and Leadership*, by John Maxwell, author of the business best seller *The 21 Irrefutable Laws of Leadership*. From a business perspective, spirituality in the workplace was seen as a way to improve productivity. From a publishing perspective, it was a marriage made in heaven because business, like religion, is a growth area in publishing.

Kids have always been an important market for booksellers of all kinds. For the Christian market, books and other materials for Sunday school and for summer Bible classes are a big part of their marketing efforts. Campaigns targeting children have expanded into the secular arena due to the success of *Veggie Tales*, the first Christian children's video series to have significant crossover sales. These videos opened the door for other marketers, including book publishers, to release products targeting the "faith-based" youth market. Some of the larger publishers have special divisions, like Zondervan's ZonderKidz, which publishes the *Veggie Tales* books, and Tommy Nelson from Thomas Nelson, which publishes NIV for kids.[2]

While *Left Behind* did little to hide the fact that its content had a Christian orientation, *Veggie Tales* was more obtuse. Unless you knew that *Veggie Tales* books were for evangelicals, it would be difficult to determine that merely from looking at the merchandising or even by reading most of the book. It is only at the end of the books that you will find mention of God and a life lesson, but even then it would be difficult to determine the persuasion of the authors. This more subtle approach was very successful for these products and aided in their breaking into the secular kids' market—a difficult category to enter. When it comes to targeting the children's market with religiously based content, publishers are competing against general entertainment companies that are better funded and more pervasive (think Disney or Nickelodeon). Further, for religious marketers producing media for kids that will be used outside a classroom is still in its nascent stages. There are few if any religious media that specifically target kids though this is rapidly changing (Packaged Facts, 2004, p. 71). Producers will likely find success by replicating the *Veggie Tales* formula: secular formats that are familiar to children, a product that appeals to the parents as well as the children, and no mention of Jesus (Warren, 2005).

Alternatively producers and publishers can alter Christian products slightly and thereby target both Christian and secular markets. *Jay Jay the Jet Plane*, a children's television show airing on PBS, has used just such a dual marketing strategy to promote its products. *Jay Jay* was created by David Michel, a producer and holder of a master's degree in divinity who wanted to spread the good word. Michel understood the value of both the Christian and the secular markets, and he did not want to miss either one. Therefore the product, with slight variation, is marketed to the groups separately. *Jay Jay* programs that have appeared on PBS are distributed to the secular market by Columbia TriStar. Programs related to specific Bible verses are distributed by Tommy Nelson. Books and toys are also separately distributed based on their level of religious content (Salamon, 2003).

Other audiences that are new for this category are the tween, teen, and 20-something religious consumer. Research shows that these groups represent a substantial prospective market. According to a University of Pennsylvania study, religion is important to close to 90 percent of tweens and teens, and two-thirds attend worship services. Similarly, Synovate, an international marketing research firm, "found that 92 percent of teens believe in God" (Packaged Facts, 2004, p. 70). Recently MediaVest, a major buyer of advertising in all media, did a study about the youth market. In the course of that work, it found that teens were spending their free time in Bible clubs. According to Jane Lacher, vice president and director of research at MediaVest, "They were admitting to it openly. That's not something that would have been cool to do a few years ago...It's cool to be religious" (Mandese, 2004, p. 10). All of this suggests that teens would purchase products if they were made available.

Offerings for this group were not readily in evidence at the 2006 Christian Booksellers Association (CBA) Retail Show, the largest international trade show for Christian retailers. Clothing—particularly T-shirts—seemed to be the primary merchandise to sell to teen consumers as opposed to books or other product options. One booth that grabbed my attention was that of C28, which I later found out stood for Colossians 2:8. The product line included goth-style T-shirts, bags, and jewelry with a logo containing the letters notw. These were far and away the hippest things I'd seen at the show. One T-shirt had the word "Blessed" emblazoned across the chest. When you got closer to the shirt you could read the rest of the text, which said, "Blessed are those whose transgressions are forgiven, whose sins are covered, Romans 4:7".

The designer of the products was at the booth and I asked him what "notw" stood for, and he told me: Not of this world. "Do people in general know this?" I asked. He said no, but that when people see the designs they want to know more about it. He explained that the company started in Southern California but they had gotten so many requests for their products that they began supplying other retailers. As I was leaving, he gave me a CD. "What is this?" I asked. It was the testimony of the company's founder, Aurello F. Barreto, a successful California businessman who became a millionaire in his thirties. When I returned home, I learned that C28 now has six stores targeted to the young Christian market. It is obvious that Barreto is bringing experience from his early success to the religious market, particularly in his knowing that he has to get his audience where they are. Says Barreto, "Our mission is to share the grace, the truth and the love of Jesus....And what better place to do it than a mall?" (Walker, 2005, p. 28).

A more difficult group to define than kids or tweens is the 20-something market. In churches, for example, there is not a specific place for them because they can be a disparate group. They are too old for youth group. They may or may not yet be married. They are becoming adults, but in many ways they have teen sensibilities. The same inability to define the 20-something market existed in the book and product category. But that is changing, in large part due to Relevant Media, a Web site and publishing company geared toward teens and 20-somethings. Their target audience is "God-hungry, mainstream-savvy 20-somethings" (Kiesling, 2003, p. 130). Relevant's tagline is: "God.

Life. Progressive Culture." This reflects its product line, which includes the best-selling books *Walk On: The Spiritual Journey of U2* and *The Gospel According to Tony Soprano*. The company's magazine, *Relevant*, is a mix of articles about faith and life issues relevant to 20-somethings. A recent issue had a cover story about the punk rock/alternative group Thrice as well as articles about managing debt, the emergent church movement, and Stephen Colbert. *Relevant* is distributed through Christian outlets as well as Barnes & Noble. Cameron Strang, founder of Relevant Media, explains the need for content created specifically for this audience:

> The church doesn't know what to do [when young people question faith], they kind of freak out because their whole thing of faith is belief so, if you start to ask questions, that's seen as doubts. But the thing is that we're not doubting, we want an authentic faith[,] we're seeking things, we want a relevant faith, a faith that matters, a faith that's worth living and dying for.
>
> (Divine Profits, 2004)

Relevant is providing for this target audience what it often cannot get at the local church—even if the services include rock music.

A number of traditional presses have created special product lines to tap this emerging market—Thomas Nelson's Transit and Tyndale House's Thirsty?, for example. Transit is probably best known for *Revolve* and *Refuel*, the Bibles that look like fashion magazines. Thirsty? has published a metal-covered Bible for teens as well as titles like *Walking with Frodo* and the *Degrees of Guilt* series, which tells the story of three high school students and their responses to the death of a classmate. Tyndale also published a tween version of the *Left Behind* series for 10 to 14 year olds.

Zondervan has gotten into the market by focusing on teen body image, with the titles *Mirror, Mirror: Reflections on Who You Are, Who You'll Become*, and *Secret Power for Girls: Identity, Security, and Self-Respect in Troubling Times*. In a very clever marketing move, "the publisher plans to distribute copies of the book to stores that have cafes so they can scatter them around the tables—and hopefully draw the attention of young readers, 'who are so much more visually oriented,' said marketing vp John Topliff" (Kiesling, 2003, p. 130).

Religious book publishing and retailing has seen extensive changes in the past decade (Borden, 2007). Broadly, the category has seen more non-denominational titles, a larger array of Christian Living titles that marry religion with popular culture, and increasing distribution through non-Christian retailers. As we can see, there is considerable segmentation in the book business, with products targeting specific audiences like women, kids, and teens and young adults. Like the secular marketplace, religious book publishers reflect the latest trends and tastes of consumers. In the wake of *Left Behind*, Christian fiction is exploding. Christian chick lit—fiction for women—is a particularly popular segment at this time. Religious diet books have also become a hot trend over the past five years. As Rapkin said, "Whatever is happening in the secular arena, it has its counterpart in the Christian arena."

Non-Christian markets

I have focused so far on the Christian book market because it is the source of many of the faith brands. Having a book and/or a television ministry are key means of creating and maintaining a brand image. However I do not want to leave the impression that books about other religions are not popular as well or that they do not use the same segmentation strategies or target the same audiences. They absolutely do. Kabbalah, for instance, has generated significant sales and interest in the last five to ten years. New Age titles continue to have large readerships. Top authors here include Marianne Williamson, Deepak Chopra, and Neale Donald Walsch. These books, too, are heavily promoted to women, but there are also titles for parents, kids, and other defined segments. Unlike the Christian marketplace where books were primarily published by independent booksellers, most of these New Age titles have been released by major publishing houses. And as we will see, these same publishing houses have also moved into Christian publishing, changing the economic structure of the Christian marketplace.

Bigger players and increasing consolidation

The Christian book industry is an amalgam of a couple of large independently owned presses, a few multinational media conglomerates, a handful of mid-sized presses, and dozens of small independents. The two major independent religious publishers are Thomas Nelson and Tyndale House, publishers of the *New King James Bible* and *Revolve*, and the *New Living Translation (NLT)* and the *Left Behind* series respectively. The major international conglomerates in this category are Newscorp (parent of Zondervan, publisher of *The Purpose Driven Life* and the *New International Version* Bible, and HarperCollins San Francisco), Bertelsmann (Random House), and Hachette (Warner Faith, which was part of Time Warner until it was sold to Hachette in 2006). Warner Faith is home to Joel Osteen, Joyce Meyer, and most recently Creflo Dollar. Mid-size presses include Multnomah Publishers (*Prayer of Jabez*), Harvest House (*The Power of Praying* series, a top-selling Christian series since 1995), and Shambhala Publications (producer of a wide range of alternative religion and New Age works, which are distributed through Random House's sales force).

New religious imprints and consolidation within the industry have occurred in response to the broadened appeal of religious products, particularly those in the Christian Living category. Large multinationals have been buying smaller religious publishers (as well as music and film divisions), and smaller religious publishers are merging to compete in a more aggressive marketplace. The earliest example of a large corporation entering this category is Newscorp's purchase of Zondervan, which occurred in 1988. Long before *The Purpose Driven Life*, Rupert Murdoch saw the value in this underserved market. Newscorp continues to visualize growth in religious media as evidenced by its creation of a new division called FoxFaith, which was formed in 2006 to produce faith-based video products. Whether movies or books, Newscorp brings significant marketing strength and the ability to cross-promote products across its media ventures. Random House has a number of divisions devoted to religious content, including Bell Tower (sacred teachings), Three Rivers Press (religious and spiritual values), Doubleday Religious Publishing (religious works), Doubleday Image (paperbacks), and Schocken (Jewish fiction and nonfiction). It also established an evangelical division called Waterbrook in 1998. As its Web site states:

> As a division of Random House, Inc.—the largest publisher in the world—WaterBrook's task is to build a major presence in the Christian Booksellers Association, competing with the top Christian publishers in our market today....We believe that our experienced leadership team in all departments brings a level of expertise and an informed and unified publishing approach that is on par with the best—while we continually endeavor to explore new tracks to take us toward increased measures of success.
>
> (Waterbrook Press, n.d.)

All of this suggests that major publishers enter the Christian marketplace fully expecting to compete—and beat—the existing players. Finally, in a major acquisition Hachette purchased Warner Faith from Time Warner in 2006. On the surface this might suggest a change in the industry—why would a large company like Time Warner want to divest itself of what appears to be a growing category? It turns out that Time Warner sold off its entire publishing division in an effort to streamline its businesses. This was not a comment on religious publishing but rather a strategy based on where Time Warner believes the media industry is headed. But for Hachette as well as the other media giants, the religion category appears to be a profitable one. Moreover, these multinational media giants bring expertise in multiple marketing and retail areas. Newscorp, Bertelsmann, and Hachette are all experts in publishing *and* music *and* video entertainment, allowing them to cross-promote products across divisions.

As for consolidation of smaller publishers, Thomas Nelson purchased World Bible Publishers (Milliot, 2003); Ave Maria Press purchased three divisions of RCL Enterprises (Holt, 2003); and Baker Book House acquired Bethany House Publishers (Milliot, 2002). These companies are not as well known as the aforementioned media giants, but the point here is that smaller presses have had to merge in order to compete.

Traditional religion publishers are not only competing with large multitargeted publishers, but also with publishers that specialize in a single target market. A good example of this is the publisher Scholastic, which specializes in children's books. This company entered the Christian market in 2006 by creating the *Read and Learn Bible*, written in partnership with the American Bible Society. Scholastic brings more than 85 years of marketing expertise, including its phenomenal success in promoting Harry Potter and Clifford the Big Red Dog. Scholastic's production capabilities would lead us to expect that they will produce video or television productions in conjunction with these titles. Thus the combination of competition with specialized publishers and large multinational publishers is forcing religious publishers to become larger and more marketing adept.

An important contributing factor in the consolidation of the publishing side of the business is the changes that have occurred in Christian retailing. Whereas once this retail segment was made up almost exclusively of independent Christian booksellers, now big box stores like Costco and Sam's Club, as well as mass-market retailers like Target and K-Mart, are key elements of any marketing plan. Wal-Mart—the retail behemoth that dominates sales in the vast majority of consumer products—has discovered the Christian market in recent years. According to *Forbes*, in 2003 Wal-Mart sold an estimated $1 billion in Christian-themed items. Wal-Mart has carried Christian-themed books and music for years, but it is only recently that the increase in consumer demand was enough to warrant additional attention and product lines. Wal-Mart's product lines vary by store, but in general the retailer has approximately 550 "inspirational" music titles and 1,200 "inspirational" books, which are primarily Bibles and best sellers. And that's just media items. According to Wal-Mart's spokeswoman Danette Thompson, "In our jewelry department, we have seen an increase in sales of inspirational jewelry such as cross necklaces and Bible charms" (Howell, 2004, p. 4).

To handle the demands of these outlets, publishers have to be larger as well.

Most publishers have established aggressive sales divisions focused singularly on the secular channel. In the mid-1990s (and before) a Christian publisher might have one or two people assigned to "work with" secular channels. It is not uncommon today to find a vice president of mass-market sales leading a large staff of aggressive sales people.

(Seybert, 2004, p. 31)

Whereas small independent retailers dominated this category even ten years ago, now their numbers are significantly reduced. These independent booksellers are members of the Christian Booksellers Association (CBA), an organization whose membership shrunk from approximately 3,000 in the 1990s to 2,370 by 2004 (Italie, 2004, p. A16). At the 2006 CBA retail show there were a little more than 9,100 attendees (CBA, 2006); this is in comparison to more than 14,000 participants in 1999 (Garrett and Tickle, 1999, p. 12).[3] Paralleling these figures is the decline in sales through Christian specialty stores. In the mid-1990s, retail sales in such stores were 70 percent of the market; by 2002 they had dropped precipitously to 40 percent (Seybert, 2004). In less than a decade secular outlets had overtaken the majority of the category sales.

In addition, competition from online outlets has affected Christian publishing. *Glorious Appearing*, part of the *Left Behind* series, was the number-one fiction title on the Barnes & Noble Web site shortly after its release in 2004. Through both online and in-store sales, the company "sold more than 48,000 copies the week it was released. At Amazon.com, 'Glorious Appearing' was the No. 14 best seller on April 8. Not far behind at No. 18 was 'The Purpose-Driven Life…'" (Howell, 2004). The advances of secular online retailers into this space is particularly hard on Christian retailers because online services are much more attractive to young consumers. Future book buyers are not establishing a habit of shopping at a Christian bookseller, which has long-term consequences for this industry.

No one is questioning the continuing value of religious publishing. The 1990s saw the start up of a number of Christian divisions within established companies and mergers among smaller ones. Consolidation and acquisitions continue. In 2006, Thomas Nelson was sold to a private equity company. The news at the 2006 CBA show was that Multnomah, the publisher of *Jabez*, was up for sale and the expected buyer was Random House. The industry is predicted to continue to consolidate in response to the changing retail environment. As consolidation increases, so too will competition and marketing.

Movies

The expansion of religious messages into the secular marketplace took off in the mid-1990s with the book industry. In the mid-2000s, a similar growth trend occurred in film. We are all aware of the phenomenal success of *The Passion of the Christ*. Beyond the box office revenues, which were in the hundreds of millions of dollars, the film sold 4.1 million DVDs on the first day of its release, making it the fastest-selling R-rated film in history (Hettrick, 2004). Like the book category, mega-retailers had a hand in the product's success. For example, Sam's Club, a division of Wal-Mart, sold bulk packs, called "churchpacks," of 50 DVDs or VHS tapes. These were marketed to churches, theological schools, and other religious organizations. "In light of the megaministry trend, and the majority of ministries having libraries and/ or bookstores with items for resale, this is the perfect synergy," said Sam's Club spokeswoman Jolanda Stewart (Casabona, 2004, p. 26). Bulk packs were also offered through record and video stores like Tower Records and Blockbuster Video.

In the wake of *The Passion*, other major studios produced movies that have generated considerable consumer interest. A number of them are employing the marketing strategies used by the producers of *The Passion*. An example of this is *The Chronicles of Narnia*, produced by Walden Media, a producer of family-friendly content, and distributed by Disney:

> Before the November opening of Walt Disney Pictures' $100 million adaptation of C. S. Lewis' *The Chronicles of Narnia: The Lion, The Witch, and the Wardrobe*, the studio partnered with faith-based outreach firm Motive Marketing to hit some of the same evangelical Christian markets as Gibson's *The Passion*. Armed with an estimated $6 million budget, the firm arranged sneak-peek religious-media screenings and launched a Web site, narniaresources.com, offering testimonials and workbooks to spur church-group discussion of the story's biblical allegories. In addition, EMI's Christian Music Group released a soundtrack of songs inspired by Narnia even before the film's secular soundtrack was complete.
>
> (Schmelzer, 2006a, p. 8)[4]

In the fall of 2006, in conjunction with Nickelodeon pictures, Walden Media released *Charlotte's Web*, which is not specifically a religious title but one that was heavily promoted at the CBA retail show. Walden Media has a tie to the Christian community via its owner Philip F. Anschutz, who is a supporter of the Christian right. Promoting through the CBA demonstrates that the company would be using religious retailers as promotional partners for this family-friendly film. This was also in evidence in the movie's marketing tagline: "This Christmas, help is coming from above." The relationship between Walden Media and Christian retailers continued into 2007, when Walden released *Amazing Grace: The William Wilberforce Story*.

As mentioned earlier, Newscorp created a subdivision called FoxFaith. This division's mission is to produce faith-based films every 18 months. FoxFaith also owns backlist titles that are appropriate for the whole family, such as 20th Century Fox musicals as well as children's videos like the *Strawberry Shortcake* series and *Garfield* (the animated series, not the live-action one). The company's Web site, www.foxfaith.com, includes a special section for films designated for use in churches. Church leaders can purchase these films and download for free accompanying church resources like video clips and pdf files of booklets that provide discussion guides to be used with the films. The guides include suggested Bible readings and questions for discussion.

A number of new movie companies have emerged to produce faith-based fare. Good News Holdings is a company that was created in 2005 specifically to produce "faith-based content in multimedia formats" (Fleming, 2006, p. 1). Its first significant project will be a film adaptation of Anne Rice's *Christ the Lord: Out of Egypt*. Another faith-based multimedia company is TDJ Enterprises, a for-profit division of T. D. Jakes, a well-known televangelist and author. TDJ Enterprises recently entered into a three-year production and distribution deal with Sony Pictures. The first project is *Not Easily Broken*, a film based on a novel by Jakes. While Sony says it is targeting African Americans rather than a religious niche, given Jakes' involvement it is hard to see how the two could be separated. *Not Easily Broken* is not Sony's first foray into religious content. Sony successfully distributed and marketed *The Gospel*, a film about an R&B singer who finds faith. The bottom-line appeal of these films is easy to see. *The Gospel* was produced for $3 million and grossed $17 million at the box office (LaPorte, 2006, p. 11).

As in the book category, subgenres for specially targeted audiences are seen as growth areas. In the kids' market, the undisputed leader is *Veggie Tales*. These talking vegetables, led by Larry the Cucumber and Bob the Tomato, started out as a video series for evangelical Christians. Like the *Left Behind* books, they found a larger audience—non-Christian children and, surprisingly, teen- and college-age Christians. Not stopping at videos, Big Idea—the creators of *Veggie Tales*—produced a movie for theaters called *Jonah: A Veggie Tales Movie*. Budget overruns of this film and a breach-of-contract dispute led to the company's bankruptcy and a subsequent takeover by secular producer Classic Media in 2003, but *Jonah* was both a box office and DVD success. When the DVD was launched, "it was accompanied by a multimillion dollar marketing campaign and joint promotions with retail and merchandising partners including Applebee's, Auntie Anne's and Chuck E. Cheese restaurants, Sea World and Curad Bandages" (Packaged Facts, 2004, p. 58). And while *Left Behind* was a book series that branched out into movies, *Veggie Tales* reversed the process by starting as visual media and then becoming a series of books published by ZonderKidz.[5]

Another subgenre is that of specific denominations. Interestingly there now exists films for members of the Church of Jesus Christ of Latter-day Saints. These Mormon-centric films include *The Best Two Years*, *God's Army*, and *The Singles Ward* (Leydon, 2004, p. 13). The films have a built-in audience through the LDS church, and when their religious message is more subtle, there has been some crossover to audiences outside the church.

Christian titles are not the only examples of subgenres. There is increasing interest in the New Age category. This has, on the face of it, a less organized audience base, but the success of one film, *What the Bleep Do We Know?*, spurred the possibility for expanding these types of films. The movie was an overwhelming success at the box office and even spawned a conference. Made for $500,000, the movie initially grossed $10 million by February 2005 through Saturday morning screenings at traditional movie theaters as well as at New Age churches. Meyer Gottlieb, president of Samuel Goldwyn Films, says that he "sees the film as part of a worldwide interest in New Age themes that generate hundreds of millions of dollars from books, videos and conferences...There's a sizable audience out there. We just have to do a better job of creating programming for them" (Higgins, 2005, p. 6). The film is heavily promoted at New Age expos and fairs, and because of the complexity of the film, many audience members have seen the film multiple times.

Books allow consumers to privately consume and sample various religious ideas, but it is movies that provide an entertaining means of learning about religion outside the home. One participant in a church course told me that she often uses movies to help clarify difficult religious concepts for herself, and she tells friends to see certain films if she feels she can not explain a religious concept on her own. Movies are important for a couple of reasons. First, they are heavily promoted and so religious content gets considerable exposure in the culture. Second, many religious films are produced inexpensively, and even a modest return makes these films profitable. This has attracted new producers to the category.

Music

While music is not a focus of this book, we cannot ignore the Christian music business completely due to its increased popularity over the last decade. Christian and gospel music accounted for $845 million in sales in 2002, representing close to 7 percent of the industry, up from only 3.2 percent in 1993 (RIAA statistics quoted in Seybert, 2004, pp. 21–2). As with the book category, Christian music has been brought to the fore by the major multinational media conglomerates. Because of this, while we may or may not (depending on our age and religious inclinations) be aware of Christian music brands, it is likely that they will continue to become more a part of our culture due to the marketing presence of the larger media institutions.

The three major labels in the category are Word Entertainment, Provident Music Group, and Chordant, owned by Time Warner, Bertelsmann, and EMI respectively. Time Warner purchased Word Entertainment in 2002, and the company is a leader in music and video, with 35 percent of the Christian video market. Provident's purchase by Bertelsmann occurred in the same year, and the company is part of RCA Nashville, which is a subsidiary of BMG music. This company, too, serves the video and audio segments of the industry as well as being a leader in children's audio. EMI has been a leader in this category for more than a decade after it released the unexpected hit *Chant* in 1994, which sold 2.5 million copies. An album of Gregorian chants digitally remixed for a younger audience, *Chant* was marketed to popular music retail outlets after another version of the CD had done surprisingly well on European pop charts. Chordant is the distribution division of the company and the outlet for EMI Christian Music Group (CMG) products. CMG was started in 1992 with the purchase of Sparrow, which was combined with Forefront to focus on Christian rock music. Bill Hearn, who sold Sparrow to EMI, says, "We've found that when you put this music in front of the masses, they will buy it. They just don't know it's there" (Peyser, 2001, p. 48). How right Mr. Hearn was. As marketing and promotion increased under the auspices of large media companies, so did Christian music sales.

These three producers dominate the Christian music industry. Word has a market share of 31.26 percent; Chordant has a market share of 29.92 percent; and Provident has a market share of 29.03 percent (Christian Music Trade Association, Soundscan 2002 Year-End Industry Report, quoted in Packaged Facts, 2004). These market shares are made up of several music genres (p. 55) including:

> Gospel (19% share) and Adult Contemporary (18% share) ... Praise & Worship (13% share), Rock (13% share), Country (7% share), Children's (7% share), Inspirational (4% share), Instrumental (4% share) and Southern (3% share).

By the early 2000s, Contemporary Christian Music (CCM) was the fastest growing segment of the music industry. Much of CCM's success has to do with bands that have branched out beyond the sappy lyrics of old. CCM runs the stylistic gamut from alternative rock to Latin to underground. The category is defined as music with "faith-based lyrics"; the sound can be anything. This less strict definition of Christian music has made this type of entertainment a vehicle for merging the religious with the secular. The success of the record label Wind Up demonstrates this. Wind Up represents a number of artists like Creed, 12 Stones, and Evanescence, none of which are dogmatically Christian. The label promotes its artists through both Christian outlets (advertising and CD samplers of the bands in *CCM Magazine*, a Christian music publication, as well as marketing via the Inspiration Network, a religious cable network) and secular ones (heavy rotation on mainstream music channels such as VH1 and MTV). Just as in the publishing industry, music companies have found the importance of a dual marketing strategy.

Another important aspect of this industry is the concerts that promote CCM artists. Christian music festivals are popular with tweens, young adults, and parents. Church groups are bused in for these events, giving them official endorsement. These events are also huge opportunities for secular marketers. Disney sponsors "Night of Joy" and Universal sponsors "Rock the Universe," both CCM events in Orlando, Florida, that attract upwards of 30,000 people. A number of brands, including General Mills, Disney, McDonald's, Target, JCPenney, Pepsi, Doritos, John Frieda, and Cover Girl, have used CCM artists to represent their products (Seybert, 2004, p. 24). This gives more exposure for CCM overall and at the same time it promotes these products to the Christian market.

And finally, not to be left out of the music download business, Christian inspiration has its own Web site, Songtouch.com. This site debuted with 15,000 songs that, like iTunes, can be purchased for $0.99. The site was created by Howard Rachinski, founder of the Church Copyright License, an organization that lets religious groups copy and distribute music for their congregations (Cole, 2005, p. 19). This was not the first such site. In 2003 LifeWay Christian Stores, the nonprofit division of the Southern Baptist Convention, began a Christian music service that sells songs for $0.99 per download.

The secularization of Christian music presents an interesting dilemma for evangelicals. Popular music is by definition for young people and most young people do not frequent traditional Christian retailers or listen to Christian media. Therefore this product had to be promoted in secular outlets. However, for many CCM fans, the music became their "church," replacing traditional religious practices.

> The lines between sacred and secular became increasingly blurry as the Christian music industry promoted a consumer-oriented culture that copied, even in some sense usurped, many functions of institutional religion. Concerts became worship services or evangelistic meetings. Consumer commodities (CDs, T-shirts, and other paraphernalia) became symbols representing religious faith. For some evangelical fans, social rituals, like going to a Christian concert or listening to a gospel recording on headphones, could qualify as a religious experience as much as attending a church service with a local congregation.
>
> All this was not without effect. Turning mass recordings and rock tours into a form of "ministry" took church pastoring from the world of local, personal relationships, premised on trust and familiarity, into the impersonal world of entertainment, characterized by the market-driven terms of production and consumer choice.
>
> (Romanowski, 2000, pp. 111–12)

As with the book market, the wide exposure in the broader culture brought CCM to the attention of the larger music industry, making the music less about evangelizing and more about business. Whether these concert goers will ultimately become churchgoers as they age is still unknown. However the trend of incorporating more rock music in the church is easily understood given the external competition.

Marketing religious products

Campaigns that target churches are a predominant form of marketing in the religious category. As we have seen, churches are a source of product and message distribution as well as being unpaid endorsers of products. This includes everything from books to films to political candidates, which will be discussed later.

The *Passion*'s church marketing campaign, discussed in Chapter 1, was hugely successful in driving sales for that film, but its producers did not invent this technique. Peter Maresco (2004), in his article "Mel Gibson's *The Passion of the Christ*: Market Segmentation, Mass Marketing and Promotion, and the Internet," outlines a history of Bible-based movie marketing beginning with *The King of Kings* in 1927. The film was prescreened by women's groups in New York and religious groups throughout the country. Children were even given time off from school to attend the film after its opening. Five years later Paramount used a three-pronged strategy to promote *The Sign of the Cross*. General moviegoers were enticed by the spectacle of the film, direct mail and church sermons were used to inform regular churchgoers of the movie, and children were marketed to through their local school districts—a strategy that paralleled what was happening through churches. Similar techniques were used in 1965 with the release of *The Greatest Story Ever Told*. In addition to church promotion, this film relied on publicity in major publications like *Life* magazine. The difference between these films and *The Passion* mostly has to do with technology. While all the films were promoted through churches and other religious institutions, *The Passion* had the advantage of television and the Internet. These allowed for inexpensive advertising (see Chapter 1 of this book) as well as national distribution of materials, including sermons with accompanying film clips.

The Purpose Driven Life was one of the first books to be heavily promoted through churches. This was done via a strategically planned publicity campaign targeted primarily at religious organizations.

The book's launch was supported by a national "40 Days of Purpose" campaign sponsored by Saddleback Church involving more than 1,550 churches representing all 50 states and nine countries. More than 500,000 churchgoers viewed a Purpose-Driven Life satellite simulcast on October 12, which kicked off the six-week campaign. Participants read a chapter a day (for 40 days) and heard a weekly sermon based on the material. A second "40 Days of Purpose" campaign will kick off on April 13. Part of the publisher's massive marketing campaign included an e-mail newsletter to retailers, in-store displays, a "40 Days of Purpose" radio blitz, a consumer email campaign, national publicity and Web site promotions.

(Maryles, 2003, p. 60)

As with other campaigns that have tapped into churches, marketing for the product is supplemented by funds from the local church. A story in the *Los Angeles Times* told of a pastor of a 300-member church who spent $3,500 of the church's money on copies of the book and another $15,000 to market the "40 Days of Purpose" event (Lobdell, 2002, p. B8). Multiply that by hundreds of churches throughout the country and you have considerable marketing support paid for by someone other than the publisher. Even if they don't go that far in their efforts, churches are a common place of endorsement. According to John Sawyer, Baker Book House's director of marketing, "[A] tactic that's been popularized by the success of PDL [*The Purpose Driven Life*] is doing grassroots marketing with churches and other religious organizations. If a title becomes part of the church buzz, the impact at retail is significant" (Kiesling, 2004, p. S10).

Because of the large media institutions in the industry, cross-promotion is now a cost-effective tool. For example, it is not unusual to see Joel Osteen's *Your Best Life Now* advertised in *Time* magazine and *People* magazine because this title was published by Time Warner books. Similarly the marketing plan for Joyce Meyer's book, *The Everyday Life Bible*, included ads in *People* magazine as well as *Charisma*, *Today's Christian Woman*, *SpiritLed Woman*, and *All You*. (It was also featured for 12 weeks on Joyce Ministries broadcasts as well as on numerous cable channels.)

Publicity or public relations, rather than advertising, is the predominant form of promotion for religious products. This entails press releases and book tours or tours by stars of a film. A book tour might also include workshops, because many religious titles have a self-help component that is readily translated into an interactive experience. Moreover, because of the rise in popularity of religion as a news topic, media outlets tend to be open to stories of these types.

Creating religious brands

Like secular marketers, religious publishers are attempting to turn their authors into brands. To be effective, authors must be associated with a single topic, which could be relationships or prophecy or leadership. More and more in all realms of publishing, editors are looking for authors who already have a following. For example, "[Thomas] Nelson editors troll the lecture/ speaker circuit for people with new ideas and growing constituencies" (Winston, 1999, p. 36). The more name recognition through ministry or media, the better.

Authors who are considered brands with the CBA, like Max Lucado and Philip Yancey, had considerable followings before their careers as book authors. Max Lucado is the pastor of the Oak Hills Church in Texas and was recently named America's Pastor (a title also claimed by Rick Warren). When forming his ministry, Lucado brought with him his listening audience, as he had had a local radio show in California.[6] Philip Yancey had been, and continues to be, a freelance writer whose articles have appeared in *Christianity Today*, *Publishers Weekly*, and *Reader's Digest*, among other high-circulation publications. These other outlets set the stage for the successful branding of Lucado and Yancey. The fact that they are also prolific is certainly helpful in their branding.

One note here: A successful brand in the Christian market does not necessarily translate into success in the secular market. For example, Doubleday tried to present Philip Yancey to the secular audience. His fifteenth book, *Soul Survivor*, was launched as a popular title. However, sales were disappointing and Doubleday released the paperback version under both a secular and a Christian imprint.

The reverse—a secular brand in the Christian market—may be more successful. One of the books heavily promoted at the CBA in 2006 was *Inside My Heart* by Robin McGraw, wife of "Dr. Phil" McGraw. Robin comes already well known to millions of viewers, having been seen on her husband's show every day for more than four years. Planned promotion for her book entailed ads in women's magazines like *O, the Oprah Magazine*, on radio programs including Dr. Laura and Janet Parshall, through a national publicity campaign that included a satellite radio tour in 25 markets, and interviews on national and Christian television. Most important, of course, is that the book would be featured throughout season five on the *Dr. Phil* show. Starting in the summer of 2006, Robin's participation in Nelson's Women of Faith tour was promoted on Dr. Phil's Web site. While the book is obviously a mass-market title, the choice of publisher (Thomas Nelson) demonstrates its Christian roots. Further setting the stage for its success is Dr. Phil's ties to the Christian market, in evidence when he plugged his most recent book on Robert Schuller's *The Hour of Power* in August 2006 (with Robin prominently in the audience).

For the *Left Behind* series, branding did not come right away. Tyndale, the series' publisher, realized it had a best seller on its hands after *Left Behind* sold between 15,000 and 20,000 copies in its first month of publication in 1996. Jerry Jenkins (the co-author with Tim LaHaye) explained that the book only covered the first two weeks of Revelation and he had close to seven years of story to go. In response Tyndale designed the book covers to be similar—black with the title in a band toward the top—and created the tagline "The Future Is Clear," which appeared on all promotion for the series. According to Tyndale's marketing director at the time, Dan Balow, the key to the brand's success was the Web site, www.leftbehind.com, which "received 4.4 million hits in January 1999 alone, many from consumers and retailers anticipating the February release of *Apollyon: The Destroyer Is Unleashed*, the fifth title in the series and the first to make the general bestseller charts in addition to religion lists" (Winston, 1999, p. 37).

Having multiple products is beneficial because one product in the brand line promotes another. The *Left Behind* movie, for example, had the advantage of having the book publicity behind it. And, like *The Passion*, this film relied on churches to help spread the word. Churches were urged to promote the film in local theaters. Even more clever was the release of the video four months *before* the release of the film in theaters. The video came packaged with discounted tickets to see the film in theaters (The "Left Behind" Phenomenon, 2001).

The most successful brand in terms of its recognition and capacity for generating brand extensions is the *Chicken Soup for the Soul* series. The ability to niche the series made it possible to target an endless list of audiences. Current titles include *Chicken Soup for the Scrapbooker's Soul*, *Chicken Soup for the Teenage Soul: The Real Deal Challenges*, *Chicken Soup for the Mother of Preschooler's Soul*, and *Chicken Soup for the Kid's Soul 2* (suggesting that the first one was so successful that it warranted a second version). There are also special series within the *Chicken Soup* series, such as the *Healthy Living* series, which targets people with specific ailments like asthma, diabetes, stress, and so on.

Here, too, books are not the only products in the line. The brand has also been applied to *Chicken Soup for the Soul* pet food products, a line of vitamins, Trends International Page-a-Day calendars and wall calendars, *Chicken Soup for the Soul* CDs produced by Rhino Records, and a card line produced by American Greetings. These last items—calendars, records, and cards—are examples of licensing, whereby other companies pay to use a brand's name or logo on a line of its products because it will help sell more of them. Since one of the goals of branding is to extend the brand name to as many product lines as possible, this is a win-win deal for all parties involved. Dan Balow, executive director of Tyndale International Publishing Services, says, "More publishers in general are creating brands, and the natural extension of that is licensing" (Raugust, 2003, p. 38).

Licensing has long been a staple in the entertainment industry so it was not surprising to see a large number of products developed after *The Passion of the Christ*. Sharethepassionofthechrist.com became a clearinghouse for a multitude of products including jewelry, mugs, key chains, and witnessing tools. These products were also available through Christian bookstores. More recently, *The DaVinci Code* movie (as opposed to the book) presented a wealth of licensing opportunities. Sony, the producer of the film, for example, "passed on a murderous monk action figure in favor of a strategic board game" (Schmelzer, 2006b, p. A15), and they also developed jewelry inspired by the film. Licensing was also used during the release of the *Veggie Tales* DVD. In this case, Veggie Tales characters appeared on Curad bandages—creating millions of opportunities for brand recognition while helping to sell more product. In addition, the *Veggie Tales* books are licensed to ZonderKidz while the rights to produce stuffed characters, puppets, scrapbooks, and T-shirts are held by various other license holders.

Probably more than any other area of marketing, licensing causes a stumbling block for Christian producers. Embracing licensing brings into question blatant consumerism. Where is the spiritual value in a *Veggie Tales* plush toy or a *Left Behind* T-shirt? Bill Anderson, president of the CBA, has found a way to get around this nagging thought. "This [the retail convention] is largely a business gathering with Christianity being the central theme. We're really an industry of one book, the bible, and all of these other products are to help us as customers understand what does the bible really say" (Divine Profits, 2004). Justification, perhaps, but not really an answer. Marketing—licensing or any other form—is a double-edged sword for most religious producers. On the one hand, the mission of Christianity is to spread the gospel. What better way to do that than through mass marketing? On the other hand, how do you enter these marketplaces without becoming secular? For all marketers, a fundamental issue is how to grow your audience without alienating your current users. It is an issue that Christian producers are struggling with, and one that cannot be easily answered or avoided.

My argument throughout this book is that religion has to be marketed in today's culture in order to remain relevant. That is how today's consumers understand what products and services are available to them. Many people no longer practice their faith within the confines of a church or synagogue, but instead get their spiritual fulfillment through interacting with religious products and events, such as books, movies, and rock concerts. For many, these things are religion, and thus religion *is* a product, which like any other product needs to be marketed in order for it to survive.

Promoting religious products—the rise of the church consultant

An area where religious products and religion itself start to blur is that of church consultancies. In helping a church to grow, consultants often come to also promote pastors, books, films, and other goods beyond the church itself.

The number of church consultancies has been growing in recent years. Since there is no formal reporting mechanism, it is difficult to put exact statistics against that statement. However *Church Executive* magazine in 2005 estimated that there were 5,000 church consultants in the United States.

The industry can be divided into two primary groups: Denominational consultants are responsible for the health and growth of many churches and have titles that include directors of missions and evangelism, church growth consultant, and director of church development. These consultants are typically salaried....Nondenominational consultants are not affiliated with a particular denomination and are compensated by the client church/organization in the form of a project fee or hourly or daily rate.

(Gopez-Sindac, 2005)

Fees for these latter services can run from $50 to $250 per hour and upwards of $3,000 a day, though some consultants provide a sliding scale for smaller institutions. It is this second type of consultant whom we will discuss here.

While most do not call themselves *marketing* consultants, that is in fact what they are. These consultants are hired to grow the ministry, and that, by any definition, is marketing. According to *The Washington Post*:

[C]ompanies in this field [consultancies] have been helping pastors incorporate multimedia technologies into Sunday services and use sophisticated marketing techniques to draw larger crowds. Some of them recommend changing the content of sermons or adding contemporary music and drama to attract young people.

(Cho, 2005, p. C1)

The marketing techniques referred to here include demographic assessments of the area surrounding the church as well as the use of surveys and focus groups to evaluate "changing religious preferences...[the level of] distaste for face-to-face evangelism, demand for intellectual challenge within the church context, and a strong tendency toward 'contemporary' worship styles and modern music" (Spiegler, 1996, p. 47). Understanding what the community wants from a church enables that organization to tailor its services to fit the audience. Research also helps to determine logistics, such as the parking and how to handle childcare. For megachurches, this may also include health clubs, food courts, sports events, and educational and singles groups. Consultants may also recommend branding the church in order to increase awareness and attention. Richard Reising, the president of Artistry Marketing Concepts, a company that works with churches on their marketing activities, says:

[T]en years ago it [branding] was met with extreme skepticism. The whole concept of promoting church was taboo. But there has been a growing acceptance over time. Now people realize what it means and what it doesn't mean. They see it is part of going out into the world to preach, promote and publish the gospel.

(Colyer, 2005)

Most churches are not versed (or were not until recently) in the language of marketing and branding, which is why a large number of them have turned to consultants for help. The increased use of consultants appears in part to be a response to the church growth movement, which was started by Dr. Donald McGavran and Dr. Robert H. Schuller. Dr. McGavran's book, *Understanding Church Growth*, written in 1970, was an important work in establishing the evangelical movement and the subsequent growth in American megachurches. In trying to find a way to grow churches, McGavran asked four questions:

> What are the *causes* of church growth?
> What are the *barriers* to church growth?
> What are the factors that can make Christian faith a *movement* among some populations?
> What *principles* of church growth are reproducible?
> (quoted in Hunter, 1992, p. 158)

In asking these questions, McGavran was initiating marketing research. To answer them, he did considerable fieldwork to try to understand why some churches succeed and others fail. A fundamental idea behind the church growth movement was one of marketing (though again they did not call it that): use psychology, sociology, and anthropology to create a message that will appeal to your audience and you will ultimately grow your church.

Dr. Robert H. Schuller, who is probably best known as the pastor for the Crystal Cathedral megachurch in California and the *Hour of Power* television show available on local television stations and nationally on cable, claims to be the creator of the megachurch. "'I launched the megachurch movement through the Institute for Successful Church Leadership in 1970,' he said, referring to his annual pastors conference at the Garden Grove church. 'There were no megachurches 32 years ago—we were the closest thing to it'" (Dart, 2002, p. 24). While others dispute this claim, there is little doubt that his teachings have had an impact on some of today's most famous megachurch leaders. Schuller says that Bill Hybels is his main disciple. Hybels, however, says that his preaching is more serious than Schuller's—he uses the "s" word (sin) (Luecke, 1997). Rick Warren has cited McGavran as being an influence on his work, and while Schuller is often described as Warren's mentor, including most publicly by Larry King when he introduced Schuller as a guest on *Larry King Live*, Warren has disavowed any connection to Schuller other than having met him. Whether mentor or not, Warren has used ideas and techniques that were created by Schuller decades ago.[7]

It should not be surprising, then, that two of the largest consultancies are tied to these megachurch leaders. Bill Hybels's Willow Creek Community Church in South Barrington, Illinois, has a nonprofit consultancy arm called Willow Creek Association (WCA). Membership in WCA costs $250 per year, and more than 10,000 congregations have paid this fee. The goal of WCA is to teach other churches the Willow Creek "brand of ministry" while simultaneously maintaining the Gospel message. The organization's executive vice president, Steve Bell, says, "We are all about values...not methods. But we do share some of the best practices that we are finding on what's working" (Cho, 2005, p. C1). WCA also holds conferences for church leaders on a number of topics including small groups and children's ministry as well as preaching and teaching. For congregations that cannot afford $3,000 per day, this provides a less expensive alternative.

As for Rick Warren, remember that *The Purpose Driven Life* is the textbook for a course that aids in creating a Purpose Driven church. What is a Purpose Driven church? One that follows the principles of *The Purpose Driven Life* with the use of materials from Rick Warren. These materials include training information for the leadership team (including for the senior pastor), timelines for the program, ideas for drama and group involvement for each week, samples of Purpose Driven products including the book, the journal, and the CD, and transcripts and PowerPoint presentations for sermons. According to the Purpose Driven Web site, more than 400,000 church leaders have participated in these teachings, which, like Hybels's WCA, is relatively inexpensive ($395). In addition to the church course, there are a number of conferences available, including ones that focus on children and youth ministry as well as conferences for recovery and HIV/AIDS.[8]

These consultancies have themselves become brands. But Rick Warren didn't get to be Rick Warren simply by being a best-selling author. He had the help of public relations specialist A. Larry Ross. Public relations is an important part of any marketing campaign, because news is more readily accepted by consumers than advertising and because of its relative cost structure (not that Ross comes cheaply). The effectiveness of these practitioners should not be underestimated. An example of this is the Atlanta courtroom shooting.

> Take the case of Ashley Smith, the Atlanta woman who became famous last year for reading passages from "The Purpose-Driven Life" to her captor, an escaped murder suspect named Brian Nichols. A problem arose when it came out that Smith had given Nichols crystal methamphetamine. "What did everyone talk about?" Chrzan [Rick Warren's chief of staff] said. "They talked about her drug use and her giving drugs" to Nichols. Ross helped Warren respond to this mainstream reaction by emphasizing their story, which was, in Chrzan's words: "God can use anybody. Here, God used a tweaked-out speed freak to get a guy to realize he'd done something wrong and turn himself in."
>
> (Saroyan, 2006, p. 49)

What could have been a stain on *The Purpose Driven Life* turned into extensive media coverage for Warren and a cover story in *People* magazine for Smith, which included a sidebar for *The Purpose Driven Life* entitled "Did this book help catch an alleged killer?" (Hewitt *et al.*, 2005).

Publicity and media relations are another type of consultancy being used by churches. It has been dubbed Christian PR and it was started by Ross in the early 1980s. As the founder of this type of marketing, he is involved in some of the most well-known Christian marketing campaigns of late and he is arguably the most famous PR man in this area. According to a *New York Times Magazine* article entitled "Christianity, the Brand," while Ross is not the only Christian PR consultant, there is only one other (Mark DeMoss, who has represented Jerry Falwell) who ranks in comparable status (Saroyan, 2006). There are a plethora of smaller marketing or marketing and PR firms that handle faith-based projects, such as Motive Entertainment, Grace Hill Media, BuzzPlant, and Renegade Idea Group. However, it is Ross who is most in evidence.

Ross works the way any PR person would except that he is specifically focused on Christian products and how to bring them more into the mainstream. "Ross characterizes part of his job as finding the sweet spot where faith and the culture intersect, because religion on its own often isn't enough, as he sees it, to generate mainstream press" (Saroyan, 2006, p. 49). For example, he positioned T. D. Jakes as a businessman because of his work with underprivileged youth. This ultimately landed Jakes a front-page story in *The Wall Street Journal*. Ross trains his clients in how to deal with the press. In particular, he tells them not to use ecclesiastical language in interviews with mainstream media outlets. The objective is to get the message out and promote the product; you can sell Jesus once you get them in the door.

Similar to the marketing plans for a number of Christian products, Ross readily thinks in terms of using a two-pronged marketing strategy—one for Christians and one for the mainstream. In marketing *The Passion of Christ*, for example, Ross had several jobs: he quelled the negative press in the mainstream media; he secured stories in the Christian press; and he introduced Gibson to high-profile pastors so that they would prescreen the film. Ross even had Gibson tape a message for pastors that could be left on their answering machines when they were out—thus the pastor gets a call from a Hollywood star and it becomes a source of viral marketing, because he keeps it and plays it for anyone who will listen.

Jonah: A Veggie Tales Movie was marketed to the mainstream as a special effects spectacular; to churches it was marketed so that religious leaders would present it to their congregations.

> Ross [and his former employee Lawrence Swicegood] created a marketing kit for the film that he distributed to about 10,000 churches.... "Veggie Tales" packets included inserts for church bulletins and Sunday-

school guides, a poster, a DVD of the trailer and a script for a pulpit announcement introducing the picture to churchgoers.

(Saryon, 2006, p. 50)

What A. Larry Ross and his colleagues are doing is not new. Some of the techniques Ross used for *Veggie Tales* are the same ones he used for Billy Graham 20 years earlier. And some of the more successful church consultancies have been around for more than 30 years. What has changed though is that consultants are no longer simply marketing churches; they are marketing religion to the mainstream through the use of popular media.

Conclusion

In this chapter we looked at the economic changes that have contributed to the increased level of religious marketing in our culture. Mergers and acquisitions have changed the face of the religious product marketplace. Multinational media conglomerates saw the money to be made in religion and turned their considerable marketing resources toward selling religious products. Suddenly Wal-Mart and other big box stores saw that they, too, could generate major revenue from books like *The Purpose Driven Life* and the *Left Behind* series. These distribution outlets also saw revenue in the movies, toys, and jewelry associated with these products. The introduction of Christian books, particularly, into mass merchandisers increased competition exponentially in this category.

Moreover, secular producers have no compunction about using churches as marketers for their products. From movies to books, churches are increasingly becoming spokespeople and distributors for secular products. Just as our schools have become endorsers of soda and junk food, churches have become endorsers of religious media, providing an implied stamp of approval for little or no compensation.

The increase in mega-corporations and retailers into this arena has pushed the drive for profits, moving sacred content further and further into the realm of the secular. But at what cost? The best-selling books have all been criticized as being lightweight Christianity, if Christianity at all. Their authors are accused of pandering to reach a wider audience.

Yet, this is the fundamental paradox of evangelicalism. Being an evangelical means you want to spread the good word, but—and this is the core issue—you have to spread the word to nonbelievers. In order to do this, you must reach beyond the protected walls of the church and into the secular marketplace. However, to compete against the ever-growing array of more fun, more entertaining, and less guilt-ridden discretionary leisure time activities, religious institutions have to match their message to the marketplace. That message needs to become simple and easily digestible in a short period of time. It also has to be palatable to people who may not be at all interested in what the evangelical has to sell. So the product—the book, the music, whatever—becomes the marketing message, for example, the book is what gets people in the door of the church.

The problem is that for most people, they confuse the advertising with the product itself. Rick Warren acknowledges that not everyone who comes to his Saddleback Church is a member (see more on this in Chapter 5). While membership in Saddleback involves considerable commitments of time, money, and mission, most of the 25 million-plus people who have read *Purpose Driven Life* do not participate at that level. Thus in the broader culture what gets understood as faith is a watered-down version of the belief system. The question becomes: Is selling a diluted form of faith in order to attract an audience worth possibly diluting the practice overall?

And because the message (particularly books and televangelistic programming) has become the marketing, the product—the church services themselves—has had to change. If seekers read one thing in the book and then go to church and see the same old, tired, boring, dogmatic services that their parents went to, they will run for the door in a heartbeat. To marry the product with the marketing, churches have learned to create services based on demographics and consumer appeal, adding more and more of the secular to their presentations.

Chapter 4

Branding faith

Nike. Apple. Coach. Why do these words make us think of sneakers, computers, and pocketbooks instead of goddesses, fruit, and ancient modes of transportation? In a fast-paced capitalist culture where we are constantly bombarded with commercial messages, product companies need to be able to communicate quickly and efficiently. Taglines, logos, and identifiable icons become shorthand for everything from cars to commodities. This, in short, is branding. To better understand why advertisers use branding, let's first look at advertising and marketing more broadly.

The evolution of advertising and marketing

Advertising has been used to sell products since at least as early as the invention of the printing press. Advertising in the 1400s primarily sold the most popular book of the time—the Bible. In this nascent stage, a straightforward sales pitch was the advertising norm. Copy would have been something along the lines of, "We have Bibles. This is where you can buy them, and this is how much they cost." These direct sales messages continued for hundreds of years, up until the Industrial Revolution.

With the advent of the Industrial Age, products began to be produced in mass quantities. For product producers, the concern became how to sell large quantities of products to people who may not have needed or wanted them. The twentieth century also saw developments in psychology from Pavlov and Freud, and later Skinner and Maslow. Thus technology and psychology changed the focus of advertising from product attributes (physical characteristics) to user benefits (what the customer gets). Soap was no longer about the ingredients it contained, but rather about how wonderful you would smell and therefore how much more effectively you would be able to attract a mate. Cars weren't about getting from one place to another, but about how masculine someone could be. The need to sell through psychology became normative as mass-produced, undifferentiated commodity products proliferated.

Therefore, to get consumers to buy mostly unnecessary products, advertisers became experts in psychology—at first through the use of surveys and other quantitative methods, and later through more sophisticated qualitative methodologies, such as focus groups and personal interviews. Today we are seeing a decided shift in the level of sophistication as marketers increasingly move away from targeting based on demographics—statistical data about consumers—to targeting based on psychographics. Psychographics is research that breaks up consumers into groups based on their motivations and attitudes rather than their age and income. "A *psychographic* segmentation covers the hopes, needs, fears, beliefs, opinions, and attitudes which shape the actions and choices a person makes" according to Carol Morgan and Doran Levy (2002, p. 30). An example they use to demonstrate this idea is that "The purchase of a high chair for a grandchild is driven by demographics, but the purchase of one made of wood versus one constructed of steel may be based on attitudes or psychographics" (pp. 5–6). Understanding how old someone is or how much money they have will not get at this deeper understanding of consumer desires.

Looked at another way, most of us know at least one example of what marketers call the "early adopter." He's the guy (and it usually is a guy) who had the cell phone, the Palm Pilot, and the iPod before anyone else. He needs to have the latest, newest thing first because it feeds his sense of being "in the know." This early adopter could be a teenage computer geek, a 50-year-old corporate CEO, or a newly minted 30-year-old MBA. Thus marketers have to target products through motivation rather than through demographic statistics.

But, you might ask, what about the iPod ads? They all showed young people dancing to current day music. How does that target all of these groups? Brilliantly, I'd say. First, the dancers were all silhouetted so that people could project themselves into the commercials. Second, younger people (teens) aspire to be older, while older early adopters (our hypothetical 50-year-old CEO) aspire to be younger, so this ad works for all three age groups because while you can't specifically see the dancers, you could guess them to be in their late twenties or early thirties. Finally, the music is just hip enough to tell some people, "This product is not for you," giving the product, at least initially, some exclusivity and cache. (Of course, that can't last for long once a company starts introducing less expensive versions of the product, because by that time the early adopter has introduced everyone else to the product and has moved on to the "next big thing.")

Michael Schudson (1984) suggests two reasons for marketing's shift to psychographics. First, women are the primary target for the majority of consumer products, and they are more emotional than men. Therefore women are "inherently" predisposed to emotional appeals. Second, as an overwhelming number of products were created, getting attention rivaled providing information. Standing out "in the clutter" became the marketer's battle cry. The best way to stand out was to have a thorough understanding of your consumers so that they could immediately connect to your message. The goal of an immediate bond became increasingly difficult as the media environment (particularly television) grew to be more complex, wherein demographic groups were sliced into smaller and smaller audiences for marketing purposes. In the 1950s, when television was first widely introduced into American households, television audiences were one mass group. This went along with the method of goods production (mass) and the distribution of the advertising messages (mass media). Undifferentiated audiences continued as the norm through the 1960s but things began to change in the 1970s, when Nielsen started calculating ratings based on demographic groups. By the 1980s, separating audiences into defined market segments based on demographic information was customary because of the widespread introduction of cable television.

While the technology of cable television was available as early as the late 1950s, it was not widely distributed until the 1980s. It was also at this time that programming networks created just for cable were first introduced. CNN, MTV, Lifetime, ESPN, and many other well-known cable brands were all established during this time period, and with them we had the beginnings of what Joseph Turow (1997) calls "Breaking Up America." Not only did these networks provide new programming, they also created specialized places where the "right people," meaning demographic groups most valued by advertisers, would congregate. And to paraphrase Schudson, marketers, unlike God, do not talk to or listen to all people equally.

As technology has become more sophisticated, the ability to break up the audience into smaller and smaller segments has increased. However, narrowly defined and fragmented audiences make it much more difficult to sell mass-produced products. Instead of airing a single commercial on a broadcast network and reaching millions of people, dozens of commercials need to be aired to reach the same size audience. Moreover, just because the number of media options has increased does not mean people's time or ability to consume more information has increased with it. In 1985, Carrie Heeter wrote, "There is controversy as to whether the limitations of the short-term memory capacity is 5-9 portions of information or 3-5, but [there is] agreement that the capacity is limited" (p. 131). Translating this to television, even in today's 150+-channel universe, we routinely watch seven channels and are aware of programming on perhaps four or five more. Our brains simply do not allow for retaining more information than this.

Heeter wrote more than 20 years ago, long before today's explosion in media outlets. Randolph Trappey and Arch Woodside (2005) assert now that changes in lifestyle and media have made it so that the twenty-first-century consumer not only has limited capacity to retain information, but also a more limited attention span to begin with. In today's environment people want information immediately. Thus we have the proliferation of swooshes, white ear plugs, and apple logos—what Robert Goldman and Stephen Papson (1998) call "sign wars." This is where branding comes in.

Branding

What is branding?

The most often quoted definition of a brand is that of David Ogilvy, an early giant in the advertising industry and founder of Ogilvy & Mather, one of the world's largest advertising agencies. He said that a brand is "the intangible sum of a product's attributes: its name, packaging, and price, its history, its reputation and the way it is advertised." As the creator of images for everything from Dove soap to the American Express Card, Ogilvy knew of what he spoke.

Branding is about making meaning—taking the individual aspects of a product and turning them into more than the sum of their parts. It is about giving consumers something to think and feel about a product or service beyond its physical attributes. It's about fulfilling a need; providing what marketers call the benefit. If we talk about something as simple as M&Ms, for instance, the tangible or physical attributes are a small piece of chocolate with a colorful, hard candy coating. The intangible attributes, that is, those associated with the branding of the product, include "melts in your mouth, not in your hand," small size, convenient packaging, and its history and reputation as a quality candy that's fun to eat. The benefit, in addition to keeping your hands—and more importantly your children's hands—clean, is good taste and perhaps a sugar buzz. As a consumer, while you do not consciously think of all of these things when deciding what kind of candy to buy, unconsciously everything you know about the brand, including your past experiences with it, comes into play at the time of purchase.

You may not think this is so, particularly when you are thinking about good experiences, but think about the last time you had a bad experience with a brand. You probably said to yourself, "This widget stinks. I'm never going to buy anything from them again." Or, "Their customer service is terrible; outsourcing is the bane of my existence." You do the same thing when you have a positive experience with a brand, though the reaction may not be quite so visceral. Instead of, "Wow! This Swiffer works great! I'm going to have to tell my friend, Susie!" the reaction is more likely to be, "This does a great job. I think I'll buy it again."

Whether we are conscious of it or not, we have these relationships with brands—good and bad. We have preferences for one brand over another. We have unconscious thoughts and feelings about products that we use (or don't use). For instance, we may buy Domino sugar because it reminds of us of "Mom." Intellectually this doesn't make sense because sugar is sugar. It's a commodity. But because we have a preexisting relationship with Domino, we are willing to pay extra money for that name and its perceived higher quality. Or, we may choose an iPod because it is easier to use than other MP3s, it has more available downloads, and those white ear plugs make us look hip while walking down the street or sitting on the bus. This is not to say that some products aren't better than others, but rather that, in the vast majority of categories, it is the brand and not the physical product that the consumer has the relationship with.

From the consumer's perspective branding is about quality and consistency, but for the company that produces a product, branding is about creating long-term profits and growing the business. According to Northwestern marketing professors Don Schultz and Heidi Schultz (2004, p. 18), brands can do five things:

- Create financial value for the owner in both the short and long term.
- Create various forms of value for customers so they are willing to seek out the brand, buy it, and continue buying it.
- Create relationships with employees and other interested stakeholders so they want to continue to be associated with and support the brand.
- Last a long time or at least be remembered a long time. That means long-term income flows.
- Become a part of culture. Cultural icons have great value. Just look at the value Michael Jordan created during his basketball career for both himself and those he worked with and for.

Branding exists to create profits. It does this by creating loyalty among its customers. Loyalty reduces producers' marketing costs, because consumers (brand loyalists) become repeat purchasers of the product. Marketers simply have to remind consumers to keep buying the brand over the long term. The ultimate achievement is for the brand to become part of the popular culture. When this occurs, the value of the product increases exponentially. The value of branding is that it makes it harder for other products in the category to thrive because the brand becomes impermeable to competition (Miller and Muir, 2004, p. xiii). And in today's global economy, branding allows products to travel around the world. Logos are streamlined—simple iconography, no words—to affect this process. Good examples here are the Nike swoosh and McDonald's golden arches.

David Ogilvy once said that he could have marketed Dove as a man's soap or a woman's soap. He just chose to market it to women. In and of themselves, products have no meaning. It is the marketers who give them meaning, and it is that meaning that is the product. It is not the soap or the car or the coffee, but the meaning behind these commodities. Much as religion created meaning for people's lives over the centuries, now marketers create meaning out of the products that fill our existence. These products come to be not just clothes to wear or cars to drive, but elements of who we are.

Brands as part of identity creation

Walk around any mall in America and there can be little doubt that brands aid in defining who we are. Yankee baseball caps. Kate Spade handbags. Abercrombie T-shirts. These are just a few of the thousands of branded products that combine to create personal identities. While this is true for most demographic groups, it is most evident in those under 20. As Juliet Schor (2004) says in her book *Born to Buy*, "more children here [the United States] than anywhere else believe that their clothes and brands describe who they are and define their social status. American kids display more brand affinity than their counterparts anywhere else in the world; indeed, experts describe them as increasingly 'bonded to brands'" (p. 13). Schor quotes a 2001 Nickelodeon study that showed that most 10-year-olds could name 300 to 400 brands and that tweens (those between the ages of 8 and 12) request specific brands more than 90 percent of the time. She concludes that "today's tweens are the most brand-conscious generation in history" (p. 25).

Teenagers, unlike children, know they are being marketed to, but this doesn't stop them from wanting to be like the marketed world they see. For her book *Branded: The Buying and Selling of Teenagers*, Alissa Quart interviewed teens about the brands they interact with and found that while the teens are acutely aware that the advertising they see is not true to life ("Can you believe this ad? No one's body looks like that!"), this does not stop them from trying to look and act just like the people in the ads. Quart says, "The personae, self-images, ambitions, and values of young people in the United States have been seriously distorted by the commercial frenzy surrounding them" (2003, p. 13).[1]

Adults, too, can't but help getting caught in the web of 360-degree "touchpoints," the numerous opportunities—from advertising to e-mail to retail—that marketers use to communicate with consumers. There is no place where you can go and not see marketing, including public restrooms! Being surrounded by advertising makes us want to buy more and more. Says Schor, "What we buy also affects who we become. Recent research suggests that the more we have, the more powerful, confident, and socially validated we feel" (Schor, 1998, p. 57). Thus we end up on a treadmill of consumerism, buying to feel better, and buying to create a sense of self.

In part this reliance on brands for identity stems from a sense of rootlessness. Americans suffer from geographic dislocation that in turn drives their need for commonalities. In the fifteenth century, if you went from place to place you could be sure that most people knew about the Bible; today, as people move from place to place, they know that McDonald's or Wal-Mart is sure to be at their final destination. Brands, more than anything else in our culture, provide consistency. While we can't count on a pension, health insurance, or a lifetime career anymore, we can count on Kraft, Apple, and Lexus.

Brands have become so much more than products to buy. Lee Clow, creator of Apple's "Think Different" campaign, states:

> Brands aren't just a way of remembering what you want to buy any more. They've become part of the fabric of our society. Brands are part of our system of ordering things—they even create context about who we are and how we live. Brands have become badges for people. They articulate who you are and what your values are.
>
> (Clifton and Maughan, 2000, p. 71)

We are not just talking here about consumer packaged goods. Think also of rock bands or sports teams or celebrities. We wear U2 T-shirts and Red Sox baseball caps and Sean John apparel, and all of those things represent who we are. Brands are not just perceptions about a product or service, they are also bits and pieces of our identity.

Clearly marketers realize that brands have power beyond sales, but scholars and social critics also clearly identify commercial culture as the source of identity creation. Naomi Klein, an outspoken critic of branding, lambastes the "marketing hype" that hides the economic hardships of third-world labor behind the glitz of the brand. In *No Logo*, she criticizes the takeover of public space, but her larger concern is the takeover of internal space. "This loss of space happens inside the individual; it is a colonization not of physical space but of mental space" (Klein, 2000, p. 66). Theologian Tom Beaudoin (2003, p. 5) is in agreement:

> For those of us who live deeply immersed in the branding economy, we make an identity for ourselves, and an identity is made for us, by our relationships to consumer goods: what and how we own, when and why we wear. Clothes and other branded products do "identity work" for us, transmitting messages about ourselves to ourselves and others.

David Lyon is more forceful when he puts this into perspective *vis-à-vis* religion (2000, p. 12).

> Identities are constructed through consuming. Forget the idea that who we are is given by God or achieved through hard work in a calling or a career; we shape our malleable image by what we buy—our clothing, our kitchens, and our cars tell the story of who we are (becoming). It is no accident that the world of fashion is seen as an "identity industry;" the idea is that self-esteem and our recognition by others may be purchased over the counter.

Or as marketer Douglas Atkin (2004) puts it, "People today pay for meaning more than they pray for it" (p. 95).

The sources of identity formation have changed. Whereas once our family, friends, schools, and religious institutions gave us a basis for understanding who we are and what we value, these groups have been usurped by marketers and mass media. As Schudson explains (1984, pp. 153–4):

> Children learn to pay attention not just to their parents but to their peer group and to the mass media…The family remains crucial, but more and more, a common culture, that includes advertising and the mass media, plays its part…If the commercial and national forces for "prefabricat[ed] identity]" through persuasion have grown, the local forces toward standard personalities through coercive religion, education, and family have weakened.

So is it really true that we have exchanged one form of socialization for another to aid in creating our identities? Is it that marketers have taken over for other social institutions? And, if we accept that as a given rather than a question, is there really any issue with religion taking on the mantle of marketer?

Given that brands contain meaning for our lives and that products become part of our identities, it is easy to see why religious organizations see the value in inventing their products and services as brands. Stewart Hoover (1996) has said that in today's culture religious practice constitutes "a situation of seekers turning to a largely commodified inventory of symbols, values and ideas out of which they appropriate those which fit best into senses of themselves." Those commodified symbols are the branded logos presented to us hundreds of times a day. If people are used to having meaning presented to them via marketing communication, then why not use what is of the culture? If people are looking for meaning, and marketers readily admit that they are, why not become the prime purveyors of the product and take back from the profane marketplace that which is sacred? Good questions indeed.

Marketing and religion

A symbiotic relationship

Here we will begin to examine the similarities between religion and marketing and start to see how the sacred and the secular are not mutually exclusive, but rather aid each other in the furtherance of their goals. Secular objects (books, material goods) are used in disseminating the sacred. The sacred must be promoted via the secular marketplace in order to recruit new members. On numerous levels, the sacred has become more secular and vice versa.[2] While critics have suggested that there is a culture war—a fight between religion and popular culture—for religion and marketing, the interaction is more of a mutually beneficial relationship than a contest. It seems that marketers have learned their craft from religion—turning diehard product users into evangelists, for example—and it is simply a situation of religion re-assimilating what is rightfully theirs.

A number of religion and media scholars have written about the intersection of commercial culture and religious objects. Some of these scholars (Hendershot, 2004; McDannell, 1995) suggest that the sacred and profane have not been mutually exclusive either in the minds of the merchandisers or the consumers. Consumers see religious products as a means of expressing their faith while merchandisers see products—including religious practice itself—as a means to spread the faith. These scholars, as well as others whose work will be mentioned in this section, have all suggested that sociology of religion researchers have relied too heavily on the secularization theory, which has obscured the reality of the intersection between religion and commerce.

Leigh Eric Schmidt (1995) provides an extensive study of the commercialization of religion and holidays. He, too, points to the symbiotic relationship between the commercial and the religious, noting that retailers were instrumental in resurrecting holidays that had become moribund, specifically Christmas and Easter. Schmidt provides historical context for this interplay, explaining that religious holidays were feast days or festivals that were regularly ringed by carts selling food and trinkets. Further, he suggests that the criticism of commercialization has more to do with America's puritanical heritage and its accompanying fear of abundance than with commercialization itself.

> A common feature of festivity is to overindulge, to eat, drink, or spend to excess, lavishly to use up resources otherwise diligently saved. The surfeit of gifts and spending associated especially with Christmas, but also with other holidays, gives expression to a kind of festal excess that is often fundamental to celebrations. In other words, festive behavior is built in large part on wastrel prodigality, on surplus and abundance, on conspicuous consumption. The critique of American holidays as consumer fetes is often an attack on festival itself, a repudiation of celebratory indulgence and dissipation out of adherence to puritanical or republican values emphasizing hard work, self-control, frugality, and simplicity.
>
> (Schmidt, 1995, p. 8)

The relationship between religion and commercial culture has long been an uneasy one. On the one hand, commercialization has made participation in religious holidays such as Christmas and Easter virtually mandatory within our culture. On the other hand, churches preach simplicity and support for those who are less fortunate. Thus while the underlying beliefs are in conflict, the institutions of religion and commercial culture do in fact support each other in staying viable. This is why walling off the sacred—no shopping on the Sabbath or holidays, for instance—has become almost impossible.

Conrad Ostwalt (2003) has written of the sacred and the secular being intertwined, and of the boundaries between the two being porous. Throughout *Secular Steeples*, Ostwalt argues that the sacred is becoming more secular and the secular more sacred. Megachurches have embraced popular entertainment forms in their services and widely used marketing techniques to attract the unchurched. The best-selling *Left Behind* book series uses secular media to transmit sacred messages. As for the secular becoming more sacred, there are numerous mainstream documentaries on everything from Jesus to the DaVinci Code, and recently there was even a reality miniseries called *God or the Girl* that showed young men making their final decisions about whether to enter the priesthood. These examples are above and beyond the increasing levels of religious content found in all types of secular media, not just television, which we discussed in Chapter 2. But whether it is the sacred becoming more secular or vice versa, the fact remains that people continue to look for religious meaning even in our rational culture. That search for meaning is less likely to happen within the confines of a church, however, and is more often now found in the form of some type of secular event, such as the Super Bowl or even a rock concert.

Dell deChant (2002) has gone so far as to say that the marketplace is a religion, and that the economy is our new God. Like Oswalt, he does not say that America is not religious—it is intensely religious. However today's understanding of what is sacred is not based on the transcendent, but on the cosmological; that is, what is of the world or the culture. According to deChant (p. 28), what is sacred is participating in the consumption process, which he defines as having three steps:

> Rather than simply consuming objects and images, postmodern culture can be understood as explicating meaning and value through a three-stage process, which begins with (1) acquisition of products, is clarified in (2) consumption of products, and finally is fulfilled in (3) disposal of products.

By defining consumption in this way, we can see that consumerism is not about just using the product or service, but also the events that occur before and after the purchase, making the process more encompassing. It is through this process that we celebrate the sacred, much as people once worshiped what was most available in their environment (deChant, 2002, p. xiv):

> As the ancients saw nature as the ultimate sacred power and worshiped it in all of its various expressions, so we today see the economy as the sacred power of our culture and worship it in an even wider array of manifestations. As the ancients participated in rituals at temples and

shrines, we participate in similar rituals at malls and department stores. Thus, rather than being functionally secular, our entire culture system begins to look profoundly sacred.

Thus even though we might not all participate in rituals within religious institutions, we still participate in sacred rites through purchasing products and watching the retelling of sacred myths of "economic success and material acquisition," as presented through the mass media, particularly television (pp. 31–2). Think of our culture's obsession with celebrity—it's the redemption story told over and over again. These myths combined with the mall provide opportunities to relate to the sacred and thus "reveals the cosmic meaning of existence, which is also the culturally normative way of life and living" (p. 36).

In their research, Russell W. Belk, Melanie Wallendorf, and John F. Sherry, Jr. (1989) break down the wall between the sacred and the profane in terms of consumer products. Through fieldwork they found that "consumers made sacred and profane distinctions in their behaviors and uses of space, time and objects" (p. 3). They agree with Oswalt, concluding that the sacred has become more secular and vice versa, and that with the blurring of these boundaries, consumption can become a means of transcendence. It is not that the world is no longer separated into these two distinct realms, but rather it is that religious objects are not the only means of interacting with the scared.

> Consumption can become a vehicle of transcendent experience; that is, consumer behavior exhibits certain aspects of the sacred...For contemporary consumers, there are also elements of life with no connection to formal religion that are nonetheless revered, feared, and treated with the utmost respect. Examples include flags, sports stars, national parks, art, automobiles, museums, and collections. Whether we call the reverence for these things religious, contemporary consumers treat them as set apart, extraordinary, or sacred, just as elements of nature are sacred in naturistic religions and certain icons are sacred to followers of contemporary, organized religions. Although the specific focal objects differ, the same deeply moving, self-transcending feelings may attend each, and the same revulsions may occur when these objects are not treated with respect. Religion is one, but not the only, context in which the concept of the sacred is operant.
>
> (Belk *et al.*, 1989, p. 2)

R. Laurence Moore (1994) and James Twitchell (2004) each deal directly with the issue of religion and marketing. In *Selling God*, a book that has been the definitive work in this area since its publication in the mid-1990s, Moore outlines the history of how religion has been marketed in the United States, from the personal selling of Jehovah's Witnesses to the more advanced and perhaps abrasive forms used by New Age practitioners, such as expos, advertising, and extensive product lines. In *Branded Nation*, Twitchell suggests that religion and marketing are virtually one and the same thing. He claims that we are all looking to be saved and it is merely the source of salvation that has changed. Both religion and marketing sell stories and "magical thinking is at the heart of religion and branding" (p. 65). We want to believe a product will make us better, just as we want to believe religion will. Twitchell adds (p. 89) that when religion is marketed, it acts just like other branded products:

> [According to old line denominations] the megachurch is the dumbing down of American religion, epiphany lite, minister as personality, service as TV with musical interludes, cherry-picking of smug baby boomers, obsession on the "front door" never minding the flood leaving the "back door," fair-weather churches feeding easy-to-digest junk food to the already overweight.
>
> Conveniently forgotten is that this is exactly the pattern not just of religion but of marketing in general. Someone develops a new wrapper or a new delivery system for an interchangeable product and overnight the market has to adjust. Brand-new brand.

Remember, religion is a commodity. Religion is personal and religion is packaged and sold the same way as other marketed goods and services.

The interdependence of religion and marketing in our culture seems almost inevitable, and there are striking similarities between these cultural forms. These institutions both rely on storytelling, meaning making, and a willingness of people to believe in what is intellectually unbelievable. Religions create meaning through myths, rituals, and practices; marketing creates meaning through advertising and shopping. Religion is the acceptance of a belief system; marketing is the acceptance of beliefs about a product. Religions have faith communities; marketing has brand communities. Religion has become a product; products have become religions.

The parallel process

Marketing is a complex problem of trying to understand the wants and desires of consumers while simultaneously factoring in the many influences—social status, gender, reference groups, and so on—that will affect their purchase decisions. The process begins before the time of purchase. It begins when you, the consumer, notice that your current state of being is not what you would like it to be. This is the first step in the consumer decision-making process. This process consists of five steps: problem recognition, search for information, evaluation of alternatives, product purchase, and post-purchase behavior (Baker, 2000, p. 58).

| Problem recognition | → | Search for information | → | Evaluation of alternatives | → | Product purchase | → | Post-purchase behavior |

Figure 4.1 Consumer decision-making process

This process is not conscious on the part of a consumer and varies depending on the importance of the product being purchased, that is, whether it is a high involvement purchase (one that warrants consideration) or a low involvement purchase (one that takes little to no thought). Let's take some examples. A low involvement product might be bottled water. The problem is that you are thirsty. Given the relatively low importance of this product within the overall scheme of your life, you don't need to search for information. You go to the store, stare at the shelf, choose a bottle of water from among the various brands offered, and buy it. For a high involvement product like a car, you will likely search for information on the Internet, ask friends about their cars, and test drive the car. Then you will need to make some decisions. Do you want an SUV or a sports car? What is the service contract? What kind of financing can you get? Where will you buy the car? Once these decisions are made, you purchase the car and hope that you are happy with your decision.

This process looks at purchasing from the consumer's point of view. There is, however, a way to look at buying through the lens of the marketer. This is the relationship marketing curve, which is based on the RM (Relationship Marketing) ladder of customer loyalty (Payne, 2000, p. 113).

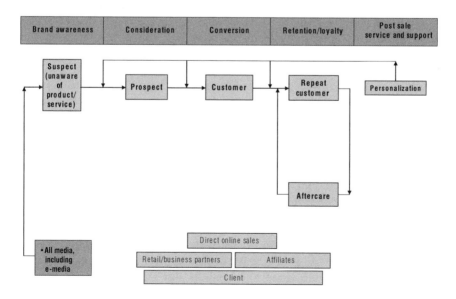

Figure 4.2 Marketing relationship curve

The marketing relationship schematic shows the path of the relationship curve between a marketer and a consumer. The process begins with creating brand awareness. This is where marketing is most important—teaching people that the product exists as well as how to think about the product. Marketers can use any number of tools, including advertising, public relations, or personal selling, to increase people's awareness of their product or service. Once a potential consumer is aware of the product, the next step is to make sure the product becomes part of the consideration set—the evaluation of alternatives step in the consumer decision-making process. When the product is still under consideration, the potential customer is a prospect. In order to push the prospect toward purchase, the marketer might do sampling—letting the prospect try the product before buying it. If it is a Web-based product, prospects may be treated to a virtual trial; or, in the case of a retailer, they might make the shopping environment one that is more conducive to lingering. That Barnes & Noble feels more like a library and Starbucks more like a comfortable place to hang out by yourself or with friends is what marketers call a "third place." A third place isn't home or work, nor is it completely public or private (Lewis and Bridger, 2001), but it is a place where people want to spend time and is conducive to buying. These are the retailer/business partners on the bottom of the chart.

The next step is conversion, when a shopper has become a full-fledged customer. This is the most straightforward step in the process—the initial marketing work has been successful and the prospect has responded to the call to action ("buy our product"). The sale is closed and conversion has occurred either through direct sales (e-commerce, for instance) or through a retailer. Once the customer is converted, he or she can be used for lead cultivation ("Do you know someone else who could benefit from this product?").

This, however, is not the end of the process. The goal in marketing, in addition to growing the size of your consumer base, is to create a repeat customer. Even though there are in fact two ways to grow your business— bring in new customers or get your current customers to buy more—it is much more cost efficient to get your current consumers to use more of your product because you do not need to teach them about your product, the category, the benefits, and so forth. Existing consumers already know about your brand and may simply need to be reminded to purchase the product.

To keep a prospect that has been converted into a consumer, marketers use a number of retention or loyalty techniques. Since most products today are commodities, it is the things that surround a product that garner retention. Saturn, for example, creates loyalty through their customer service. Gerber, a producer of premium products for babies and toddlers, creates retention and loyalty through providing information about child development and coupons for products that are appropriate for the child's age. Amazon.com "remembers" your purchases and provides suggestions for future purchases based on your past preferences ("Joe, last time you bought *The Passion of the Christ*, so now you might be interested in *The Da Vinci Code*"). Providing other spaces where the consumer can interact with the brand furthers brand attachment. Starbucks, for example, has branched out into supermarkets and even movie theaters with the 2006 film *Akeelah and the Bee* (affiliates in the chart). These exchanges between consumer and producer help lead to a bonding between the two. There is consistent reinforcement that the purchase decision is a good one and the brand can increasingly become a source of identification, for example, "I am a Coke drinker."

The final stage is post-sales service and support. This is where further personalization occurs between producer and consumer. The more the producer knows about the consumer, the better it is able to fulfill the consumer's needs. Using the Gerber example, if Gerber knows the age of your child, the company can send you the appropriate information and coupons that correspond to your child's age. Another example is the expanded use of the Internet, which has become an important space for personalization. A major part of that is the creation of places within a company's site where consumers can interact with each other, such as on bulletin boards or in chat rooms, creating opportunities for positive reinforcement of their purchase decisions. Through these interactions the company can continue to cross-sell (getting consumers to buy more products) and up sell (getting consumers to buy more expensive products) the convert—all in the hope of creating positive word-of-mouth, which is the most effective form of marketing.

Conversion career

Having examined the marketing relationship curve, we will look now at the conversion career and how it parallels the marketing process. While they are not exactly the same, there are some decided similarities between product acceptance and the framework of conversion for religious seekers.

Building on the work of conversion theory, Henri Gooren (2006a, 2006b) has developed the taxonomy of the conversion career. Under this theory the religious seeker or shopper goes through a multistage process in coming to accept a religious practice. The steps are: (1) pre-affiliation (potential members who have not yet committed to a group); (2) affiliation (formal membership); (3) conversion; and finally (4) confession (committed membership). I add to this framework the initial step of *spiritual awareness*, as people do not become involved in the process of becoming a member of a religious group unless they have determined that this is something missing in their life.

In the spiritual awareness phase, religious seekers become aware of a need for spirituality. They may have experienced a trauma in their life or it may be that they are in the period in their life cycle when they have children whom they believe should have religious instruction. It may even be that they have

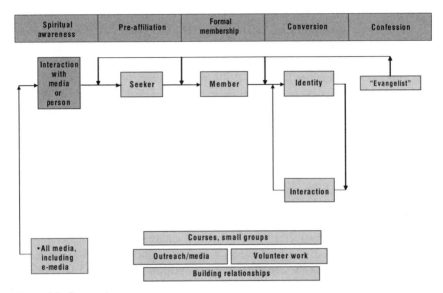

Figure 4.3 Conversion career

not specifically thought of seeking out religion or spirituality, but instead it has come to them either in the form of some type of marketing—advertising, direct marketing, or personal selling, for example—or through the media.

The next step, which is where Gooren's theory begins, is the pre-affiliation stage, or what I call the seeker stage. This phase is a trial period. The institution trying to woo potential members uses a less hard sell approach than that of traditional marketers. At this point the main objective is to allow the seeker to sample the "product" without scaring him or her away because of negative associations in their past. The organization makes information about its services readily available, but it does not require seekers to identify themselves to the organization. Seekers are allowed to go at their own pace. They are not forced to accept anything they are not ready for. We will see this in subsequent chapters when we discuss the Alpha Course and the Kabbalah Centre.

After spending time with a religious organization, the seeker may decide to become a full-fledged member. This is the first step in making a commitment to the religious institution. While committing to membership, the religion or spiritual practice has not yet become integral to the person's identity, but religious identity is likely to build over time as the new member moves from being anonymous to being identified, and in the case of megachurches, from merely attending services to participating in small groups, such as Bible study or recovery groups. As participation increases, this may also lead to volunteer work, which also increases a person's attachment and identification with the organization (see bottom of chart).

Increasing commitments of time, and also money, lead the member to the next step, which is conversion. At this point, the member has become fully identified with the religious group ("I am a follower of Kabbalah" or "I am born again.") This self-identification comes with a change in worldview and a change in the representation of the self as religious. As with the marketing relationship, identification is supported by interaction with other individuals. Being part of a community that supports your belief system is what is most likely to keep you believing. Starting from pre-affiliation and moving through conversion, an important support for the system is the building of relationships. The more connected people become to other people, the more likely that they will be committed to the institution—religious or secular—because by walking away, you are abandoning not just the institution, but also everyone with whom you have established a relationship.

The final step is confession, or what I call the "evangelist." I put this in quotes because I am not referring to Evangelicals per se, but rather the movement of the member from his or her own belief to wanting to share that belief with others. At this stage, the member has become fully immersed in the beliefs, rituals, and myths of the institution and participates regularly in services and other activities. Because such members feel so strongly about their newfound beliefs, they want to tell others, making them missionaries or evangelists for the belief system.

Parallels and repercussions

Broadly, the parallels between the marketing relationship curve and the religious conversion process are arresting. Within the marketing context, the seller of the product is trying to become part of a person's consideration set once that person has decided that there is a need in their life (problem recognition). In the marketing relationship curve that need could be religious or secular, it really makes no difference. In the conversion career, it is strictly religious or spiritual. In order to fill that need, the person needs to become aware of the alternatives available. In both cases, marketing and advertising are instrumental in informing prospects or seekers of their various options. A wide array of marketing tools is used, from billboards to personal selling to the store or church building itself. In both cases personal selling is the most effective means of creating "buy in" on the part of a prospect, because personal connections generate the highest levels of acceptance. Once acceptance occurs, the ultimate goal is to turn your loyal customer, your convert, into an evangelist for your product—whether that product is religious or not.

The key difference between religion and consumer products occurs at the point when the need is first recognized. A consumer need like buying a car, a computer, or a cell phone can be driven by external forces. This is the whole point of marketing—to generate a need or want for a specific branded product. But for the majority of people, the choice to pursue a religious practice tends to be an internally driven decision. The choice of *which* church or synagogue may be external, but the choice *to pursue* a faith practice is internal.[3] It is at the point when a person begins to look for a means to fill that recognized need that the conversion process becomes the same. That initial step is the search for information, which is aided by marketing methods, from advertising to PR to direct mail.

I would suggest here that the increase in religious shopping directly relates to religious consumers' ability to learn about alternatives during the search process. As discussed earlier, it is not enough that you be sociologically released from your ties to a religious institution; if there were no means to find out about something you would prefer, you would stay where you are. However, with the wealth of media alternatives available, a person need only turn on the television or search the Internet and hundreds of religious and spiritual alternatives become available, some virtually, some physically. For many consumers, it really doesn't matter if the religious message is through a communications medium; if a person is looking simply for an uplifting message and doesn't care about community and fellowship, online and televised churches may suit this religious shopper just fine. In sum, it is the combination of no fixed ties to a community and readily available information about alternatives that creates the increasingly popular shopping mentality around religion.

Pre-affiliation is identical to consideration. In both cases the prospect is still anonymous to the product company or religious institution. While marketers may be more blatantly aggressive at this point, religious institutions take the soft sell approach. We will see again and again that religious organizations do not push seekers to join the church or to commit to a belief system before they are ready. Membership is cultivated through small increments. Take a class and if you like it, you can take another. What happens between the first and second class, however, is that relationships are formed so that the person is committing not just to the study of the belief system, but also to the friendships he or she is developing. However, whether hard or soft sell, both marketers and religious organizations are attempting to cultivate a long-term user for their good or service. In support of this, different methods are used. Churches may use outreach programs as an attempt at establishing relationships. Open houses and free books are popular tactics used in this regard. This might be followed up with asking people to attend an additional meeting or to sample a small group. For marketers, it may be requesting more information like e-mail addresses or phone numbers, so that a more personalized, subsequent interaction can take place.

Conversion is different in the marketing sense than in the religious one. Marketers consider a person converted once they have made a purchase, not when they have become a repeat user. But in the religious framework, conversion does not usually occur until the belief system has become part of the person's identity. In both cases, the ultimate goal is for the convert to take on the identity of the product.

The final step in marketing is the most important, particularly in these times of easily available, virtually identical alternatives. That step is converting someone into an evangelist for the product—religious or otherwise. For consumer products this entails providing customer service, product information, and branded events. For religious groups this starts with confession (the final step) and then providing opportunities to evangelize.

Overall the psychological, if not physical, steps in both of these processes are identical: the seeker/consumer becomes aware of a choice, makes it part of his or her consideration set, purchases the product, and then wants to feel good about having made the decision. There are obviously larger considerations when choosing a truth/belief system than when choosing a computer or a bar of soap, but recognizing that the underlying process is the same aids in our understanding of why purchasing a product feels on some level like a religious experience, and how religion could become just one more product to fulfill consumers' needs.

The process of conversion is nothing new. What is new is that over the past 50 years it has been applied to consumer products. Consumers take on brands as part of their personal identity and in turn become evangelists for the product. The irony is that conversion and evangelizing have traditionally been religious processes, and now that religious institutions are reclaiming the concept of self-promotion, they are being chastised for being marketers. Thus it is not religious conversion that has changed, it is that consumer goods have taken ownership of the experience. In writing about missionaries and monetary fund marketers, Russell Belk (2000, p. 343) has come to a similar conclusion.

> The conversion experience…marketers seek is brand, store, or place loyalty. But while the goods and services marketers offer may be real, the paradisal bliss they promise has proven equally as ephemeral as the parallel promises of missionaries and monetary funds. In each case these change agents hold out images of material utopias that create, enlarge, sustain, and nurture, but ultimately dash human hopes. The one perhaps redeeming feature of the consumer goods marketers' promises of paradise is that we largely recognize the puffery and have few illusions that the goods promoted will actually bring us bliss. This is not to say that we have entirely given up the hope that they will. But we have been fooled so often in the past that we are no longer surprised when the acquisition and possession of a new car, clothing outfit, or fragrance fails to make us the popular and successful person shown in the ads. And alternative attributions may locate the fault less with the product than with our selves. A lingering doubt remains whether we have such incontrovertible flaws that even our latest acquisition, with

all its magical power, cannot help us. And if we ultimately fail to find nirvana with our purchases, we may still be grateful to the marketer for having tried to help us achieve it. For our parts, at least we have tried to find material happiness, and with luck next time we will succeed. For with the help and encouragement of marketers, we can always hope.

Whether we are talking about religion or brands, what we are searching for is a sense of hope, a sense of satisfaction, perhaps even nirvana. Today that sense is as likely to be generated by a product as it is by a preacher. However, as Roof (1993a) has said, "Deeply influenced by a culture of consumption, boomers have grown up with religion made into a commodity and have looked on it in much the same way as other purchasable goods" (p. 195). Thus the product and the preacher may just well be the same thing.

The marriage of marketing and religion

Brand communities and brand cults

> Generation Y is a new kind of consumer...Looking for community, these 78 million young people...want their brands to express a new reality—one in which they're interactive, interconnected and involved. These findings...have particularly significant implications for children's business retailers: change your goal from selling a product to creating a hip, community experience.
>
> (Children's Business, March 1, 1999)

The goal of marketing is to transform products into objects with meaning, not just for Gen Y, but for all consumers. This is particularly in evidence when we examine brand communities and brand cults. Marketing cultures fill in the void left by social structures that have abdicated their position in society. Just because people are not attending church doesn't mean that they do not value community. Just because people are not professing faith to a single religion does not mean that they do not trust or have faith in other institutions. Robert Putnam's now famous *Bowling Alone* thesis demonstrated that old types of community were no longer robust, but that newer ones, like the Sierra Club and women's groups were growing, and had replaced traditional communities. Now brand communities are yet another new method of coming together and these, too, are replacing traditional forms of community.

The idea of a brand community was first espoused by Albert M. Muniz, Jr. and Thomas C. O'Guinn (2001). According to their research, "a brand community is a specialized, non-geographically bound community, based on a structured set of social relations among admirers of a brand" (p. 412). Brand communities, unlike traditional communities, coalesce around a manufactured product, which makes the community specialized. The product is geographically dispersed because the media that advertises the product is dispersed, and because the users of the product are dispersed. These product users do, however, have multiple points of contact that may or may not occur in a physical space. And, as we will see, these communities demonstrate a number of social interactions similar to those of a physically based, traditional community.

Muniz and O'Guinn explain that, to date, the discourse of community has centered on the idea that modernity and consumerism have contributed to the demise of community. They argue, rather, that community has not disappeared, but exists within the commercial culture as brand communities. These communities are "most likely to form around brands with a strong image, a rich and lengthy history, and threatening competition. Also, things that are publicly consumed may stand a better chance of producing communities than those consumed in private" (p. 415). Thus history and competition (with its ominous sense of doom) aid in generating meaning and a sense of purpose in these communities.

The authors support their thesis with sociological theories about other types of communities. The first idea is that of neotribalism, which suggests that individualism is declining and in its place are neotribes that "are characterized by fluidity, occasional gatherings and dispersal" (Maffesoli, 1996, p. 76, quoted in Muniz and O'Guinn). Brand communities are fluid in that they regularly meet in cyberspace, but there are no regulations on participation. They meet in person for periodic events sponsored by the product company and these gatherings are usually the only time that members come together physically. Brand communities are also similar to "communities of limited liability" (Hunter and Suttles 1972; Jannowitz 1952); that is, they are like urban neighborhoods, which are "intentional, voluntary, and characterized by partial and differential involvement" (p. 414). Both of these theories suggest that communities do not require intense, consistent interaction on the part of members.

Muniz and O'Guinn claim that these groups are communities, and not simply a mass of people, because they "exhibit three traditional markers of community: shared consciousness, rituals and traditions, and a sense of moral responsibility" (p. 412). Shared consciousness, or what Joseph Gusfield (1978) calls "consciousness of kind," describes how members feel connected both to the brand and to each other. This connection, often forged by a quality that members cannot articulate, delineates users from nonusers. The authors include two underlying aspects of shared consciousness: legitimacy—someone who really knows the brand and thus legitimately belongs in the community; and oppositional brand loyalty—demonstrating opposition to opposing brands. In the study, which examined Ford Broncos, Macs, and Saabs, community members expressed disdain for those who drive Broncos for "the wrong reason," for example, because they happen to be trendy. For Mac users, expressing contempt for IBM and Microsoft is an ongoing theme.

Rituals and traditions, for any community, reproduce meaning for the group both internally and externally and aid in maintaining the community culture. For brand communities, these rituals and traditions center on product experiences. For Saab owners, one ritual is to wave or honk to one another when they pass on the street, almost like a secret handshake. Tradition is perpetuated through "celebrating the history of the brand." For Mac users, this manifests in having intricate knowledge of Steve Jobs, the company founder, and knowing the importance of January 24, 1984—the day Macintosh was introduced. Being aware of such rituals and traditions defines true believers. Moving from a marginal community member to an insider becomes a strong incentive to become more involved with the brand, and learning rituals and traditions is part of that process. Another important aspect of ritual and tradition is the sharing of stories.

> Storytelling is an important means of creating and maintaining community. Stories based on common experiences with the brand serve to invest the brand with meaning, and meaningfully link community member to community member. Communities traditionally create and retell myths about what happens to those who leave the safety of the community to venture out to the unknown world. The telling of these stories has a ritualistic character about it, and certainly represents a strong tradition within the brand communities.
>
> (Muniz and O'Guinn, 2001, p. 423)

These stories fall into a number of categories. For Saab users they may include "odyssey" stories, which include tales of traveling adventures and sleeping in the car. Others talk about life saving stories, which support Saab's safety attribute. For Mac users, stories include "Mac immunity" stories, which tell of how viruses do not attack this brand. Interestingly these myths or stories may initially come from a "commercial text." Marketers help perpetuate stories "by publishing and distributing community socialization materials such as histories, important brand stories and myths, and insider talk in the form of marketing communications such as brand magazines" (p. 423). However the community does not swallow this information whole hog, but rather acts as an interpretative community (Fish 1980; Scott 1994), adding their own input about how the brand should be presented to those both inside and outside the community.

The final aspect of community discussed by Muniz and O'Guinn is moral responsibility. This manifests in responsibility to the whole community as well as individual members. Two missions are included in this responsibility: "(1) integrating and retaining members, and (2) assisting brand community members in the proper use of the brand" (p. 424). Integrating and retaining members means helping others learn about proper behaviors with the brand. For example, if someone is a Mac user, it would be blasphemous to also use a PC. Assisting others may include offering basic help and guidance in using a product as well as providing information on additional sources that will assist them.

James McAlexander, John Schouten, and Harold Koening (2002) further developed the concept of the brand community. One key additional concept is that the relationships in the community are threefold: community member to brand, community member to firm, and community members to each other. Within these complex interactions, community members share "essential resources that may be cognitive, emotional or material in nature" (p. 38), but most of all they create and negotiate meaning, which the authors suggest is true of all communities.

McAlexander *et al.* initially thought to base their ideas on Daniel Boorstin's (1974) invisible consumption communities—communities based on what people consumed as opposed to interpersonal, geographically tied groups. However, their fieldwork suggested that there were "subcultures of consumption" (Schouten and McAlexander, 1995), groups in which people were more tightly connected than Boorstin had assumed. They found this to be true in their study of brandfests, events that "provide for geotemporal distillations of a brand community that afford normally dispersed member entities the opportunity for high-context interaction" (McAlexander *et al.*, 2002, p. 41). More specifically, these are events put together by marketers as a means to provide more personal interaction with the brand, the people who produce it, and other brand owners.

McAlexander *et al.* did some of their fieldwork at Jamborees and Camp Jeep, events that allow consumers to learn how to drive their Jeep off road and to talk with the maker of the vehicle. Learning to drive with an expert helps move consumers toward being "legitimate" brand community members because they are more versed in the correct use of the product. These brandfests also allow for interaction between more and less experienced brand users. McAlexander *et al.* also suggest that communities are solidified through inviting friends and family to share their brand experience, which is promoted by the brand company. This helps to integrate the community because users have continuous reinforcement of their brand beliefs. "Sharing meaningful consumption experiences strengthens interpersonal ties and enhances mutual appreciation for the product, the brand, and the facilitating marketers. Virtual ties become real ties. Weak ties become stronger. Stronger ties develop additional points of attachment" (p. 44). Moreover, these personal relationships act as exit barriers to the community, making it more difficult should someone decide to leave or switch.

Further developing the idea of communities and then relating it to religion can be seen in subsequent work that Muniz did with Hope Jensen Schau (2005) in examining the Apple Newton community. The

Apple Newton was the predecessor to the Palm Pilot, and though it was discontinued by Apple, this did not stop avid fans of the product from building a community to support and perpetuate the use of the product. The narratives that this community uses most reflect that of a religious community, including stories that contain themes of persecution, miracles, and resurrection.

Adding to his earlier work, here Muniz with Schau suggests that brand communities are defined "by their capacity for powerful and transformative experiences. Many of these experiences have religious and magical overtones" (2005, p. 738). These experiences become shared through community myths, which in turn further solidify relationships within the group. Within the Apple Newton community, the myths surround "survival, the miraculous, and the return of the creator" (p. 739). The authors state that these themes not only stem from the context of the community, but also are "indicative of the very clear and resilient need humans have to believe in something or someone outside mundane reality" (p. 739). Like a religious community, Newton enthusiasts feel compelled to explain their brand. Oftentimes this comes up when defending themselves against conversion to other products. These members fight back by demonstrating the wonders of Newton. Muniz and Schau see this as a fundamental religious aspect of the community—the use of these stories is an effort to create a world where Newton flourishes and nonbelievers are converted.

Religious aspects are in evidence in other ways as well. Community members are empowered through their faith in the brand. A slogan often used by the group is "keep the faith," and myths exist about how faith in the product was rewarded. Online community members share tales of how wireless technology, which did not exist at the time of the Newton's creation, can be configured to work with the Newton. Community members see this as a magical element of the product. Survival tales are legion. Community members often talk about the product being indestructible, thus suggesting that Newton has become a religious totem. Tales of miraculous recovery—data once lost is recovered—are also common. Such stories are often responded to in the online community with religious affirmations such as, "Hallelujah, I believe!" (p. 742). Finally, tales of resurrection—that some day Apple will see the error of its way and bring back the Newton—is a recurring theme in this community. All of these myths and the reactions to them suggest a strong similarity between this brand community and more traditional religious groups. In fact, the authors state, "Our findings reveal important properties of brand communities and, at a deeper level, speak to the communal nature of religion and the enduring human need for religious affiliation" (p. 737).

Taking the community analogy still further, the symbiotic relationship between religion and marketing has been adopted by the marketing industry under the rubric of the brand cult—the new gold standard for brand success.

There is little discernible difference between brand communities and brand cults other than as a way to further equate products with religion and, perhaps, the level of commitment by cult members.

Brand cults are self-selected groups that surround a particularly powerful branded product. A good example of this is Mac users (as mentioned earlier, this group was also researched as a brand community). People who use Macintosh computers are devoted to the brand. Mac users share information, use a special language, and even have their own trade show (Macworld). Products become a form of religion for these brand cult members, providing rituals, traditions, and a shared worldview.

While Apple has come up repeatedly as an example, it is not the only brand cult. Schouten and McAlexander (1995) studied Harley Davidson users, and while they do not refer to them as a cult, they do say that the brand is "in effect, a religious icon, around which an entire ideology of consumption is articulated" (p. 50). In *The Power of Cult Branding*, Matthew Ragas and B. J. Bueno (2002) list nine different successful cult brands, including Apple and Harley Davidson, but also Linux, the Volkswagen Beetle, Jimmy Buffett, and Oprah.

Douglas Atkin (2004), a strategic marketer for an advertising agency and the creator of the cult brand concept,[4] found in his research (p. xiii) that:

> [T]he same dynamics are at play behind the attraction to brands and cults. They may vary in degree of strength (although not always), but not in type…When research subjects were recounting their reasons for joining and committing, they were describing the profound urges to belong, make meaning, feel secure, have order within chaos, and create identity…The sacred and profane are being bound by the essential desires of human nature, which seeks satisfaction wherever it can.

Atkin, too, studied Apple and Harley Davidson users along with eBay and JetBlue consumers, among others. His conclusion was that as commercialism increases, so, too, will the commercialization of organizations that sell "community, meaning and identity" (p. xiv).

What we can learn from this examination of brand communities and brand cults is that as our physical communities have become more fractured, other social agents have stepped in to fill the void. Online communities have been popular among different demographic segments and now brand communities provide an opportunity to come together through products that engender shared interest. As Howard Rheingold (2000) noted in his examination of online communities, these groups seem to function best and are more cohesive when physical interaction occurs in addition to other forms of interrelationship. Thus annual marketing events aid in maintaining the online interaction.

These groups are true communities with shared experiences, rituals, and myths and a sense of responsibility to the community. That they occur in relationship to a marketed product does not diminish the importance of these communities for their group members. If we think about religious groups as "brand communities," we can see where religions have taken on some aspects of these product groups. For instance, less face-to-face meetings are acceptable and are supplemented with mediated interaction. Big events, like Christmas and Rosh Hashanah, become similar to the brandfests of the brand communities—a few key times a year in which community members interact and repeat their myths and rituals is enough to perpetuate the group.

Intimacy is also an important aspect of community. The obvious question becomes: how does a brand create intimacy? In part it occurs through the elements that we have been talking about—shared experiences, the development of myths, and the acting out of rituals. Intimacy is also fostered by the relationships within the community, and as marketers have advocated, bringing family and friends to the brand is the most effective means of connecting consumers to the community. At the ultimate (from the marketers' perspective), product purchasers will become "community-integrated customers [who] serve as brand missionaries, carrying the marketing message into other communities" (McAlexander *et al.*, 2002, p. 51)—the very essence of the marketing relationship curve.

Faith brands

There are numerous similarities between marketing and religion, and the line between the two has become increasingly blurred. Evangelicals are marketing by using demographics and psychographics; marketers have learned the value of creating brand cult members—users so enthusiastic for a product that they become product evangelicals. Religions and brands create myths for understanding the world. Products and faiths are both sources for identity creation. From the marketing side, there have come brand cults; now, religions are faith brands.

Faith brands are spiritual products that have been given popular meaning and awareness through marketing. They have a readily recognizable name and logo, though there may or may not be a tagline. These products may be books, religious courses, a spiritual practice, a pastor, or some combination of all of these. More so than with consumer products, spokespeople—pastor, rabbi, or television personality—are an important aspect of the brand.

In the next section of this book, I will present some of the most popular and profitable faith brands. Church courses, like 40 Days of Purpose and the Alpha Course, which has significant brand recognition in England and is becoming increasingly known in the United States, are important marketing products for bringing prospects into a church. These brands are highly associated with the people who created them—Rick Warren and Nicky

Gumbel respectively. These pastors are important elements of the brand, just as the new televangelists—Joel Osteen, Joyce Meyer, T. D. Jakes—are faith brands with line extensions that include their ministries, their books, and their conferences for believers as well as church leaders. Note here that it is the televangelists that are the faith brands and not their churches. Joel Osteen, for example, is the pastor of the Lakewood Church in Houston, and promotion for the church is conducted under the "Joel Osteen Ministries" logo rather than a separate logo for the church.

Joel Osteen will be examined, as his is the country's largest megachurch. We will also look at Oprah Winfrey as part of this group, because while there is no doubt that she is a major brand, I believe that she is also a faith brand. Her show is an important example of the secular becoming more sacred, just as Joel Osteen is an example of the sacred becoming more secular.

Kabbalah, too, is on the list of faith brands because it is now widely known throughout the world as the result of a well-orchestrated marketing campaign through the Kabbalah Centre. This is the most product-oriented of the faith brands, and it also has its own popular spokesperson in Madonna, even if she is not the leader of the organization. Many of the organizations discussed in the next section are part of megachurches, but they will not be separated out because it is usually not the church itself that makes up the brand. These organizations will be discussed, however, within the context of the other faith brands.

As we will see, faith brands act like other consumer products. They are repackaged and retooled to appeal to consumer tastes. This means changing the product as well as the packaging. In the case of religion, this means changing the content of religious services to appeal to specific target audiences. For many this has meant shorter, more entertaining weekly services. It also means marrying the product to the faith brand message. For example, if Joel Osteen is "the smiling preacher," then the content of his sermons must match this image in order to perpetuate the brand. Therefore, sermons are overwhelmingly positive and uplifting without mention of sin or salvation.

Faith brands, as marketed products, take on the ultimate goal of all marketers—growth. Growth is measured in terms of attendance as well as in terms of the number of products sold. While some may measure growth in terms of the number of actual members added to their church or synagogue, simply getting people in the door seems to override this goal. Growth can also be measured in terms of brand extensions or franchises.

That faith brands and brand cults exist demonstrates the full extent to which marketing and religion have taken on aspects of one another. In a culture where we spend more time with media than any activity other than working and sleeping, and that media is supported by advertising and marketing, it should not be surprising that religion would need to take on aspects of the market in order to stay relevant within the culture. It is at its base a product, competing against an overwhelming number of other products in the consumer marketplace.

If religion is to win the marketing war (and marketing is a war as evidenced by the terminology—objective, strategy, tactic), it has to fight with every tool available.[5] If a religious institution wants someone to get up out of their Barcolounger, drive through traffic, sit for an hour or more during a service, and then drive home again—all this when the person could be engaging with a plethora of media and entertainment options—then that religious institution needs to offer a product that's worth the effort. If it means changing the message and the way it is packaged to get people in the door, so be it. Moreover, in order for a religious institution to be noticed by people, it has to find a way to "stick out in the clutter," that is, be heard above all the other noise of the culture. That's what branding does. But taking on the mantle of branding means also taking on the mantel of marketing. This means pandering to audience tastes, no matter what the consequences are, all in the quest for the elusive goal—growth.

Chapter 5

The course to God

While other denominations are declining, evangelical Protestantism is growing. So much, in fact, that evangelicals are now the largest religious group in the United States, representing 36 percent of all practitioners (Symonds, 2005, p. 81). Much of this increase can be attributed to the success of seeker churches. These churches, also known as megachurches, now total more than 1,200, up from 600 since the turn of the millennium.[1] Megachurches minister to more than 2,000 congregants but can serve as many as 20,000 to 30,000 people—or more—on a weekly basis. According to *Religion & Ethics Newsweekly*, "Megachurches that have grown the fastest report almost two-thirds of their members are involved in outreach and evangelizing their friends, family and neighbors" (Megachurches, 2006).

One of the most important tools to turn church members into faith brand evangelists—or personal salespeople—is the church course. While there are virtually hundreds of such courses, there are only a few that have risen above the rest to become branded, readily recognizable products that turn a "commodity church" into a branded one. Purpose Driven (or 40 Days of Purpose) and the Alpha Course are two that have come out of megachurch environments to help spread the good word around the world.

Purpose Driven®

The creation of a brand

It's unusual for someone not to have heard of *The Purpose Driven Life*. It is the best-selling hardcover, nonfiction book of all time—second only to the Bible. It has been translated into more than 50 languages. Its author, Rick Warren, founder of the Saddleback megachurch in California, is a ubiquitous presence in the media. However, Purpose Driven is more than a book. It is a brand and the primary means of perpetuating this brand is a church course called 40 Days of Purpose. This is the story of how this course came to be.

The Purpose Driven phenomenon started not with *The Purpose Driven Life* but with *The Purpose Driven Church: Growth without Compromising*

Your Message and Your Mission, which is a guide to creating a healthy church by tending to the needs of the people, rather than to the needs of the church.[2] The principles of *The Purpose Driven Church* became the foundation for subsequent products and services offered by the Purpose Driven brand. To understand this brand, it is necessary to understand the tenets of this initial work.

The way to focus on the needs of members and potential members (a fundamental marketing principle) is to manage a church based on five New Testament purposes, which are:

> Love the Lord with all your heart.
> Love your neighbor as yourself.
> Go and make disciples.
> Baptize them.
> Teach them to obey.
>
> (Warren, 1995, pp. 103–6)

By balancing worship, ministry, evangelicalism, fellowship, and discipleship, Warren asserts that it's possible to create a healthy, thriving church.

The most important question a church has to ask is, "Why do we exist?" Out of answering that question, the church develops a "purpose statement," similar to a corporate mission statement.[3] Like corporate mission statements, the purpose must be winnowed down to one line. For example, Disney's statement is "To make people happy," and Wal-Mart's is "To give ordinary folk the chance to buy the same thing as rich people" (BRS, n.d.). For Purpose Driven organizations, the purpose statement must be biblical (the key difference from a corporate statement), specific, transferable, and measurable (stated in terms of results and not activities). After defining the purpose statement, it must be communicated to the church regularly, the church must be organized around its purpose, and the church's purpose must be applied to all aspects of the church.

To implement the purpose, it is necessary to have a process, or what marketers would call a strategy. Saddleback's process, for example, is: "We bring people in, build them up, train them, and send them out. We bring them in as *members*, we build them up to *maturity*, we train them for *ministry*, and we send them out on *mission*, *magnifying* the Lord in the process" (Warren, 1995, p. 109). This straightforward method means that the organization can stay focused on its goal—to increase the number of people who "are being mobilized for the Great Commission."

Warren created his Purpose Driven philosophy based on what he learned from visiting successful churches and applying those strategies to his own church. In starting Saddleback, Warren determined that the best way to increase the ministry was to focus on the unchurched—those who do not attend services on a regular basis, if at all. In order to find the unchurched, he analyzed demographic and census data about cities around the United States. He learned that one of the least churched areas of the country was Orange County, California, and at the time (in the late 1970s), it was the fastest-growing region in the nation. That combination—an unchurched populace and high population growth—has become crucial in determining where many new megachurches will be established. Thus the marketing strategy is defined: target unbelievers and turn them into new users. This is as opposed to stealing regular churchgoers from the competition, a strategy that does not deliver on the overriding goal of increasing believers and creating new missionaries.

To move people through the process of being a seeker to becoming a missionary takes several years—a key difference from consumer product marketers, who must live by quarterly financial statements. Warren uses a diagram of concentric circles to illustrate the path that seekers take from Community (seeker) to Core (lay minister). The outermost circle is made up of the unchurched community within which the church resides. Inside that circle is the crowd, or regular church attendees. Within that is the congregation, which is made up of church members. The fourth circle is committed or maturing members. The innermost circle is the core, which is made up of lay ministers (Warren, 1995, p. 130). In this way, Warren distinguishes between "the Crowd," the large outer circle made up of seekers who come to see what the church is all about, and "the Congregation," members of the church who have taken courses, signed a membership covenant, agreed to tithe, and have committed to daily quiet time and weekly small group participation (p. 54). While it is important to continually bring in new prospects, the most important goal takes into account the church's purpose—converting seekers to members and finally to lay ministers. This is why Warren cautions that "the church should be *seeker sensitive*, but it must not be seeker driven" (p. 80).

Another defining element of the Purpose Driven church is the use of small groups. Warren claims to have stumbled upon this idea when he realized that he couldn't do everything himself.

> He had hit upon an organizational structure that has allowed Saddleback to get big and stay small. Today it has 3,300 small groups organized by neighborhood, interests, or experiences: men, women, teens, mothers of preschoolers, people who speak Korean, wives of unbelievers, fitness buffs. ("How can you serve the Lord to the fullest if your body is rundown, tired, and not functioning as God designed it to function?" says an ad for an aerobics group.)…a key function of its [Saddleback's] website today is to organize the groups, which typically meet weekly to pray, study the Bible, and do good works.
>
> (Gunther, 2005, pp. 112–13)

Whether fitness- or family-related, groups are separated based on their purpose. There are seeker groups, which allow newcomers to explore and ask questions;[4] support groups that deal with life stages such as parenting for the first time, loss of a spouse, and divorce; recovery groups, which assist in overcoming addictions to alcohol, drugs, sex, and food, among others; service groups, which are for ministry outreach; and growth groups, which create the discipleship classes and other educational programs (Warren, 1995, p. 146).

The Purpose Driven Church was the penultimate step in the process of creating a network of church leaders to change the world for Christ—what Warren has called his "stealth strategy" (Stafford, 2002, p. 42). Before the book, Warren gave seminars to church leaders for more than a decade. These had started as "brown-bag lunches and church tours....[and] morphed into conferences about church-building" (Nussbaum, 2006, p. 1).[5] Purpose Driven seminars and conferences became Purpose Driven Ministries, a nonprofit organization through which pastors could learn from Warren how to replicate the success of Saddleback. Purpose Driven conferences are given on an annual basis and are attended by thousands of pastors. By 2002 the number had reached 3,800 pastors for a two-day event (Stafford, 2002). Through the combination of conferences, book sales, and sales of tapes and sermons, Warren amassed a considerable following of tens of thousands of church leaders—all of whom would be a primed audience for the next step, *The Purpose Driven Life*.

The Purpose Driven® Life—the course disguised as a book

The Purpose Driven Life had an initial print run of 500,000 copies. This large, and what people might have thought optimistic, printing was possible because the book was pre-sold to pastors based on Warren's long-standing relationship with them. Supporting the book launch was a public relations campaign entitled "40 Days of Purpose," which was in essence Sunday school for adults. In conjunction with the release of the book, congregations would follow the text of *The Purpose Driven Life* for 40 days. Thousands of pastors, who had read *The Purpose Driven Church* or had signed up for pastors.com (Warren's Web site for church leaders) and were already predisposed to the Purpose Driven concept, signed up to be part of the 40 Days campaign. In order to participate, churches had to buy the book by the caseload (at a discount) so that everyone in the church could follow along for the 40-day program.

The Purpose Driven Life is 40 days of spiritual exercises that are based on the concepts of *The Purpose Driven Church* but reconfigured to suit the individual seeker rather than an entire congregation. *The Purpose Driven Life* consists of basic tenets of Christianity, repackaged into 40 easily digestible chapters. The book begins by explaining the importance of 40 days—Moses on Mount Sinai, Noah and the Flood, and so on. It also includes a covenant to be signed by the reader that establishes a commitment to "discover God's purpose for my life" (Warren, 2003, p. 13). Each chapter contains one day's worth of simple spiritual exercises for the reader to follow. The chapters are short—usually four to eight pages—and end with a box entitled "Thinking About my Purpose." In this box are "points to ponder" (ideas such as "It's not about me" or "I am not an accident"), "verses to remember" (biblical verses related to the thought for the day), and "questions to consider" (questions that are meant to help the reader in delving deeper into the idea of the day). The Purpose Driven philosophy is based on five tenets: worship God, join a church, study the word of God, serve others, and bring others to Christ. These points are the teachings of the *Purpose Driven Church* translated into ones that an individual practitioner can relate to and endeavor to practice.

The 40 Days of Purpose campaign was launched in October 2002. This ambitious book promotion reached an estimated half million people in 1,562 churches around the world. The teachings began with a sermon by Warren that was available via satellite. Throughout the campaign churches had access to videos of Warren via the Internet (Lobdell, 2002, p. B8). There were also classes and Bible study focusing on Warren's five purposes. It was never expected that this would be a one-shot promotion, though no one could have known that 40 Days of Purpose would turn into multiple national campaigns to turn local churches into Purpose Driven churches. By the end of November 2003, 1.5 million people in 4,500 churches in the United States and 20 countries had taken the 40-day course of study (Gorski, 2003, p. A1).

Since then 40 Days of Purpose has morphed from a PR campaign into a full-fledged church course. In addition to the satellite feeds and the books, congregations have access to the 40 Days of Purpose Resource Kit, which contains videos, songs, sermons, and reading materials (Purpose Driven, n.d.c). It has also spawned 40 Days of Community, a new initiative that takes the Purpose Driven concepts out of the congregation and into the surrounding community. Warren explained the magnitude of this course at a Pew Forum in 2005.

Ten percent of the churches in America have now done 40 Days of Purpose....We will take another 10 to 15 thousand through it this year, and on and on and on. And there's a little story of how that got started in churches and then it spread to corporations like Coca-Cola and Ford and Wal-Mart, and they started doing 40 Days of Purpose. And then it spread to all the sports teams. I spoke at the NBA All-Stars this year because all of the teams were doing 40 Days of Purpose. LPGA, NASCAR, most of the baseball teams—when the Red Sox were winning the World Series, they were going through 40 Days of Purpose during the Series. So the story of the 40 Days of Purpose is more than the story of the book. And maybe we can get back to why that touched such a nerve around the world, because *The Purpose Driven Life* is not just the best-selling book in American history; it's the best-selling book in about a dozen languages....

The next phase that you're going to see is we're actually doing citywide 40 Days of Purposes. We've already done one in Chattanooga; we're going to do one in Philadelphia this fall with 250 African-American churches. We're doing one in Orlando.

And it doesn't stop there. 40 Days has also made an impact on the American military. According to the *New York Times*, a recent Air Force-sponsored Spiritual Fitness Conference offered U.S.-based chaplains workshops based on the book (Kaminer, 2005, p. 28). And, finally, Rwanda has now been dubbed the first Purpose Driven country (Bergner, 2006, p. 44), learning the ways of this brand through the book and the course.

There can be little doubt as to the success of the Purpose Driven brand. Its breadth can be seen in "300 community ministries to groups such as prisoners, CEOs, addicts, single parents, and people with HIV/AIDS" (Berkowitz, 2006, p. 1). According to the Purpose Driven Web site (purposedrivenlife. com), ABC News reported that the Purpose Driven Life is "the epicenter of a spiritual shockwave taking root across America in unlikely places like offices and university campuses. It has become a movement" (Purpose Driven Web site, n.d.a).[6] According to purposedriven.com, the Web site for Purpose Driven churches, Warren has helped train more than 400,000 church leaders throughout the world in the ways of Purpose Driven. There are Purpose Driven lives, Purpose Driven churches, and now Purpose Driven countries.

Marketing Rick Warren—the creator of the brand

Everything about Rick Warren is disarming. Whether by default, and almost undoubtedly by design, Warren is presented as an approachable Everyman who just happens to have written a best-selling book. He often dresses in Hawaiian shirts, and he doesn't wear socks. People call him Rick, or Pastor Rick. He has a monthly column called "Purpose" in *Ladies Home Journal*. He talks and preaches like he writes, in an easy, relational style, using simple words and concepts. He has been quoted as saying that he doesn't know how to do things, yet somehow he'll figure it out. But don't let any of that fool you. *Forbes* magazine called Warren a "spiritual entrepreneur" and stated that if Warren's ministry were a business, it "would be compared with Dell, Google, or Starbucks" (Karlgaard, 2004, p. 39). He is as much Bill Gates as he is Billy Graham.

Warren has been called "the most prominent face of evangelicalism," and he's been dubbed America's pastor.[7] In a 2005 *Time* magazine cover story entitled "The 25 Most Influential Evangelicals," Warren's picture graced the opening page (the article did not list the evangelicals in rank order, but the first-place listing was certainly implied). According to this article, "when 600 pastors were asked to name the people they thought had the greatest influence on church affairs in the country, Warren's name came in second only to Billy Graham's" (Van Biema, 2005, p. 35). With Graham having all but abdicated the religious throne due to age and health, Warren has taken up the mantle.

His status has been achieved as a result of years of cultivation. Rick Warren has been marketing and promoting Christianity for close to 30 years. He started out in 1980 by selling sermon transcripts, books, and Bible lessons to churches around the world. He did not limit his reach to church leaders, however. He faxed messages to thousands of business leaders as well (Gold, 2000, p. B1). By 2000 the entrepreneurial enterprise was transported to the Internet as pastors.com. While initially created as a portal with e-mail, chat rooms, and online auctions, the site now offers a plethora of products from books (*The Purpose Driven Life* is featured) to Bible study (which leads you to a page where you can purchase CDs) to sermons (which are available for $4 apiece). The centerpiece of the site is a "pastors only" area, which gives church leaders access to bulletin boards as well as the ability to sign up for a free newsletter called "Rick Warren's Ministry Toolbox." The Toolbox is a weekly e-mail that includes an opening note from Rick, a section on ministry perspectives, recommendations for books (many written by Saddleback ministers), "Saddleback Sayings," "Bible Bytes," and hyperlinks to pastoral resources. Recently the Toolbox added a link to a 20-part series on Rick Warren in the *Orange County Register* (Warren, 2006).

The Toolbox is not the only e-mail that Warren sends out. One e-mail sent in May 2006 contained the following message:

Dear friends,

I recently created a short video to explain exactly what it means to be a follower of Jesus Christ and posted it on our Purpose Driven Web site. It's a simple presentation you can pass on to anyone you care about.

You can place this link on your own Web site http://www.purposedriven.com/salvation and copy and paste it at the bottom of all your e-mails, like I do below. You also can download it and place it on your Web site, too. http://www.purposedriven.com/salvation.zip

My only desire is to help you share the Good News with the people in your life.

I thank God for you!

Rick Warren

This e-mail is the very essence of viral marketing. With one simple communication, Warren has distributed this video to thousands of pastors, who in turn will e-mail it to their congregations and/or put it on their Web sites. Moreover he has provided a highly produced video that can be used to improve the overall image of a small, local church, much in the same way churches connected their advertising to *The Passion of the Christ*.

Starting in August 2006, there was another new monthly e-mail distributed to pastors. Called the Purpose Driven Monthly e-mail, it contains three sections—resources, conferences, and 40 Day Campaigns. The first and most prominent section is the resource area, which lets recipients know about products such as DVDs for small group leadership, books, and new products from Celebrate Recovery, an addiction recovery Web site. The conferences section promotes things like "Race Against Time" (Warren's HIV/AIDS initiative) and a couples retreat. The 40 Days Campaign section provides links to the 40 Days of Purpose and 40 Days of Community campaigns.

Pastors.com is not Warren's only Web site. There is www.rickwarren.com, which interestingly is the smallest of the sites. It provides links to several others Web sites including a site for the Saddleback Church, purposedriven. com (which is pastor-directed), purposedrivenlife.com (which is targeted to the individual seeker), Acts of Mercy (which talks about the PEACE and AIDS/HIV initiatives), Celebrate Recovery (similar to a 12-step program though more strongly focused on a commitment to Christ and his teachings), Saddleback Family (a site for church members), and the PEACE Plan (a site dedicated to Warren's current project to eradicate poverty).

The PEACE Plan is Warren's latest campaign, an effort of mobilize Christians around the world to fight what he considers to be the planet's biggest problems: spiritual emptiness, corrupt leadership, poverty, disease, and illiteracy (Purpose Driven Web site, n.d.b). PEACE stands for: plant churches, equip leaders, assist the poor, care for the sick, and educate the next generation. The most visible part of this plan of late is Warren's mission to address the AIDS crisis in Africa. While AIDS has been a thorny issue for evangelicals in the United States due to its connection with homosexual lifestyles, overseas the issue more directly affects women and children, thus making it more palatable for evangelicals. With this new initiative, Warren has generated considerable publicity—both for himself as well as for the Purpose Driven brand. The most significant piece of promotion was a one-hour, primetime Fox News special called *Purpose Drive Life: Can Rick Warren Change the World?*, which aired in the summer of 2006.

Say what you will about Rick Warren, he is an entrepreneur, a skilled leader, and a brilliant marketer of himself and the Purpose Driven brand. He has helped create a brand that is being perpetuated through a combination of marketing elements. First, there are the e-mails to pastors that work synergistically with the numerous Web sites connected to Purpose

Driven, Rick Warren, and Saddleback. Second, there has been traditional promotion. For example, in late 2005 quotes from *The Purpose Driven Life* appeared on cups at Starbucks (Grossman, 2005, p. D8). Third, the books themselves perpetuate more sales in that Warren encourages people to buy the book for partners, neighbors, and friends while he encourages churches to buy it in bulk for their members. Finally, there are the church members themselves who have become evangelizers for Purpose Driven. If someone accepts a Purpose Driven life, they have committed to continually bringing new people into the church creating an unending supply of new prospects.

According to Geoff Tunnicliffe, head of the World Evangelical Alliance, Rick Warren is "rebranding…American evangelism" (Gunther, 2005, p. 120). That brand is Purpose Driven, and Rick Warren is its icon.

Putting Purpose Driven in perspective

Before there was Rick Warren and Saddleback, there was Bill Hybels and Willow Creek. So why is Purpose Driven ubiquitous and there is no well-known brand associated with Hybels or Willow Creek? The difference is in the marketing, both in terms of target audience and packaging. Warren started with pastors but had the expectation of ultimately reaching individuals. While Hybels has the same ultimate goal of converting individuals, he has continued to primarily target church leaders without having crossed over to speak to individuals directly. Moreover, his church course, which is directed at pastors, is called "Becoming a Contagious Christian." This title is viscerally less accessible than the phrase "Purpose Driven." And it highlights the difference between these two preachers: Hybels has a propensity to flaunt his Christian faith, while Warren is willing to obscure his beliefs (at least initially) in an effort to bring more believers to the church. By looking at these and other similarities and differences between these two men, their megachurches, and their courses, we can see the ultimate impact of marketing.

Willow Creek was founded in the mid-1970s. Started in 1975 by Hybels—then only 23 years old—Willow Creek grew from 150 members to 2,000 congregants in a mere three years. Now Willow Creek is firmly planted on a campus in South Barrington, an affluent suburb of Chicago, and ministers to 20,000 weekly attendees.

It was Bill Hybels—not Rick Warren—who pioneered the concept of an upscale, youthful "seeker" church. He used consumer-focused techniques popularized by management guru Peter Drucker (just as Warren did). "What is our business? Who is our customer? What does the customer consider value?"—these questions, provoked by Drucker, are listed on a poster outside of Hybels's office. Employing these techniques, Willow Creek grew rapidly and drew the lion's share of media attention in the late-1980s and early

1990s. In 1989 *Fortune* magazine claimed that "the paradigm of customer orientation is Willow Creek Community Church" (Stewart, 1989, p. 117), not only for churches but for any type of consumer-oriented organization. In 1991 a Harvard Business School case study was written about the organization, marveling at how, in 15 years, the church had grown from nothing to a thriving church of tens of thousands of members with a multimillion dollar budget.

In these pieces and elsewhere, the church was noted for its consumer-friendly religious services, which contain highly produced dramas, use live contemporary music, and are of short duration. Willow Creek was also noted for its lack of traditional Christian accoutrement like crosses and hymnals, for its casual dress code, and for its free childcare. Most importantly, it was noted for its size and for its marketing acumen. (All of these things could ultimately be said about Saddleback as well.)

Bill Hybels conducted his door-to-door survey in the mid-1970s (Stewart, 1989, p. 117), and not surprisingly the story sounds almost identical to that of Rick Warren. He asked, "Do you actively attend a local church?" If the person said yes, it was on to the next. If the answer was no, he asked, "Why not?" Just as Warren did a few years later, Hybels found that non-churchgoers thought churches were about money, and that the services were boring and irrelevant. Based on the information from the surveys, Hybels developed a psychographic profile for Willow Creek's target audience. He named this person "Unchurched Harry." Unchurched Harry is white, upscale, and male. He is also defined by the fact that he "wants to be left alone. He wants to be guaranteed that he's not going to have to sing anything, sign anything, or give anything" (p. 120).

Willow Creek and Saddleback both targeted the unchurched, but only Willow Creek made the decision to specifically target men because studies showed that if you got men to attend church, women would readily follow (Lewis, 1996, p. 14). Moreover, we know that women attend church more than men, so targeting a campaign at women is going to be less effective in terms of generating new users.

To that end, Willow Creek was designed with this consumer in mind. Seeker services are held on Sunday and believer services occur during midweek, a schedule that Saddleback also uses. This fits the consumer-friendly model because the seeker services occur when the unchurched expect to attend church (so there is no conflict with a preexisting belief) and when busy, upscale men are most likely to be available. To increase relevance, Hybels presented sermons that were personal, understanding that these men would relate to the issues and problems going on in his life because he was one of them. According to Twitchell (2004), "Hybels is forever referencing his own family, neighborhood, history, and experience" (p. 95). Finally, attendees are not asked for money, nor are they pushed into accepting Jesus until they are ready.

Hybels stresses the use of the soft sell in promoting Jesus to the unchurched. He understands that "Harry" (and now sometimes "Mary") doesn't want to be banged over the head as soon as he walks through the door. For that reason, there is a deliberate process (much like that at Saddleback) that seekers go through—attending church services and then attending small group sessions, followed by seminars to deepen church commitment, and finally a meeting with a counselor to determine which one of more than 100 ministries would most benefit from that member's gifts. In addition to the steps to develop in faith, there are also groups and activities that may or may not be specifically related to religious practice, such as marriage enrichment and recovery groups. Participation in these groups acts to enmesh the person with the church. The process is slow and deliberate, and very effective. The beauty of it is that like all evangelizing institutions, once there is a base of believers, the church becomes a sales pyramid, helping itself to grow exponentially.

Willow Creek's strength has been in its approach to pastors and others in the church growth movement and not in terms of its branding beyond the Christian market. Pastors soon noted the success of Willow Creek, and Hybels (yet again like Warren) began holding conferences for these church leaders. Conferences occurred three times a year and were attended by upwards of 500 people (Gilbreath, 1994, p. 23). Hybels has continued to give conferences and in August 2006, he held a leadership summit that was attended and/or viewed via satellite by 50,000 pastors and volunteers. His appeal to church leaders is evident in Willow Creek's having been recently chosen as the most influential congregation in the United States in a survey of 2,000 non-Catholic pastors (Brachear, 2006, p. 1).

Willow Creek's influence on the church leadership community comes from its longstanding consulting arm—the Willow Creek Association (WCA). Formed in 1992, the WCA was started to reach a larger audience of church leaders than could be handled through on-site conferences. Today 11,700 churches from 90 denominations are members of the association. The association (www.willowcreek.com versus .org for the church) is a not-for-profit institution that has "attracted 110,000 fee-paying church and lay leaders in 2004" (*BusinessWeek*, 2005, p. 84) and generated $17 million in conference and membership fees.[8] Member fees provide access to, among many things, a monthly audio tape about strategies to "maximize their church's impact," online discussion boards with other members, discounts on conferences, and educational items such as books and small group study materials as well as Web-based ministry tools. These last elements include what WCA calls the "Service Builder," an online tool that helps church leaders put together church services using materials provided by Willow Creek. As the WCA Web site (Willow Creek Association, 2007) states:

You choose: the topics your service will address; the types of media you'll need for your service; and your target audience; Service Builder will search from an extensive selection of music, message transcripts, dramas, and multi-media to create your own unique, life-changing service. Or search through Willow Creek Community Church's archives of the past ten years worth of services to see examples of how WCCC has put together their services over the years.

Hybels, like Warren, has a seminar for pastors based on one of his books. This is a one-day event that churches can book at any time through Outreach, a marketing company that provides a plethora of outreach products for churches; or churches can order materials through Willow Creek. The difference between this course and Purpose Driven is significant from a marketing perspective. First, the name Becoming a Contagious Christian eliminates the possibility for crossover—either in terms of book sales or seminar implementation. Since we know that seekers want to be gently eased into their belief, this title would scare them away because it asks them to proclaim a Christian identity at the outset. We might also question the use of the word "contagious" within this context. Do consumers really want to become a Christian through contagion, which is a word usually associated with something you *don't* want to get? Second, it is a one-day event as opposed to a sustained campaign supported by the entire church community. Compare that to the 40-day Purpose Driven course, which provides for sustained acceptance of the concept. Moreover, since Purpose Driven is done as a church, there is community acceptance and buy-in of the product, providing consistent support to individuals who might waiver. Finally, the Contagious Christian is designed for leaders, not for individuals, thus limiting the number of people who ultimately become salespeople for the product.

All of this helps explain why Hybels and Willow Creek have not gotten the same level of attention that Warren and Saddleback enjoy. For example, Hybels, too, was on *Time*'s list of influential evangelicals, but he was on the last page while Warren was on the first. More recently Hybels released a new book in the summer of 2006, and other than a piece about it in the *Chicago Tribune* (Willow Creek's local paper), it was barely noticed by the media—Christian or otherwise. This is not to say that Willow Creek is less successful than Saddleback by almost any measure—in fact, it is comparable in size and has numerous parallels to Saddleback in terms of its evangelical work. Willow Creek, however, has achieved neither the secular crossover nor the level of *consumer* brand recognition that Purpose Driven has. Instead, its brand recognition exists at the level of the distributor—the members of the Association.

Hybels (and it seems his publisher, Zondervan) have recently tried to change this with the release of his latest book. Entitled *Just Walk Across the*

Room: Simple Steps Pointing People to Faith (another title that lacks the same branding ability as Purpose Driven), the book was marketed with some of the same promotional tools as *The Purpose Driven Life*. First and most importantly, the book was launched with a four-week church campaign. Like the 40-Days campaign, the book is the basis for the course so that everyone in participating churches will need a copy. Materials for church leaders include a CD that contains "outlines, summaries, and transcripts for four 35-minute weekend sermons; interactive campaign timeline; marketing materials; implementation guide; and links to the campaign Web site" (Just Walk Across the Room, n.d.). The campaign, which ran twice—once in October 2006 and once in January 2007—began with a satellite broadcast by Bill Hybels (free if the church starts its campaign on the dates prescribed by the publisher).

There is no data available to assess the course's success, but it appears that Hybels is looking to expand his influence. In a recent article in the *Chicago Tribune*, it was said that Hybels considers "himself [to be] first among equals in the fraternity of evangelical pastors" (Brachear, 2006, p. 1). While that may be his goal, if he wants to expand the Willow Creek brand and the brand of Hybels outside the Christian community, he will need to reframe the message to be more accessible and less Christian.

The Alpha Course

Introduction

While the 40 Days of Purpose is practiced within the confines of the church, churches have been increasingly utilizing courses that take place outside of a traditional church setting. These informal gatherings—including everything from small Bible study groups to "Theology on Tap" (scripture at the local bar)—are particularly appealing to younger congregants who have negative associations with a church building or structured religion. One of the most popular manifestations of this type of worship is the Alpha Course.

Alpha is better known in Europe, where it began, than it is in the United States. However, that is changing rapidly as company statistics suggest. According to information supplied by Alpha, the organization has run more than 31,000 courses in 155 countries since its founding more than 30 years ago, and it is estimated that eight million people worldwide have attended an Alpha Course. Alpha has full-time offices in 28 countries around the world, and the course is available in 54 languages and Braille (Alpha, n.d.). In the United States, the number of courses has grown from just over 200 in 1996 to more than 8,000 by the end of 2006, with attendance leaping from 3,610 to a cumulative total of more than 1.6 million participants.

The Alpha Course began in England in the 1970s (Bendis, 2004).[9] The course was started at the Holy Trinity Brompton Church, an evangelical church in London, as a class for new Christians. In 1986, Nicky Gumbel, a former lawyer turned pastor, took responsibility for the course. Noticing that most participants in the classes were not churchgoers, he revised the curriculum to be introductory in nature—targeting not only the unchurched, but also the newly churched. Growth from that point on was exponential.

In format, Alpha is a 10-week, 15-session course that is promoted and presented to be nonthreatening in nature. Classes are primarily given in the evening and follow a prescribed format. The gathering starts with a one-hour meal during which participants can casually get to know one another. Following dinner, announcements are made and a hymn or two are sung. Next comes a 45-minute lecture, given either by someone from the church[10] or via DVD, which is the preferred method in most groups. The lecture is followed by a 15-minute coffee break and finally small group discussions that last approximately 45 minutes.

Just as the megachurch has repackaged the Sunday service, Alpha has repackaged small group study into dinner, video, and discussion—or as one participant described it to me, "It's like dinner and a movie." Religion is not discussed during the meal. It is a time to create connections between participants. Moreover, Alpha stresses for its group leaders that the atmosphere be nonthreatening, and this is supported throughout the evening: at dinner, the focus is on getting people to talk about their week; the DVDs have a "Did you ever consider this?" attitude to them and present basic topics as broad questions, such as "Who is Jesus?" "Why did Jesus die?" and "Why and how do I pray?"; and during the question period at the end of the evening, participants are encouraged to share their thoughts even if they disagree or have hesitations about the discussion topic. In 2006 I interviewed Kimberly Reeve, Alpha's director of marketing and development, who said that the course is "fairly unique [in this approach]…We are not your typical Bible study. The leader is not here to say that this is the right answer. He is really there to facilitate discussion. That is pretty different from what we have seen."

The prerecorded DVD lectures are by Nicky Gumbel, the founder of Alpha and for many as much the logo for Alpha as the guy with the question mark and the baggy pants (more on him later). Gumbel's style, while benign and welcoming, is still very much upper-class British (more like Hybels than Warren). There is no doubt that he is highly educated, as further evidenced in the intellectual nature of the lectures, particularly the initial ones. This is a smart tactic to use, because many of the people who come to the course may be skeptics, and most are well-educated. As the course progresses, Gumbel uses a combination of humor and argument to present his case. He becomes increasingly affable and cajoling as he asks participants to invite Jesus into their lives, and at various times when he invites people to pray. He is the face of Alpha and the embodiment of the storyteller—the mythmaker.

In addition to the 10 weekly evening sessions, there is a weekend event. This is a two-day affair wherein the charismatic aspect of the course is demonstrated. Participants are encouraged to participate in the laying on of hands, to profess their commitment to Christ and the Holy Spirit, and to speak in tongues. This aspect of the course is not heavily promoted and several organizations have chosen not to include it in their course offering. When asked about the hesitation in using the Holy Spirit, Kimberly Reeve said:

> Well, a lot of churches don't talk about it, and don't want to talk about it...The Holy Spirit is the fruits of the spirit, and there is controversy over whether or not one of the spirits is speaking in tongues...One of the talks says that when you ask to receive the Holy Spirit one of the things that could happen is that you speak in tongues...and some churches think that speaking in tongues is no longer a present day gift...they have issues with that. And we say well, so you won't talk for that one. That's fine.

This flexibility for how to use the course is part of its appeal and has allowed for it to be used by multiple denominations and in various settings from colleges to prisons.[11]

Marketing the Alpha Course—pastors and laypeople

Alpha has three target audiences: pastors and lay people who are currently running the course, pastors and lay people who are considering running the course, and "religious consumers," who may already be Christians or they may be seekers. In this section we will focus on Alpha's marketing to the distributors of the course—the churches—whether they are current users or prospects. We will focus on churches and church leaders as a single group because as a target they are the same and therefore they can be reached via similar methods.

Like the other marketing programs discussed in this book, Alpha depends on the workings of local churches to support and promote the product. Therefore senior pastors are the target for these campaigns. These church leaders must create buy-in within their congregation and then must sell it to the lay constituency, who by and large are responsible for running the course. Most of the marketing to this group is reminder marketing as opposed to explication. According to Reeve:

> Looking at the different presences that we already had, we determined that if you wanted to run Alpha, there were enough ways, enough information out there that you can already contact us....For marketing to existing Alpha users we have *Alpha News*, which is published three

times a year and it is a newsletter which has testimonies, some tips, and we have a column where people can write in and ask questions, and there is always an update on our mission....Then we have e-mails that we send out reminding people of conferences or special resource orders. We do advertising in *Christianity Today* and some of the publications like that. And then a lot of it is word of mouth.

This last strategy is also true of end users and confirms our understanding of the marketing curve discussed in Chapter 4. "It is almost as if everyone has to go through it once to kind of buy in, and then once they have been through it and realize that it is a great experience, they are more willing to invite their friends and neighbors." For a church community, word of mouth tends to take a little longer. According to Reeve, the church must run a course five times before it begins to take hold within a community.

Alpha News is now primarily distributed via e-mail. It promotes ways in which Alpha leaders can expand and improve on their use of the course. The resources available are similar to those used by Purpose Driven and Willow Creek. For example, a recent issue highlighted AlphaConnected (www.alphaconnected.org), a new Web site through which users of the course can access "training resources, and local and national networking opportunities...[and] we're rolling out our superb online training resource, Building Better Alpha Courses (BBAC)" according to Kim Swithinbank, Director of AlphaConnected (Alpha, 2006c, p. 9).

The networking area is like Rick Warren's pastors.com, providing bulletin boards for exchanging information and learning about best practices. BBAC is similar to WCA's service builder because it includes the ability to "create your own Alpha library of articles and online videos" (Alpha, 2006b, p. 1). In order to aid in finding the needed information, the site divides the information into seven sections (p. 3):

- Mission and Values—the underpinnings of the Alpha Course
- Course Launch—helpful information for starting a course
- Course Improvement—information for growing or improving a course
- Specialty Alpha—the course as it looks in settings outside of a church
- Week by Week—behind-the-scenes steps for each week of the course
- Marriage Courses—two more wonderful resources, just for couples
- Frequently Asked Questions—the place to go for answers and insights.

In August 2006, expanding on BBAC, Alpha tested its first interactive conference call for Alpha leaders. In this free 45-minute call, an Alpha leader provided information about presenting and promoting the course and answered questions from those who called in. The test must have been a success because additional calls were held later the same year and continued into 2007.

The Fall 2006 issue (as well as previous issues) of *Alpha News* also included inspiring stories of people who had used or taken the course, articles about how to integrate Alpha into church life, information about workshops for leaders, and a plug for the "Alpha Advisor" program, which pairs more seasoned leaders with newer ones, as well as news from around the world, a directory of Alpha personnel, and a number of pages of advertising for the course and course materials. Interestingly, at the end of the newsletter, on one of the last pages, was a section called, "What Church Leaders Are Saying about Alpha." One of the leaders quoted was Rick Warren, who said, "It's great to see how Alpha has been used to reach people with the good news of Jesus Christ, who wouldn't normally come to church. This resource is very complementary to helping seekers connect with *The Purpose Driven Life*" (Alpha, 2006a, p. 17). This is very high endorsement from what would normally be perceived as the competition. It's possible that Warren does not see Alpha as threatening to his own work, and he may even believe that it is effective in bringing more people to Christ and therefore an adjunct to his work. For Alpha, it is obvious kudos.

E-mails are sent to pastors and course leaders several times a month and are much more promotional in nature than, for example, Rick Warren's Toolbox.[12] One e-mail with the subject heading "A New Way to Tell Guests about Alpha" promoted a pamphlet called "Explore the Questions of Life"; another promoted a new pamphlet by Nicky Gumbel called, "The Da Vinci Code, a Response." There are reminder e-mails about upcoming conferences for Alpha leaders as well as for specialized courses like Alpha in the Workplace and the Marriage Course. There are also monthly prayer newsletters that include a quick note from Alpha (the June 2006 e-mail, for example, was about attending the Alpha International Week at Holy Trinity Brompton, Alpha's original church), followed by "Points for Praise," a day-by-day description of what is to be praised over the course of a week, and finally "Points for Prayer," a day-by-day outline of prayer for Alpha conferences, courses, and its "core team" of pastors and church leaders. There was even an e-mail from John B. Donovan (February 23, 2006), Alpha USA's national youth coordinator, who encouraged churches to "connect with local schools by offering Youth Alpha on the basis of Released Time, the practice by which students are released from the campus legally to take a religion class."[13]

One e-mail that seemed less promotional in nature was sent in the fall of 2006. Alpha courses tend to run on a schedule—one in fall, one in spring, one in early summer. Since many churches start a new course in the fall, Alpha sent out an e-mail outlining 10 steps to prepare for their latest course. These steps were: pray, educate the congregation, extend invitations, advertise, train your team, arrange the weekend away, plan the meals, inventory your supplies, register the course on the Alpha course directory, and finally, attend an Alpha conference. While all of this was likely helpful to the Alpha leader, all of the steps just happened to be reasons to access Alpha materials or conferences—from prayer ministry training resources to brochures, invitations, posters, and banners to training DVDs and conferences, not to mention the *Alpha Cookbook*, a resource for recipes suitable for large groups.[14]

The Alpha Web site (www.alphausa.org) is an important resource for course leaders and prospects. When prospects go to the Alpha Web site, they can find a tremendous amount of information about the course, the materials available to teach it, and the services provided by Alpha. Upon request, Alpha will send out free of charge a package that includes *Alpha News* and some marketing materials such as postcards and pamphlets as well as a promotional tape about Alpha including the first lecture for the course. In addition, information about local Alpha offices is available. Alpha has centers in 15 cities throughout the United States from which they send out representatives to meet with local churches and encourage them to use the course. The goal of these meetings is to get church leaders and laypeople to attend an Alpha conference. The Alpha conference is a two-day event in which organizations interested in Alpha learn how to present the course. Most churches send five to ten people. Alpha strongly emphasizes attendance at these conferences, and according to Kimberly Reeve, approximately 75 percent of people who run the course attend a conference. However, if attendance is not possible, Alpha recommends purchasing a number of books as well as video and audio cassettes about how to run the Alpha Course.[15]

Once a church or other organization decides to run an Alpha course, the company provides a breadth of materials, all at a fee. To promote the course to participants, there are postcards, flyers, and registration forms, all of which can be customized for the individual church. Signage is available that can be hung outside the church. The signage is very obscure so as to pique the interest of passersby. For example, one sign says "Jesus who?" and has the Alpha logo underneath. Another says, "Alpha is coming" with no further explanation as to what it is or when. There are even buttons that leaders can wear that say, "Ask me about the Alpha Course." Beyond these promotional materials, there are the educational tools necessary for presenting the course itself. These include the videos or DVDs of the Nicky Gumbel lectures, course manuals, manuals for leaders, individual pamphlets, and the aforementioned *Alpha Cookbook* for recipes for pre-lecture dinners and post-lecture desserts.

Marketing the Alpha Course—seekers

The consumer target for Alpha consists of young adults, particularly those in their 20s and 30s. This is highly evident in the marketing materials for the course. Be it the Web site, pamphlets, or registration cards, the marketing materials are created with people in their twenties prominently displayed. On the "Everyone's invited" page of the Alpha USA Web site, for example, there is a picture of an African-American male flanked by an Asian woman and a Caucasian male. This page leads to an overview of the course, which is a slide show of sorts. All of the pictures show young people of various ethnicities, some carrying heavy boxes (to represent life's problems), and many dressed in suits to appeal to the upscale consumer. This target audience is also highly evidenced in the videos for the course. Throughout the videos, we see reaction shots of 20- and 30-somethings of all races who have attended Nicky Gumbel's lectures. This brings up another defining point about Alpha's target audience—*all* races are prospects for the course. This feels self-conscious in its execution because every promotional piece has a mix of ethnicities. Whether intended or not, there is what I call the "cheese factor" in much of Alpha's marketing—there's something just a little too happy about it. This is particularly true of the ubiquitous logo.

The logo is an illustration of a man carrying a question mark. The man appears to be young because he is wearing a pair of blue jeans and a baggy, nondescript yellow shirt, as is the current fashion. He has no defining facial characteristics and his skin color is such that his race is indeterminate. The man is carrying a red question mark that is the same size as he is, and he is falling backward under the weight of his load. What is particularly interesting about the logo is the use of light. While the question mark is red, the front and top are white, indicating a light source coming from above. Then there is a shadow under the man, though it is small—again suggesting the light source from above. The symbolism is obvious, but it is meant to be so. The Alpha Course is not esoteric; it is nothing if not simple and straightforward, and the logo reflects that. Moreover, this logo communicates who the course is for (young people) and what it is meant to do (shine a light on life's big questions).

Cheesy or not, Alpha's marketing has been very effective as evidenced by the numbers cited earlier. The broader marketing initiatives over time have led to the most important and effective means of selling the brand—word of mouth. Said Reeve:

> Most people find out about Alpha through a friend...if you are a pastor, you find out through another pastor; if you are a lay leader, you find out through a friend of a friend who ran Alpha at their church; if you are a course guest, you found out because someone invited you to come. So really it is primarily through friends.

My discussions with attendees confirmed this. A number of people heard about Alpha when they were in college. The experience of Bruce,[16] a white male from the southwest, was typical. "When I was in college I would come back to lifeguard during the summers, and a co-worker and I were talking and the fact that we both went to church came up and she was actually having Alpha at her house at the time so she invited me to come and I just completely loved it." Another attendee found out about Alpha through her church in New England and then again when she moved to New York, "I heard about it also when I started going to the Vineyard."[17] People find out about it through multiple forms of promotion. At one of the courses I attended, most people were there because they knew of others who had taken the course; some were taking the course for a second time; and some had simply seen a flyer in their church and decided to come to the course instead of a typical Bible study class. A pastor who runs an Alpha course regularly summed it up like this:

> It has to be word of mouth. You see, there are two ways to promote it: members inviting friends to go and over the Internet. But in order for someone to find out about it over the Internet, he/she has to have been tipped off to it in the first place, and usually that is through a friend that has already taken the course. But the Internet has become such a big part of this. I would say about 20 percent of the people who come found out about it through the Internet, without prior knowledge of the church or relationships with anyone inside the church.
>
> (personal interview, 2006)

I asked Kimberly Reeve about the Alpha Web site, because I noticed that it had changed quite a bit in the last year. She explained, "We did an overhaul and really redesigned the site so that it would primarily appeal to [seekers] who want to know something about Alpha, maybe a friend had mentioned it…[and they] would not have any other means of accessing us." After word of mouth, then, the company's Web site is the main source of information for seekers. In addition to providing general information about Alpha—what it is, who it is for—there is a map through which seekers can find a course in their area. The information is just enough to pique a prospect's interest, but not so much that the person would not want or need to seek out a course.

Alpha uses a combination of traditional marketing techniques and more sophisticated methods. In England, Alpha uses billboards, Web sites, television, and radio campaigns that were developed by Saatchi & Saatchi, one of the world's largest advertising agencies. Alpha also relies on word of mouth to reach its under-35 target audience. The last night of the course is actually a sales event wherein guests are asked to bring friends to the closing night dinner. However, to supplement word-of-mouth promotion, Alpha employs stealth marketing techniques, a sophisticated form of word-of-mouth advertising. According to Laura Haynes, a brand consultant, the company uses "plants" at bus stops or pubs (*Brand Strategy*, 2003). These plants start a conversation about Alpha and create a one-on-one relationship with the customer. Thus the product is introduced in a nonthreatening manner in accordance with the brand's philosophy. In fact, prospects don't even know they are being sold. Similar techniques have been used to introduce new and sophisticated products into the marketplace, such as picture-taking cell phones and, since much of this type of marketing happens in bars, vodka.

These promotional tools have been used recently in Canada but have not yet expanded into the United States, according to Reeve.

> The reason why it hasn't been used in the U.S. is mainly because it is just cost-prohibitive for us at this point. If you want to broadcast in the UK, you run an ad campaign in London. It is expensive but it is very manageable. So one of the things we are looking at is if we can do something similar in a targeted geographic area like the Twin Cities or Houston, where it is a fairly contained geographic region. But looking at doing a campaign across the U.S.—that is easily $25 million, and that is not going to happen.

The Twin Cities—Minneapolis and St. Paul—and Houston are where Alpha has had a presence for the longest time. Other possible areas, according to Reeve, might be New Orleans, St. Louis, Phoenix, or Chicago.

> I would love to see us do a national initiative similar to what the UK does. I just saw when Canada did it. They now have, it's crazy, something like sixty percent of all people in Canada know what Alpha is, which is phenomenal. The courses increased over a hundred percent the year that they did their national campaign. So just building that awareness and…establishing an alumni network…would really help us build more awareness and just get people questioning, because our message is great. Who doesn't want to explore the questions of life? I think that could be huge.

To expand its reach with various audiences, Alpha has created brand extensions along demographic lines. Specialized Alpha courses now exist for Catholics, prison populations, youth, executives, and college students on campus, among others. These courses are specifically tailored for the special needs of these target audiences. The Alpha for Youth course is illustrative of the customization for these courses. Alpha USA provides a page of information to organizations that may be interested in presenting a youth course. On this one sheet, they explain the best way to run this specialized course. For example, in the adult courses videos are the primary source for the lectures, but in the youth course, live lectures are recommended. These lectures "should be quick hitting, and should feature visual and interactive communication techniques. Unlike adult Alpha, where the message is verbal and linear, in Alpha for Youth the message should be shown, not told, and experienced, not explained." It is also recommended that Alpha for Youth be conducted with seekers, rather than making them feel separate from the presentation. Guests are encouraged to:

participate and own most aspects of the course. For instance, allow the students to design the menu and prepare the food. Allow the students to pick the time, place, and layout of the course (such as in a home or at the church). Have the students choose the music and lead the songs.

This is a prime example of creating individualized programs for individualized consumers. While adults want to be catered to, teens want ownership and control in their lives. It is important for teens to be part of a group and to feel that they are not "sticking out." As Alpha suggests, "for the most part, we do not find that students are very interested in attending a church program. However, we do find many students would love to gather at the home of a ringleader student for a series of evenings of making a meal, singing some songs, and discussing 'spiritual' issues." The materials used are also different. The adult course uses a subdued booklet that is given to each participant and contains areas for writing notes about the DVD while watching the lecture. The booklet for youth is like a teen magazine, similar to *Revolve* and *Refuel*. The book consists primarily of photography and graphics and has a limited amount of written text.

The success of these brand extensions is evident in the statistics. The most popular course is the youth course, which has been run close to 3,000 times worldwide. Alpha on Campus, another popular course, ranks second worldwide and third in the United States. The marriage course rounds out the top three, and this version of the course has been getting more marketing since it was launched in the United States in 2006. In terms of upcoming plans, "[We are] translating all of our products into Spanish…Then the next big thing down the pipe is a parenting course that is currently being run out in the UK. That will logically come to us in the next 18 months or so as well," says Reeve.

As of now, there is no concerted effort to move attendees from one course to another. There is an Alpha 2 that some churches run, which tends to involve more traditional Bible study and lasts six to eight weeks. As one Alpha leader explained:

> We do make an announcement, especially toward the end of the course, saying if you like this and you want to continue, you can take Alpha 2. Because a lot of people make friends and they miss hanging out so there is that opportunity. It is a 6 to 8 week course. It is shorter and a lot more flexible.

However there is no coordinated effort nationally to do this because the focus is more on the churches than the end user. Reeve explained:

> We do virtually nothing because we do not know who takes courses at individual churches, so we don't have lists of course participants,

and at this point we are really not able to do anything. Also, just philosophically, and this comes out of Nicky Gumbel's views and beliefs and our desire to support that, we don't want to be asking who just graduated from Alpha for money, because that kind of is what people are expecting, and so we don't want to even go down that path at all. What we are piloting this year is just trying to start up an Alpha Alumni Network, so that if people are engaged, they have an opportunity to sign up via e-mail to receive a monthly update and that would be an e-mail from Nicky or whatever, and really looking at how we can help them continue their faith journey. But as of right now, we know the churches that run Alpha, but we have no connections with any of the course guests.

Conclusion and analysis

> One of the miracles of modern capitalism is its ability to stimulate demand for the most banal products (bottled water, for instance) simply by crafting it [sic] a new image. Something like this appears to be behind the revival in demand for Jesus Christ.
>
> (Lewis, 1996, p. 16)

Church courses have helped craft this new image by creating a consumer-friendly forum through which people can learn about Christianity. While these courses may be disparaged for being bad theology, they are by every measure good business.

The success of the Alpha Course can be explained in the packaging and promotion of the product. It is soft sell evangelicalism. Dinner, a video, and a chat with friends feel like an evening at home, not a Sunday at church. Kimberly Reeve explains, "I think we are different from many ministries in that we are really not in your face...we hear time and time again that 'someone invited me to come and I went for the food and stayed for ten weeks.' That is the approach that we like to take." In attending courses, I did not initially understand its appeal, nor could I determine what was so compelling as to keep people coming back week after week. I found Nicky Gumbel a bit dry in the first couple of DVD lectures I saw; certainly he was not as charismatic as some New Age speakers, like Marianne Williamson, or a televangelist like Joel Osteen. However, over time I realized that it was the camaraderie that led seekers to return. The dinner, the conversation, the fellowship with other seekers in a nonthreatening environment—all of this is the unique selling proposition for Alpha.

Continued commitment to the course by guests is further supported by the Alpha helpers and reinforcement within the videos themselves. Throughout the videos there are cutaways to people in the audience—all young and, interestingly, not all happy, suggesting that it is okay to continue to question, to wrestle with life's big questions as the logo suggests. *The Economist* stated in 1998 that "Alpha's success appears to lie more in its structure than its content," and my experience bears that out.

Ultimately, however, church courses are an important means of inculcating new church members. Because of the small group aspect of most church courses, they are the best means of converting new members because we know from both marketing and religious conversion that one-on-one selling is the most effective means of creating buy-in. Thus a religious course—or any other small group session—has the biggest opportunity for evangelistic payoff and is therefore the most important to promote. And promote these courses have done. For both Purpose Driven and Alpha, a long-term, step-by-step strategy was used. For both, it was over the span of a decade that these brands began to make inroads. It was the steady building of the pyramid and the development of evangelists that allowed these brands to reach the so-called tipping point.

Both Alpha and Purpose Driven have been criticized for being simplified theology in the face of marketing, though Purpose Driven is the larger target because of its popularity. Conservatives criticize Warren for watering down the faith; liberals fear he is a wolf in sheep's clothing. "The Purpose Driven ministry is a marketing strategy," says Dennis Costella, pastor of the Fundamental Bible Church in Los Osos, California (Steptoe, 2004, p. 55). Wendy Kaminer, a liberal author, has said, "Rebranding won't change the fact that he [Warren] is part of a large, influential conservative movement that threatens the rights of others" (Gunther, 2005, p. 120). While Alpha has not been so publicly lambasted, the course does have its detractors, particularly those who are concerned with its focus on the Holy Spirit. In either case, the critics are correct in saying that these products promote what will appeal and hide what may lead to prospects hesitating at the door. Also, promotion through evangelizing is difficult to disentangle. Once surrounded by "friends" who make you want to come back again and again, it becomes harder to question the theology when doing so means you might have to give up the friendships.

Responding to critics, Warren has said that what others call commercialism and marketing, he calls evangelism. "I believe I have the key to meaning and purpose in life with God, and I'm trying to share it with as many people as possible," he says. "That's what evangelism is—sharing good news" (Steptoe, 2004, p. 55). For Alpha, 58 percent of the churches that use the course attracted new members (Taylor, 2001 p. 28). Reeve discovered that other churches are also finding Alpha an effective assimilation tool. "I just did a focus group on this in Houston and about half the churches said that they wanted it to be an outreach, but it ended up being more of an assimilation thing just because it so clearly presents the basics of Christianity." What we are seeing here is these courses reclaiming the marketing tool of evangelism for the church—and they can call it whatever they want to.

Rick Warren takes much more offense to these accusations than does Alpha. In fact, Alpha is not averse to talking about their marketing programs. But if you call Warren a marketer, it is as if you've called him the devil, or worse. This is particularly interesting since Rick Warren is more blatantly promoted than Alpha. On the subject, he recently said this:

> The myth [is] that mega-churches grow by marketing. I'm so tired of this story; I've heard it over and over and over—the latest being the most recent issue of *Business Week*, where it basically says the mega-churches are big business. Now that is just such a superficial, unrealistic view of what actually goes on. The implication is that if a church is this big, it must be because of marketing. No, it's because of changed lives. When peoples' lives are changed you'd have to lock the doors to keep them out, because they want to go where their lives are changed. We put people in a tent for three years where we would freeze in the winter and it would rain on us all spring and we'd burn up in the summer and the howling winds could come through—and people would walk about a mile through the mud to get to this tent. I mean, everything was inconvenient. And why did they come, why did they show up? Because their lives were getting changed; that is what was happening. So they put up with inconvenience.
>
> The only guy I know who got this was a *New York Times* reporter who did an article on Saddleback a while back. And I like the way he said it. He said, "Marketing creates a message in order to sell a product. But Warren's doing the exact opposite—he's creating products in order to push a message." Well, it's true. I plead guilty to that. But that's not marketing, that's taking the message and trying to get it out as many ways as possible instead of creating a message to sell your product.
>
> (Pew Forum, 2005)

This quote misses the point: the product *is* the message. Purpose Driven is the message *and* the product. While changed lives and belief in Christ, God, and so on is the product and that is what church courses—or religion generally—is selling, that is a long-term goal. The short-term goal, however, is to get bodies in the door. And that's what these products are expediting. Is that a bad thing? Inherently there is nothing wrong with exposing people to religious messages, and if someone takes the time and makes the effort to explore these courses, then they probably have at least a mild interest in the product. But what we can and should question is whether the product delivers on the marketed message, which as presented suggests that changing your life can be simple. I would argue that no life can be fundamentally turned around in 40 Days of Purpose or 10 weeks of Alpha.

Chapter 6

The new televangelists

On-air evangelists have been around since the inception of broadcasting. First in radio and then television, preachers have been spreading the gospel through these most mass of mass media. As we saw in Chapter 3, outlets for preachers today have proliferated at an unfathomable rate as digital technologies have expanded to every corner of the nation and the far reaches of the planet. But even before the explosion in communications technologies, televangelists were masters in the art of marketing. Early religious programs were, in reality, promotion for live religious rallies (Bruce, 1990). As religious programming expanded, additional marketing tools became necessary. In a saturated market with a large number of choices and where prospects lack technical knowledge, consumers come to rely on marketers to inform them about what is available in the marketplace. According to Edward Shaffer (1993, p. 640):

> Sellers therefore constantly attempt to gain the confidence of consumers by building up brand loyalties. They boldly proclaim the alleged superiority of their products...TV evangelists have used these same marketing techniques...Playing on fears engendered by lack of knowledge about the future and the hereafter, they offer viewers hope and salvation, promising them a place in Paradise in return for contributions.

In other words, a small price to pay for such a large return.

With the changes in technologies, salvation is sold using ever more sophisticated marketing techniques. Now media work synergistically to perpetuate the preacher's marketing message in a way that was never before possible. Televised sermons are again advertising in and of themselves. More importantly, television in conjunction with the Internet has allowed the television programming to become almost exclusively a marketing message (what we can do for you), while the Web site closes the sale (what you can do for us). Whereas earlier televangelists adapted television genres such as talk shows (Pat Robertson) and variety shows (Jim and Tammy Bakker), today's tele-religious program is an infomercial—the sermon sells the product

(Jesus, salvation, the pastor) while chyrons rotate at the bottom of the screen announcing tour dates and promoting the sale of DVDs of the broadcast, the latest best seller, or its accompanying journal or devotional. Shows end with additional appeals to purchase these products, to visit the Web site, and, of course, to donate money.

It is not just the packaging that is different with these modern day Oral Roberts. Today's televangelist delivers a more subtle message than his or her early day counterparts. Instead of fire and brimstone, these preachers sell fine living and abundance. This type of preaching—which goes under a number of names, including prosperity preaching or Name It and Claim It, among others—has made the evangelistic message attractive to a wider audience. Just as secular television is decried for appealing to the lowest common denominator, so, too, religious programming panders to prospects for broader appeal. In order to draw in the masses, preachers must include what will attract the largest number of people—ideas about how their lives will be better, more prosperous, more fulfilling—and exclude those things that will lead viewers to reach for the remote control—mentions of Jesus, requests for contributions, suggestions that they are going to hell.

Explains David Lyon (2000), "The American Dream, rather than reference to conventional Christian creeds and confessions, is its [televangelism's] popular epistemological touchstone" (p. 63). Highly sophisticated production values combined with positive messages to improve your life make these television programs both entertaining and effective. People who would never think twice about Tammy Faye Bakker or Jimmy Swaggart are watching Joel Osteen, T. D. Jakes, and Joyce Meyer. Is it because they are better preachers? Perhaps. But more likely it is because the audience finds the product—the message, the pastor, the branding—more appealing.

Not only is the message affirming, but these preachers also don't ask for money! At least, not initially or as an inherent part of their programming. Early day televangelists had to support their on-air ministry through private donations, just as preachers today have to. However, preachers now can pitch the product on air and then ask for the money online. Thus the existence of new technologies and the interaction between media allow for a more subtle preaching style.

While the 1980s saw the scandals of Jim Bakker and Jimmy Swaggart, televangelism in the new millennium is riding high on prosperity preaching and feel-good sermons. Fueled by multiple television outlets, multinational publishing companies, and a growing trend in American evangelism, televangelism has exploded, with sermons available at any hour of the day or night (see Chapter 3). This also correlates with the recent rise in megachurches (Goff, 2006, p. W11). Televised sermons have replaced the more intimate church setting. Watching a preacher at home is not much different from watching a preacher at a megachurch. In these super-sized religious houses of worship, the preacher is projected onto a screen so that people in the back of the auditorium (or even outside of it, in the case of a church like Saddleback) can see the preacher's face.

> The way worship is conducted in growing numbers of evangelical congregations now replicates what once was confined to the TV screen. Sitting in your living room, you may feel just as close to the pastor as you would at the 5,000-person megachurch down the street. Unless you join one of the megachurch's cell groups, these institutions can be as impersonal as mass media.
>
> (Goff, 2005, p. W11)

Given this scenario, what does it matter then if you watch the preacher on television or see him from the back row of a 16,000-seat former basketball stadium?

Along with the dramatic proliferation of available media outlets and the replication of the televisual element within the church building has come a contemporary breed of on-air preachers that I call the new televangelists—Joel Osteen, T. D. Jakes, Joyce Meyer, and Creflo Dollar to name a few. Each one is a brand supported by television, books, national tours, and their own congregations. One of them, T. D. Jakes, even has his own entertainment company. But the undisputed superstar of the group is Joel Osteen—"Joel"—whom we will examine in this chapter as the prototype of the new televangelist, a faith brand subset.

These religious celebrities—and there is no doubt that they have been methodically developed into celebrities—are not the only promoters of faith. Secular celebrities, too, have become televangelists, or minimally, spokespeople for God. Think about Madonna and Kabbalah, Mel Gibson and Christianity, Tom Cruise and Scientology. However, just as in traditional televangelism, there is one person who stands above the rest in the secular television sphere: Oprah Winfrey. As the sacred has become more secular, here we see the secular become increasingly sacred as Oprah presents guest after guest giving their "testimony." She, too, is a new televangelist and she, too, is most definitively a faith brand.

Joel Osteen™ [1]

The brand mythology

The brand of Joel Osteen is made up of a brand name (Joel Osteen), some key phrases ("discover the champion in you," "be a victor not a victim"), and a humanizing icon ("the smiling preacher," as he has been dubbed). Then there are ancillary elements that add to the brand mythology. These include Joel's wife, Victoria, a tall Texas blonde who is included in most marketing materials, as well as other members of his family, particularly his children and his mother, Dodie, who miraculously recovered from liver cancer 25 years ago. But the brand itself is Joel Osteen: the Web site is Joel Osteen; the television show is Joel Osteen; the "concerts" are "An Evening with Joel." While that might not seem strange within a traditional consumer context, remember that this man is the pastor of a church—the country's largest megachurch, Lakewood Church, whose name is in little evidence when talking about this faith brand.[2]

As with all brands, the product is supported by mythology. The story doesn't begin with Joel Osteen, but with his father, John. John Osteen was a Southern Baptist minister who preached love, salvation, and prosperity. The theme with which he became most closely identified was "It's God's will for you to live in prosperity instead of poverty. It's God's will for you to pay your bills and not be in debt. It's God's will for you to live in health and not in sickness all the days of your life" (Martin, 2005, p. 110). This approach was antithetical to preaching fire and brimstone, which was the convention of his denomination at the time. Moving further from Baptist teachings, in the late 1950s John preached the "gifts of the Spirit." This charismatic tradition promotes speaking in tongues and raucous prayer services.

Practicing faith in this way caused a split between the elder Osteen and the Baptists. Breaking out on his own, John held his first Lakewood service in an abandoned feed store with 90 members in attendance. This church, located in a predominantly black neighborhood in Houston, was founded as an "oasis of love" (Dooley, 2004; Martin, 2005; Mathieu, 2002). Son Paul (Joel's brother) would later say of John: "He wanted the people nobody else wanted. He didn't want to preach a gospel of condemnation" (Mathieu, 2002). The combination of charismatic services, an open-arms policy, and reaching multiple races led to a steady stream of growth for the Lakewood Church.

In 1983 Joel, the youngest of John's six children, called his father and said he wanted to drop out of Oral Roberts University and create a television ministry for his father in order to help facilitate spreading the good news and to help grow attendance at Lakewood. While Joel didn't call it marketing, he knew that this is what the television ministry was—even from its earliest time. Joel's affinity for promotion is evident in an interview in which he said, "I think the possibility of going into someone's living room, in their own environment, it's such a great tool…When Coca-Cola wants to reach a generation, man, they go to TV and the people are watching" (Mathieu, 2002). The only restriction that John put on Joel's idea was that the show would never be used to ask for money.

The position of television producer seemed to serve Joel well. He could help grow the church while honing his craft of production and marketing, which he did for almost 20 years. Initially the show aired locally in Houston as well as nationally on the Family Channel, which at the time was owned by Pat Robertson.[3] "'We don't have much drive-by visibility where we are,' says Osteen. 'So TV was a big impact. That's when the church really began to grow'" (Mathieu, 2002). Under the stewardship of John Osteen, Lakewood grew into a successful megachurch attended by 6,000 parishioners weekly with a television ministry—produced by Joel—that was broadcast in 100 countries (Lockwood, 2006).[4]

Another element of the Joel Osteen myth is that Joel was always a behind-the-scenes person—shy, withholding, not someone who craved the limelight. That's why, as the story goes, everyone was surprised when, in January 1999, John Osteen fell ill and called Joel to ask him to preach for him the following week. Because of his retiring manner, Joel refused, hung up the phone, and began to eat dinner. However, after hanging up the phone, Joel believed he got a call from God to do what his father asked. Joel called John back and agreed to preach. The following week, John Osteen passed away and Joel took over as Lakewood's preacher. There is one last piece to the legend of Lakewood: because Joel was so unsure of his ability to fill his father's shoes, he literally wore John Osteen's shoes for a number of years whenever he would take to the pulpit.

Building on what his father started as well as his experience in the television ministry (and with the help of God, as the myth goes), Joel quadrupled the size of Lakewood. Today the church boasts weekly attendance of 35,000 to 40,000 attendees, with some people claiming that the church could grow to as high as 100,000 regular congregants. In addition to the tens of thousands of people who attend the Houston church, there are an estimated seven million viewers who watch Joel on television every week, making it the highest rated show of its kind.

The brand message

The overriding message of the Joel Osteen brand is one of happiness, success, and prosperity. This almost overbearingly positive message is presented in all communications related to Joel. The books and the television show present this positive message through words. The book cover, Web site, and marketing materials are covered with smiling pictures of Joel alone or with his wife Victoria. The success of the books and the television show and the growth of Lakewood solidify this message by demonstrating Joel's ability to put his words (and God's favor) into action.

"God's favor" is a key element of the brand message. As Joel once said:

> I believe God's favor is something intangible where you've got God's blessings on your lives...God works where there's faith. And faith to me is having a positive outlook, believing that things are going to get better, and expecting good things in life. God's given you the strength to endure a tough time. God's there for you. Call on him, believe in his strength.
>
> (Sheahen, 2004b)

Thus the way to having God's favor is by having a positive attitude, and everything Joel Osteen does works in the direction of that goal. In his television show he encourages viewers to "discover the champion in you." (This is also Lakewood's theme song, as well as the theme song for the television program.) He endlessly evokes the mantra "You are a victor, not a victim," and chides his viewers to stop having a pity party. A half-hour with Joel—and he is always called Joel—is like a half-hour with Dr. Phil—a feel-good, get inspired, easily digestible dose of entertaining television. It is the power of positive thinking on steroids.

The message is not only positive, it is also practical. According to Joel, "When I speak, I try to make it a point to talk about something people can take home and use that day or tomorrow at work" (Butler, 2005a, p. 57). His talks are as often about good relationships, healthy eating, and financial responsibility as they are about remembering to keep God in your life.

As with other brands examined in this book, the message of faith is simplified and undemanding in order to improve its marketability. Most Christians don't believe that what Joel is teaching is even Christianity because there is no mention of sin or sacrifice.[5] Here is an excerpt from an Easter Sunday edition of the news show *Meet the Press* with Tim Russert wherein Joel explains his preaching philosophy:

> PASTOR JOEL OSTEEN: I don't believe in going around condemning people and telling them all what they're doing wrong....We try to present the truth to them and present the biblical ways that we see it, but no, Jesus didn't come and condemn people...when you show love, when you open your heart, it seems like that's where people respond. So that's what our message is, has been about all these years....the Bible also talks about how it's the goodness of God that leads people to repentance...[We] let people know that God is a good God...that he's on your side. And, yes, we have to obey and, yes, we have to be obedient, but when we do, I believe we can rise higher....It doesn't bother me a bit that people criticize us for people leaving the church here on Sunday feeling better than they were before. But I want people to go out challenged and inspired to know that you know what, you can rise higher, you can overcome bad habits, you can beat addictions, you can be a better person, a better husband, a better wife. So, you know what, I like the fact that they come, they get challenged, get your heart right, find the areas you need to change, but then go home knowing you can do something about it.
>
> (*Meet the Press*, 2006)

What we see here is a marketing pattern of the faith brands. Prospects are "brought into the tent" with messages they want to hear but are not presented with their responsibilities until later. If you just heard the positive message of Joel, you would assume that following his faith simply means being positive all the time—certainly a difficult task in and of itself. But Joel's message is not only about this. Beyond the smile and upbeat words, it is about accepting Jesus as your Lord and Savior and accepting the Bible as the inerrant word of God. It is about joining a good Bible-based church.

Marketing Joel began with marketing Lakewood

Like Saddleback and Willowcreek, Lakewood is a megachurch that follows the successful patterns of these oversized churches. There are several services during the week and four on the weekends, including one in Spanish that is not officiated by Joel. Seekers can choose to be as involved or as anonymous as their worship style allows. Lakewood targets the unchurched with a particular emphasis on attracting men, as is the strategy of other megachurches (see discussion of Willowcreek in Chapter 5). There are also small group ministries in myriad categories. Thus from a marketing perspective, Lakewood employs the same strategies as other megachurches.

Unlike Saddleback and Willowcreek, however, Lakewood is also a television ministry. Says Joel, "'I'm a big believer in the media...That has always been my passion'" (Leland, 2005, p. A1). With the strength of that passion, the show has become widely distributed and is now available nationally on ABC Family (formerly The Family Channel), Discovery, BET, TBN, and USA as well as locally on network affiliates in 30 U.S. cities, including top markets like New York and Los Angeles. Getting carriage on these major market stations is no small feat, nor is it inexpensive. The television ministry is a large part of Lakewood's budget and in 2005, the church reportedly increased its spending on television by 60 to 70 percent (Dooley, 2004, p. 1). But from the beginning, Joel created the show to be an evangelizing tool—a marketing tool.

Television is not the only means of promoting Lakewood. Even during John's time, the church used local marketing. Because the church was situated in a predominantly African-American, sparsely inhabited area, the church had to use advertising to increase awareness of its existence.

It was hard to drive on a Houston freeway without seeing John Osteen's smiling visage shining down from strategically placed billboards. Not everyone knew exactly where Lakewood was, but few Houstonians were unaware that it existed. This point was brought home to me one evening around that time when, riding around with two of my granddaughters, then about six and four years old, a radio commercial began with "We believe in new beginnings," and the girls immediately chimed in with "and we believe in yoooooouuuuu!!!" (The Houston Press would later assert that the jingle ranked as one of the most successful marketing campaigns in the city's history.)

(Martin, 2005, p. 111)

Through these marketing and media efforts, which have largely been credited to Joel, Lakewood grew significantly. By 1987 the church needed to increase its capacity, so it built a 7,800-seat facility to accommodate its expanding congregation.

Joel's experience with television was not limited to religious media. Lakewood Church, under the licensee name Humanities Interested Media, bought KTBU Channel 55 in Houston and programmed it with family-friendly content. Launched in July 1998, the station was marketed as "The Tube." It was run by Joel, who acted as president and general manager, and his brother-in-law Don Iloff, who was the vice president of marketing. Iloff said at the time, "We like to think of it as attitude branding" (Larson, 1998, p. 16).[6] This marketing expertise would be translated to Joel himself after he took over his father's pulpit.

The program

In television, a program's formula is what makes a show successful. On *Law & Order* there is invariably a murder, an investigation, and a trial. On *Grey's Anatomy* there's going to be an unusual medical case and Meredith is going to run into Dr. McDreamy so there will be a thread of sexual tension throughout the episode.

Joel Osteen is also based on a formula. It is even more predictable than these dramatic series, which makes this show a brand its viewers can count on time and time again. The show always begins with a joke related to the Bible or religion. The joke is usually pretty corny and often makes fun of Joel and his family. A favorite of Joel's is the story of two men who debate all of their lives whether Jesus is white or black. The two men die on the same day and go to heaven. When they get to the Pearly Gates, they ask God who was right—is Jesus white or black? Just then Jesus walks up and says, "Buenos Dias." This joke fits well with Lakewood and its tradition of diversity—something Joel claims does not come from him but from God.

The joke is followed by everyone in the audience raising their Bibles and repeating:

> This is my Bible: I am what it says I am; I have what it says I have; I can do what it says I can do. Today, I will be taught the Word of God. I boldly confess. My mind is alert; my heart is receptive; I will never be the same. I am about to receive the incorruptible, indestructible, ever-living Seed of the Word of God. I'll never be the same—never, never, never! I'll never be the same, in Jesus' name. Amen.

Not seen by the television audience is the incantation on video screens throughout the church so that everyone can follow again. When this is completed, Joel says something like, "You sound terrific as usual."

Behind Joel is an oversized golden globe that spins slowly throughout the sermon. Flags also grace the stage, but crosses and other Christian symbolism do not as is the case with other megachurches. The new home of the Lakewood Church as of July 2005 and the source of the broadcast is the former Compaq Center, a sports arena that used to be home to the Houston Rockets basketball team. Throughout the show the cameras give a wide shot of the audience so viewers can see the vastness of the congregation. There are also periodic close-ups of people in the arena—opportunities for audience members to find someone like themselves—old, young including children, and every color imaginable.

After the incantation Joel moves on to stories about his family. His wife Victoria, especially her penchant for shopping, is a recurring source for teaching and good-natured ribbing. Sermons run 20 to 25 minutes. Recent topics include: Giving your dreams a new beginning, Improving your self-image with words, Being passionate about life, Being grateful for the gift of today, and Eating healthier. All of the messages are upbeat and the sermons are interwoven with stories and examples, making the messages positive and practical—the essence of the brand. Scripture quotes pepper the sermon, but they are kept at a minimum compared to other on-air preachers. At the end of the sermon Joel asks, "Did you receive it today? I know you did," which is followed by audience applause.

Each broadcast ends with a virtual altar call from Joel:

> We never like to close our broadcast without giving you an opportunity to make Jesus the Lord of your life. Will you pray with me? Just say, Lord Jesus, I repent of my sins. I ask you to come into my heart. I make you my Lord and Savior. Friends, if you prayed that simple prayer, we believe you are born again. Get into a good Bible-based church. We love you and hope to see you again next week.

More than a sermon, *Joel Osteen* is an infomercial. The product is Joel, and tangentially the Lakewood Church, and this is hit home by the structure of the program. The show is presented in a widescreen format so that there is a black band on the top and bottom of the screen. In the band at the top, on the left-hand side, JoelOsteen.com is continuously displayed. Throughout the course of the show, chyrons appear on the bottom of the screen promoting everything that is Joel. During one program shown in 2006, the promotional text included the following items:

1   "Lakewood Church" (so viewers are situated).
2   "Sign up for Daily Inspiration from Joel [e-mails; described later in this section] at JoelOsteen.com."

3 Graphic for "An Evening with Joel" with "On sale now" and a list of cities and dates for Joel's tour.
4 "The New York Times Bestseller!" with a picture of Joel's book, *Your Best Life Now*—everywhere books are sold or at JoelOsteen.com.
5 Mailing address for Joel Osteen in Houston.
6 Bible quote (shown 8 minutes into the show).
7 "To purchase 'Being grateful for the gift of today' [the sermon being broadcast] visit JoelOsteen.com or call the 800 number."
8 "Sign up for Daily Inspiration..." again.
9 Bible quote.
10 Bible quote.
11 "Lakewood Church."
12 Bible quote.
13 Another plug for *Your Best Life Now*.
14 Information on how to purchase the sermon, again.
15 "Sign up for Daily Inspiration..." again.
16 "An Evening with Joel" and its tour dates, again.
17 Joel Osteen mailing address.
18 *Your Best Life Now*, again.

Out of 18 pieces of information shown to viewers, four were Bible quotes, two were for the Lakewood Church, two were the mailing address, and 10 were to sell a product or service related to Joel—a key indicator of what is being marketed and sold.

After Joel's sermon, a commercial comes on with Joel and Victoria thanking viewers for their prayers and support. This is followed by another commercial to sell tickets for "An Evening with Joel" and then ads for *Your Best Life Now* and *Your Best Life Now Devotional*. The program ends with a female voiceover inviting viewers to "visit us at JoelOsteen.com."

Like any good infomercial, *Joel Osteen* is also good television. This is no surprise given Joel's experience producing his father's program. For almost two decades he watched his father preach and edited his sermons, thus honing his production skills. Joel is well aware that he is competing with other television options in the marketplace, and not just with other religious programming:

> It's important to me that the production of our broadcast is very high quality. I realize that you've got to have good cameras and lighting and good presentation if you expect your message to be received, because you're competing with people that are doing the Grammys and local news, and you can't be subpar.
>
> (Butler, 2005b)

The Web site

JoelOsteen.com is the heart and soul of the Joel brand. Every television show prominently displays the site's URL throughout the course of the program. It appears on all correspondence and is the endpoint for promotion on daily devotional e-mails and weekly calls to view Joel's latest sermon.

In 2007 JoelOsteen.com was redesigned, resulting in a new streamlined version that is much improved over its previous incarnation, which was notable for how cluttered it was. Now the home page is easy to navigate, and the essence of the Web site—what it is trying to accomplish—is easy to discern. On the home page there is a static blue rectangular banner at the top that contains just the Joel Osteen Ministries logo. Below that is a narrow horizontal band with standard Web site links: Home, About us, Events, Broadcast, Ministry Support, Bookstore, and Contact us. The rest of the page contains promotions for one product or another.

What immediately catches your eye is a band that changes content every couple of seconds to promote five items in rotation: An Evening with Joel (the tour), Meet Joel! (a promotion for Joel's book signing schedule), Free podcasts (available for download), Inspiration in your inbox (the daily e-mails from Joel and Victoria), and an ad for the broadcast schedule that says, "Don't miss a minute!" To the right of this box are quick links to viewing Joel online, the event schedule, submitting prayer requests, giving donations, and the site for Lakewood Church. If you've opted in to the Web site (i.e., submitted your name and e-mail address), you'll see below the rotating promotions, on the left of the screen, a media player that visitors can instantly click to view one of Joel's sermons. (Within the site Joel can be watched live when services are occurring or through previously recorded broadcasts—you need to opt in to view these.)

The middle of the home page is an area called "News & Events," which contains three boxes for exactly this purpose. Recently these boxes showed: a link to a *Publishers Weekly* article about Joel's upcoming book, *Become a Better You: 7 Keys to Improving Your Life*, which will be launched in October 2007 with a three-million copy press run; a plug for Joel's next tour date and a link to buy tickets; and a picture of Barbara Walters with the headline "Most Fascinating" and a link to the ABC News Web site of the ten most fascinating people of 2006, of whom Joel was one.

To the right of New & Events are three more promotional boxes. One promotes "A Night of Hope," Joel's tour to the United Kingdom. Another box says, "Share the best news ever," which leads to the Easter Story. The final box is for "Inspiration in your inbox," which links to a page where you can sign up for Joel and Victoria's daily inspirational e-mails. These boxes change regularly to reflect the organization's marketing needs.

The Web site is more of a promotional tool than an assistant to faith. Yes, Joel's sermons can be viewed on the site, but that is pretty much the only teaching or ministry aspect of it. Books are sold. The television program is sold. Tour updates are promoted. Joel is promoted. Scripture or opportunities for sharing faith are in little evidence here.

The marketing elements—e-mails and direct mail

Given his marketing savvy learned from years of television production and traditional advertising, Joel's use of the Internet, and particularly e-mail, as a marketing tool is not surprising. E-mail is used to promote Joel's tour dates and his latest book offerings as well as any missions that are of particular focus to the church at any given time. For example, people who signed up for e-mail updates via the Web site received requests for donations for victims of Hurricane Katrina.

These e-mails contain promotional elements. For example, when Joel was in Philadelphia, an e-mail went out announcing that he and Victoria would be at Sam's Club for a book signing. In October 2005, *Your Best Life Now Journal* had just been published so this was promoted in a banner down the side of the e-mail. The e-mails for the Joel concerts contain a button to "Invite a friend," and with the click of a button, you can send an e-mail to a friend to "Join Joel Osteen's Team," also making the recipient part of the e-mail database. The only e-mails that do not promote products or events are ones that are specifically asking for money for Joel Osteen Ministries. These are sent monthly and are usually sent from Joel and Victoria, though Joel has also appeared solo in these donation requests.

According to an e-mail sent early in 2006, "After months of requests from friends like you for e-mail inspiration from God's Word," Joel (and Victoria) began offering daily e-mail devotionals beginning in March of that year. These e-mails are delivered Monday through Friday under the subject line "Today's Word with Joel & Victoria." The e-mails were recently redesigned to reflect the revamped Web site. So above a picture of Joel and Victoria is the blue bar with "Joel Osteen Ministries" and below that is a gold band containing links to the broadcast schedule, events, and the bookstore, thus creating more consistency across the brand.

Each e-mail follows a prescribed format. It begins with the title of the message. Some examples include: "God wants us to be happy!"; "Magnify the Lord!"; and "You are God's Masterpiece." In line with Joel's preaching, these e-mails are endlessly hopeful and uplifting and are based on themes from Joel's preaching elsewhere. They include victory, having a positive attitude, calling on God, and living a Christian life.

The message title is followed by a section called "Today's Scripture," which is a single Bible quote. Here examples include: "I have come that they may have life, and have it to the full" (John 10:10), which is a favorite among prosperity preachers; "You must each make up your own mind as to how much you should give. Don't give reluctantly or in response to pressure.

For God loves the person who gives cheerfully" (2 Corinthians 9:7); and "If anyone sees his brother in need yet closes his heart of compassion, how can the love of God be in him?" (John 3:17).

The middle section of the e-mail is "Today's Word from Joel and Victoria." This section is a Joel mini-sermon. It is positive self-talk with many of the sentences ending in exclamation points. "He came that we might have and enjoy life, and have it to the full-until it overflows!" or "We know that God's plan always leads to peace, health, and prosperity in every area of life. And that is something to praise Him for!" The e-mail ends with "A Prayer for Today" based on the scripture reading. Just below this is a hyperlink to past e-mails under the heading "Read Another Word with Joel & Victoria."

On each e-mail there is approximately a two-inch column that is used for promotional purposes. While initially this space was used to advertise a number of products such as videotapes of past sermons, music CDs by Lakewood's in-house music directors, or copies of Joel's latest books, of late it only promotes Joel's book. There is also a single button asking people to "support God's work. DONATE NOW."

Once a week, an e-mail from only Joel comes under the title "Live Like a Champion," playing off the brand tagline. These e-mails are promotions for the television show. They start out with a description of that week's sermon. In the middle there is a picture of Joel with his hand balled in a fist raised in victory. Next to the picture is a button to "Watch this week's Live Like a Champion," which is a hyperlink to the corresponding television program. There is also a link on the bottom of the page that directs readers to "Look for Joel on TV this week." By clicking on this link, readers are directed to a map of the United States. When a state and then a city are clicked, readers are then directed to when and where they can see Joel on television in their local markets.

Demonstrating the extent to which religion and marketing have merged was an e-mail under the subject line: "Joel Osteen Ministries Wants to Bless You so You can Bless Others." This was an announcement for the 2006 Christmas sale, for which Joel products were available at 50 percent off, which was the biggest element on the e-mail. The text went on to say: "Discounted so that you can bless your friends, family and neighbors with the greatest gift of all. Share the hope, encouragement and worship from Joel Osteen and Lakewood Church with everyone on your Christmas list." And, to make sure that it was perfectly in line with the market, the sale ran from November 24—black Friday—until December 3.

As with traditional televangelists, Joel readily uses direct mail as part of his ministry. When you contact the church, you receive in return a package in a simple envelope that has the Joel Osteen Ministries logo on it. It is addressed to "Dear Friend," and besides containing a letter from Joel, has a number of marketing elements in it. First, it has a bookmark that on one side provides the network listings for *Joel Osteen* and on the other side contains the "This is My Bible" confession. Second, there is a small booklet by Joel called *30 Thoughts for Victorious Living*. The format is identical to that of the daily e-mails—scripture, mini-sermon, prayer for the day. Finally there is a donation sheet that contains an area to put in a prayer request. Mailings usually contain a letter and a donation request, though periodically a "gift" is also included—stickers similar to address labels given by charities are a popular item, however, these stickers contain Bible quotes. At the bottom of each sticker is "Joel Osteen Ministries," providing a constant reminder of Joel with the inspirational message. Prayer cards are another common item. These contain a list of scripture quotes that relate to the card's theme, which might be "Your Life Has a Divine Purpose and Destiny," or "Children are a Heritage and Blessing from the Lord." End-of-year mailings request donations as well as provide a way for you to have your best life in 2006—that is, by purchasing a copy of *Your Best Life Now* calendar.

Postcards and magazines are also used as promotional tools. These announce where Joel will be having a book signing in a local area or when he will be in a city for a live event. Lakewood's magazine is called *Life Now!* In addition to mail distribution, these promotional pieces are handed out at Joel's tour dates. On the cover of *Life Now!*, as with most of the promotional material, is a picture of smiling Joel and Victoria. The magazine always includes stories by Joel, Victoria, Paul (Joel's brother), and Dodie (Joel's mother). It is chock full of advertising for tour dates, the television program, and *Your Best Life Now* as well as other products such as the brand's videos and music CDs.

Mail—whether snail or electronic—is not used simply for donation requests. It is used to promote the brand of Joel and to keep his face and his message top of mind. Almost every communication with a member or a prospect is an opportunity to get that person to purchase a book or videotape or to attend an event. The mailings (snail) contain small gifts, which direct marketers know help generate increased donations. These gifts are not just ways to remember Christ, but ways to remember Joel, because his likeness or name is always incorporated into the gift.

The Joel tour

In 2004 Joel Osteen went beyond the confines of the Lakewood Church for the first time. Having already established a national presence with his television ministry, he began a 15-city tour. The tour, "An Evening with Joel," began in Atlanta's Philips Arena (capacity 18,000) and included stops in Anaheim, California, New York City, and Chicago. According to Duncan Dodds, the executive director of Joel Osteen Ministries and a close friend of the pastor, this was simply an opportunity for people to see Joel live. "Our ministry goes pretty broad…We are in the major markets across the country. This is a chance for us to go out and see our viewers on a face-to-face basis"

(Dooley, 2004, p. 1). Since then, these tours have become a staple of the ministry, with Joel having had 14 tour dates in 2006 and nearly 20 dates in 2007, including in locations outside of the United States.

Joel is a celebrity, a rock-star preacher. He sells out arenas in major cities throughout the United States and has done so for several years. When the tour first began, there was no charge for the events. However, so many people showed up at the first locale that the crowd was unmanageable and many people had to be turned away. At Madison Square Garden, some audience members were accommodated by being seated in an adjoining theater where thousands watched Joel via live video feed. After those first missteps, Joel began to charge $10 and to assign seating so as to manage the crowds. In cities around the country, additional nights are added to accommodate seekers. In Dallas, scalped tickets went for $100 (Martin, 2005), which is amazing considering that Joel can be seen for free in Houston every Sunday morning. Through all of this, Joel has achieved status as a celebrity beyond just the world of the sacred, and the sell-out crowds for "An Evening with Joel" reflect this.

"An Evening with Joel" is more like a rock concert than a church service, much like the services at Lakewood and other megachurches. These shows are highly produced, from the music to the promotional videos that are projected onto screens throughout the oversized arenas where these events take place. At the start of one "show" at Madison Square Garden, the stadium goes dark. The audience anticipation is palpable. Slowly the music builds, the audience stands, and rhythmic clapping fills the auditorium. The lights come brightly on, the choir of 80 or more (plus orchestra) begins a rousing number, and Cindy Cruse-Ratcliff and Israel Houghton, musical directors of Lakewood, lead the audience in singing praise. The songs are rock tunes with simple lyrics, which are flashed on overhead video screens so the audience can sing along. Music is an important element in these evenings. It underlies most of the show, functioning as a soundtrack and cuing audience members about appropriate emotional responses.

Joel and Victoria appear on stage to welcome the audience. The welcome is upbeat—"We love you guys" is a popular greeting. Joel goes on to say, "God loves you," "God is great," and that the night is a celebration—"We're gonna have a good time tonight!"—to which the audience whistles and applauds. These are themes that will get repeated again and again throughout the night. Joel is followed by Victoria, who tends to be more flagrant in her use of religious language, saying "God" and "Jesus" continuously. She builds on the theme of the evening by letting people know that God cares about them: "God's not just interested in the big things. He's interested in the details of your life—your marriage, your finances, your children, success in the workplace."[7] The welcome continues with Joel reminding people to enjoy the evening. "Get your mind off your problems—lots of people wanted to be here but couldn't be. We have lots to be thankful for...Give God praise first and then he can change your circumstances."

After another song, Joel gives a prayer, then another song is sung, and then Dodie Osteen, Joel's mother, takes the stage. Dodie is another carrier of the myth. She embodies the legacy of John Osteen. She tells the story of how she was given just a few weeks to live after her diagnosis of liver cancer. She and John went home and lay down on the floor and John spoke to the cancer and it disappeared. She says that God is a loving, merciful, and compassionate God. "Do not go home the same way tonight...Go home in faith, believing God will do what you need" (Dodds, 2004). This story acts as an introduction for Joel to give a prayer of healing. He speaks of a "supernatural God"—another term in his lexicon and code for a charismatic belief system. "You may not see it, but the moment we pray the tide of the battle turns." The prayer continues. "I pray for promotion among your people. Give them bonuses, increases, raises, inheritances. Father, favor them on the job, favor them wherever they go." The music crescendos and the band begins to play.

There is more talk, another song, and then Joel shares "a little bit of my story." Here the myth is reviewed for anyone who doesn't yet know it—father in the feed store, coming back from college to start the TV ministry, John trying to get him to preach, Joel finally acquiescing as his father lay dying. To lighten the mood, Joel then talks about his first date with Victoria—a story that is frequently retold.[8] Victoria returns to the stage and proclaims, "Joel is exactly what you see on TV in his personal life," thereby adding to the audience's feeling that they know Joel, that he is a personal friend.

The auditorium goes dark again and a video plays on monitors through-out the arena. "The critics all said it couldn't be done" is the theme of the presentation. This is in part a reference to the starting of Lakewood, but primarily it is about the construction of the Compaq Center and its refurbishment into the new Lakewood Church. The video goes on to tout the television ministry, claiming that it is the most watched inspirational program in America, according to Nielsen, and it can be seen in 150 nations around the world. The video also includes testimonials of people who were saved by watching the television program—they are no longer depressed; one woman decided not to commit suicide. The video ends by showing the helping ministries around the world. As the video ends volunteers begin to pass large white buckets around the auditorium for offerings to help the ministry.

With the collection complete, Duncan Dodds, executive director of Joel Osteen Ministries, comes on stage to present Frederick Lewis, special assistant to Virginia Fields, Manhattan Borough President. October 21 and 22, 2004, are proclaimed Joel Osteen Day in New York. At this time, the head of Time Warner Books comes to the stage to announce that Joel's book had made the *New York Times* best-seller list.[9]

Finally, almost 90 minutes into the event, Joel gives his sermon. In format, it is just like the TV program—joke, incantation, "you sound awesome," positive sermon. The theme is a page from Norman Vincent Peale—in order to change your life you must change your thinking. You must start the day by putting your mind in a positive direction. "This is the day the Lord has made." "Don't magnify your problems. Magnify your God." "Expect good things. Expect God's supernatural power." The sermon ends with "How many of you received it tonight?" which is answered with thunderous applause.

Paul Osteen, Joel's brother, comes on stage to tell a parable that is acted out both through the audience and on video screens overhead. It is the story of coming back to your "father." Music plays in the background and again guides the emotional impact. This story is a setup for the altar call. "We're here to help you find a new beginning," says Joel. "Stand where you are if you are not at peace with God. Take a step of faith. I'm not talking about finding religion. I'm not talking about finding a church. I'm talking about finding life and peace and true fulfillment. There's a void in you that only God can fill." As most of the audience members stand, Joel begins the prayer, "Lord I repent of my sin." a prayer known by most of the audience through his television show. He then urges people to get into a good Bible-based church and not to "hang out" with friends who will pull you away from the Lord.

The show ends with Victoria and their children joining Joel on stage. Joel talks about "how everyone has lots of negative people in your life that put you down." At this point, Joel stops as he begins to tear up. The audience applauds to show their encouragement. "Tonight is a night of new beginnings…Everyone under the sound of my voice is blessed." and the band begins to play "I Am a Friend of God," a song now familiar to the audience because its simple lyric and melody were played earlier in the evening. The show ends with song and applause and Joel saying, "We'll be back next year. Good night. We love you," much like a rock star would at the end of a concert.

While some might call these evenings a crusade, in reality it is nothing more than an extremely elaborate, highly produced book tour. Each city of the tour has a book signing in conjunction with the evening event. Reports are that people get up at five in the morning so that they can be the first in line at his Joel's signings. They wait for hours to have 10 to 15 seconds with the Smiling Preacher (Brown, 2006). Viewers of the television show became prospects for the book, just as members of Rick Warren's Web sites are prospects for purchasing *The Purpose Driven Life*. The tour simply provides the "personal touch." Using this strategy Warner Faith sold close to 2.5 million copies of *Your Best Life Now* in the first 28 weeks of its release, plus another 200,000 in audio book form (Hilliard, 2005, p. S12). When asked who the audience for the book is, Joel told Beliefnet (Sheahen, 2004b), "I don't want to just preach to the church and I just feel like I have a broader message. I'd like to think that I can help everyday people who don't necessarily go to church."

Oprah—talk show as televangelism

Oprah, the media brand

Someone else who is looking to help everyday people is Oprah Winfrey. As the sacred has become more secular in Joel Osteen, the secular has become more sacred in Oprah Winfrey. Over a 20-year span, her daytime television talk show has fluctuated in its religious/spiritual content, rising to its current mission-based, intention-filled version of pop religion. Content has been blatantly spiritual, as when the show ended with "Remembering Your Spirit," a short video segment about how to connect to your spiritual side, and today's more coded religious content, which slips spiritual principles into the discussion under the guise of self-improvement. For example, when guests tell their stories of redemption, Oprah calls this their "testimony," or she asks guests, "What did you learn?" attempting to illicit the intention behind their actions. This comes from the mission of the show, as Winfrey explained in O, The Oprah Magazine, "I'm proud of how we evolved from a TV show to an hour filled with purpose and intention. The show is a force for good. Good information. Good entertainment. Goodwill" (Kogan, 2005, p. 279). Within this context, Oprah is not afraid to talk about God and miracles or offer praise to Jesus, though she often does so with a joking attitude so as not to appear overtly religious. According to Christian Today, "To her audience of more than 22 million mostly female viewers, she has become a post-modern priestess—an icon of church-free spirituality" (Taylor, 2002, pp. 40). So it should not be surprising that Oprah makes the list of cult brands in The Power of Cult Branding (Ragas and Bueno, 2002); she is the very essence of the intersection of marketing and religion.

Unlike Joel Osteen, Oprah started as a brand and the televised faith came later. The brand was built out of the media empire Oprah created, much as Joel created his. Her daily talk show has been on the air for more than 20 years, and she has a contract to continue for several more, at least through 2011. Harpo, Oprah's production company, also produces Oprah After the Show, a mini-version of the regular talk show that appears on the Oxygen network. Oprah is a co-founder and co-owner of Oxygen with Gerry Laybourne, an originator of Nickelodeon, Carsey-Werner, producers of such shows as Cosby, Roseanne, and That 70s Show, and Vulcan Ventures, Paul Allen's investment company. Beyond her television enterprise, there is O, The Oprah Magazine—a women's publication that features Oprah on the cover of every issue and is a joint venture between Hearst and Harpo Print—and the Web site Oprah.com.

Oprah's talk show is the highest-rated talk show on television, reaching more than 20 million viewers weekly (Granatstein, 2004, p. SR13). While the majority of daytime shows average a 2 rating, Oprah achieves a 7 rating or better, which is equivalent to the rating of a prime-time show. *Oprah* is the most successful daytime talk show in history. So, too, O magazine, a sort of print version of the show, was the most successful magazine launch in history, starting with a circulation of half a million in 2000. By 2006, the magazine's paid circulation was 2.3 million and its newsstand sales were more than 850,000 copies per month (ABC Statement, 2006).[10] The company recently launched *O at Home*, a spin-off publication about home decorating, and there are plans for *O Girl*, a publication targeting teen girls. Meanwhile, Oprah's Web site attracts two millions users per month who generate 30 million page views (Oprah.com).

Like Joel's media outlets, Oprah's are in and of themselves forms of publicity. They serve to promote the brand of Oprah, her beliefs, and her products and services. This includes cross-promoting each other (the magazine promotes the television show, which promotes the Web site, which promotes the magazine, etc.) as well as providing multiple platforms for Oprah's pet projects, the most recent of which was the Leadership Academy for Girls in South Africa. Oprah's media outlets also promote the people and things that Oprah chooses to present in these forums, an act that creates an implicit endorsement.

Other than perhaps Martha Stewart before her jailhouse travails, there is no other media empire—moreover no other media brand—so associated with an individual. Unlike Martha Stewart, however, Oprah is a brand that represents honesty, integrity, and, yes, spirituality. Because of this she is able to influence her viewers in multiple spheres, and not just their media choices.

The brand mythology

While brands can be positioned in the minds of consumers based on attributes (physical characteristics), benefits (what the product will do for me), or beliefs and values, the most effective position is based on the last one. Oprah is a brand based on her passions, values, and beliefs. Oprah is not just a talk show host; she is perceived by many viewers as a friend, a confidant, a teacher, and a role model. The basis of the Oprah myth is that she is a wise friend whom you can count on.

Oprah has come into America's living rooms on almost a daily basis for more than 20 years. No other television personality has had this longevity or consistency with their audience. Oprah is as dependable as, well, God. She is there every day, day after day, with words of encouragement and support. Consistency is at the heart of the Oprah brand.

The myth of the Oprah brand has been built over years of storytelling in the most intimate of settings—the viewer's own living room. Sharing your home with someone in that way creates a significant connection on the part of the audience, what researchers call a para-social interaction. To viewers, Oprah is a dependable friend even though she has never been physically closer than appearing on the television screen. In addition, Oprah has revealed herself at a level not seen with other celebrities. Fans are well-versed in her rags-to-riches story, which Oprah openly talks about on her show and which appears as her biography on her Web site. Born in Kosciusko, Mississippi, Oprah was raised with outhouses and was shuffled among family members throughout her youth. She has often talked about being raped as an adolescent and has had a lifelong battle with her weight (a problem shared by millions of Americans, both men and women). Viewers have seen Oprah laugh and cry. She, unlike most other personalities, appears to let down the wall between herself and her audience. Oprah (everyone is on a first-name basis with her, just like with Joel) has risen above all of this to be included on the *Forbes* list of wealthiest entertainers, with a fortune estimated to be over $1 billion. Even so, viewers tend to think of her as "one of us," even though she isn't even close.

The program

Broadcasting & Cable, a leading television trade magazine, called *The Oprah Winfrey Show* a virtual ministry. When asked about that moniker, she said:

> I sincerely believe that it [the show] is a platform that has been given me from a power that's greater than myself. I look at my history and my background and how this all sort of happened. I understood somewhere, after '98–'99, that it wasn't mine to play with. It wasn't mine to say, "Oh, I don't know if I feel like it." It was a calling bigger than a job on television.
>
> (Bednarski, 2005, p. 52)

Oprah sees her show as a conduit for providing information and entertainment to serve a higher power. While she is not professing to provide viewers with the ultimate truth, nor does she quote scripture, she has, according to Oprah.com, "enlightened and uplifted millions of viewers" a statement that could be applied to religious contexts, if not certainly therapeutic ones. She presents shows that are about creating positive changes in her viewers' lives. As she told O magazine, "I don't do any guests who represent the dark side: Satanism, the KKK, etc. I realize everything is about energy. Dark energy—whether it's called Satan or not—creates more of its kind when given a forum" (Kogan, 2005, p. 279).

In 1994 Oprah made the decision to move away from what other talk shows, like Jerry Springer, Ricki Lake, and Maury, were doing, that is, trash TV. This was in response to criticism from Vicki Abt, a professor at Penn State and author of *Coming After Oprah: Cultural Fallout in the Age of the TV Talk Show*. Oprah conducted a six-hour interview with Professor Abt, and out of that conversation she decided that if she was going to stay on the air, she was going to use television to improve the lives of her viewers—similar to how Rick Warren sees his ministry. Over the next several years her program would change to reflect a service orientation, so much so that Oprah has come to call her show "my ministry" (Taylor, 2002, p. 42).

Oprah's Angel Network, an organization created to raise money for people doing good works, began in 1997 "to encourage people around the world to make a difference in the lives of others. Oprah's vision is to inspire individuals to create opportunities that help underserved people rise to their own potential" (O Philanthropy, 2007). In 2000 the Angel Network established the "Use Your Life Award," which appeared as a weekly segment on the show. People doing good works appeared on the show and were given a check to aid in their missions. The Angel Network continues to raise money today, though it is now a less obvious part of the television show. Following the Angel Network in 1998, Oprah dubbed the season "Change Your Life TV." During that time each show ended with a segment called "Remembering Your Spirit," presenting some type of meditation or practice that would allow viewers to connect with their spiritual side. Oprah was criticized for this overt presentation of spirituality, and she often had to defend her choice on air. Eventually the segment was dropped, though the sentiment was not.

Spirituality is still an integral part of the show, but it is enmeshed within the show rather than highlighted separately. A great example of this is the Christmas giveaway show. For years, Oprah would give members of the studio audience expensive gifts from the "O List," a monthly list in O magazine of Oprah's "favorite things." Three hundred audience members would scream for an hour as they received package after expensive package of consumer products. In 2006 Oprah changed the concept by giving everyone in the audience $1,000. But there was a catch: the money had to be used to help other people. A few weeks later, Oprah brought back these audience members and demonstrated how $1,000 could be turned into much more. One woman, for example, raised more than $70,000 for a man with brain cancer who was the sole supporter of nine children and one grandchild. Working with her small community, she was able to eliminate this man's hospital bills, get donated groceries, and even create a college scholarship for one of his sons.[11] This program demonstrated two spiritual concepts key to the Oprah brand: (1) the belief that if you give, you will get abundance back in return, and (2) gifts of the spirit are better than material gifts—though material ones are not to be eschewed (this is television after all).[12]

This show also demonstrated two of Oprah's popular themes—gratitude and the alleviation of suffering. Gratitude is a staple of the show. Oprah often recommends keeping a gratitude journal, basically a daily list of things to be thankful for. She got this idea in the late 1990s from Sarah Ban Breathnach, author of *Simple Abundance.* In the pursuit of happiness, the first step is to be grateful for what you have. And, when you do have things to be grateful for, it is incumbent upon you to help out others who are less fortunate and thereby alleviate suffering. In showing suffering of any sort, Oprah does not do so without providing viewers with a way to help. Oprah's spirituality—like Joel's—is very practical. Whether it is the victims of Hurricane Katrina or the AIDS crisis in Africa, action steps are offered. Again and again Oprah will say, "So what can we do?" The answer might be donating to the Angel Network or it could be helping someone in your hometown. Whatever it is, the ultimate goal remains the same—personal happiness. It is happiness through empowerment. As people feel empowered, they feel more in control, and then they feel happier.

Roads to empowerment come in different guises. For some it might be forgiveness—another important theme on *Oprah.* She has done numerous shows about people who have forgiven others in the direst of situations. For example, one mother forgave the man who killed her daughter. Another woman who was hideously deformed by a car accident forgave the man who hit her car while driving drunk. For others, empowerment comes in the form of learning to take better care of yourself through weight loss. For still others, Oprah shows examples of how people have turned their lives around, whether it is through conquering addictions or teenage prostitutes getting out of "the life." In talking about these topics, Winfrey readily evokes her faith. In a show in May 2005, for example, Oprah's guest was a woman whose husband had burned her almost to death. Said Oprah:

> This is what's so amazing to me and I'm sure to a lot of other people who are watching. Okay, so you were obviously a woman who didn't have very much self-esteem if you allowed yourself to be told what to wear and who to talk to and whatever. And then you can come from that—this is how great God is, I think—is that you can come from that to sit here with half of a face, in the process of rebuilding your face and rebuilding your life with greater self-esteem than I've ever seen from anybody. That's amazing. Isn't that amazing?
>
> And my words to everybody is so that's what it took for Carolyn. That's what it took for her to get the lesson. But there is a divine order to things, and God always whispers first. And anybody who's ended up in a crisis or tragedy or some kind of dramatic situation, you can look back, and you can hear the whisper, and many of you who are watching and those of us who are here have lessons that are coming in your own life that don't have to do with particularly necessarily physical abuse,

but because you have seen this, the reason why you saw this today isn't so that we could all stare at her face, but it's so that you can look inside your own life and the lives of people you know and to hear your own whispers. Hear your own whispers.

(The woman without a face, 2005)

Oprah's shows become parables; her guests become lessons. It is through seeing these dramatizations—more highly produced, more real, more personal than at any megachurch—that people learn about what Kathryn Lofton (2006) calls the "Religion of Oprah" (p. 18).

God has been evoked increasingly more often on *Oprah* over the last few years. In a show in May 2006, for example, Oprah talked to women who hate themselves. One woman had gained more than 100 pounds and was drinking heavily. Oprah told her not to drive drunk. Here is part of the discussion:[13]

WINFREY: God works through people.

DR. SMITH: Right.

WINFREY: God—God—you're waiting on God and God's waiting on you. ...You think you hate yourself now, you kill somebody else's child, you maim somebody, you cause brain damage, not to yourself, because you wouldn't care if it was yourself, but you do that to somebody because I—the way the universe works is it keeps trying to show you, keeps trying to show you. And I know a lot of people might not understand this, but it's true, you go out and you cause damage to somebody else would be another way for God to get your attention. In the meantime, somebody else's life is destroyed...

LAUREN: Because of my...

WINFREY: ...because—because of you. And maybe that's what it would have to—and then you would say, "Well, now I seen what I've done." Don't let that happen. Just don't get—just let that be one of the rules of your life. As you're figuring out—and that alone will be a positive step for you. Don't do that to yourself, because you don't need another lesson. You don't need another lesson. OK? You promise?

LAUREN: I promise.

...

DR. SMITH: ..."I'm doing this because I'm—it's my first step...

WINFREY: Yeah.

DR. SMITH: ...in loving myself. It's my first step in being worthy. It's my first step in hearing from God that I am good enough. And so because I'm good enough, I don't want to harm myself and I don't want to cause pain." So it's a step of loving you to not drink and drive.

Again the communication is that God is sending you a message. Here, too, it is not just Oprah, but also the psychologist Dr. Robin Smith who invokes the name of God, giving further credence to these assertions because she is a therapist, a doctor. In summing up the show, Dr. Smith explains what all of the self-loathing guests have in common: a belief that they are less than what God created us to be.

> DR. SMITH: …As kids, we believe what is told. "You're beautiful. You're smart. You're dumb. You're ugly." Whatever it is you were told, we all took it in. And it's now [time] to say "I'm going to break that lie and I'm going to create that which is true about me. That which God says about me."
>
> (Why I hate myself, May 11, 2006)

God is an integral and accepted part of *The Oprah Winfrey Show*. He is the power behind her. What we come to think is that if we act like her, which includes accepting her faith in God, then we can be like her too—happy, wealthy, accomplished, well-loved. That's a very compelling message given Oprah's success.[14]

Part of Oprah's appeal comes from her seemingly whimsical approach to spirituality. This is not to say that her faith is whimsical, but that the medium through which she presents it requires that it be so. Like Joel Osteen, she presents a practical spirituality—meditating will make you calmer with your kids; listening to your intuition can save your life—tips that people can use even while they are spiritually based. And, like the gospel of Joel, if you do make these changes, you can be successful too. It is the very essence of materialist spirituality.

Impact on spirituality

Beyond the show itself, there are two key ways in which Oprah has had a significant impact in bringing spirituality into the popular culture. One is through her choice of guests and book selection, and the other is in her making it acceptable for celebrities to openly discuss their faith.

Oprah has become one of the most influential forces in the publishing arena. The books she recommends for her book club become immediate best sellers. Book club selections have included Elie Weisel's *Night*, *The Rapture of Canaan* (Sheri Reynold), and *The Book of Ruth* (Jane Hamilton), among many others. All books selected for the club have strong moral themes that reflect Oprah's beliefs and sensibilities. An important element of the club is having people who have read the book write in and explain how it has changed their lives. Oprah had typically selected a handful of viewer/readers and invited them to a dinner with the author. This dinner with the author becomes another show, which demonstrates the power of reading and its ability to change people's lives—yet another tool in the spiritual arsenal.[15]

Authors not part of the book club have also been staples on the show and they, too, receive a significant sales boost. This trend started in the 1980s, when Oprah recommended *Creative Visualization* (Shakti Gawain), an early New Age best seller. Other guests, including Marianne Williamson and Deepak Chopra, became household names after appearing on her show. The importance of this is in what media scholars call "agenda setting." This theory explains that while the media does not tell us what to think, it does tell us what to think about. For example, what is on the front page of the *New York Times* is going to set the agenda for what people will be talking about that day. So, too, through her selection of books and authors, Oprah sets the agenda of what millions of women (and their families and friends) will be discussing—at home, at work, at the gym, in book clubs, and in countless other settings.

Oprah does not present the spiritual message by herself. Her supporting cast—a rotating group of specialists/authors—have become helpers in transmitting the faith. While now she has her XM Radio "friends," in the past she has also had a core groups of regular guests like life coach Cheryl Richardson, financial advisor Suze Orman, and New Age authors Gary Zukav and Iyanla van Zandt, to whom she gave weekly platforms for presenting their spiritual lessons. The most famous of her specialists was Phil McGraw, now known familiarly as Dr. Phil. His first appearance featured Shannon, "a laxative-gulping, heavy drinking suicidal rape survivor" as described in the *Washington Post*:

> "Dear Oprah," Shannon wrote, as if entreating a higher power, "I really need your help."
>
> Winfrey employed Dr. Phil, who grilled Shannon. "How did the rape make you feel?"
>
> The good doctor had her stand and repeat after him, church-service style: "It is my time, and it is my turn." Then he entreated the audience: "If you think this girl has hurt long enough, if you think she's felt dirty long enough, if you think she has paid long enough, then stand up for her right now."
>
> "Go, Shannon!" Winfrey said, cheering for the cure. "You go, girl! Let the healing begin!"
>
> (Copeland, 2000, p. C1)

The involvement of these psychologists and life coaches on *The Oprah Winfrey Show* has helped to blur the line between spirituality and therapy. Spirituality is about getting happier, as Oprah's tagline ("Live Your Best Life") suggests. Whether it is letting go of the past through therapy, reading spiritual books, meditating, or a combination of all of these things, Oprah offers a spirituality that reflects the cafeteria style of seekers. And Oprah herself has said, "One of the biggest mistakes humans make is to believe there is only one way. Actually, there are many diverse paths leading to what you call God" (Taylor, 2002, p. 45). It is obviously a spirituality that her viewers relate to, or she would not have the sizable audience that she does. Oprah's religion is one that doesn't take too much effort; it is created by the consumer, and just like the American Dream, if you keep on working it, it will cure whatever ails you.

Televised religion as entertainment...and vice versa

What Oprah Winfrey and Joel Osteen are presenting is the simplest of marketing messages: problem/solution advertising. My breath smells lousy—I'll use Listerine—my breath will smell sweet. Of course, what is also implied is, if I fix my bad breath, I will also find a husband or wife. Similarly, my life is a mess—I watch Joel or Oprah—presto, everything will begin to fall into place. Well, just like Listerine won't get you a mate, watching television won't fix your life. Life is complex and difficult and not always happy. Alas, unhappy endings do not make for good television, particularly television that needs to compete in a marketplace of entertainment. Instead success, happiness, prosperity, empowerment, redemption—these are the messages of televised religion. To compete in the marketplace, faith brands like Oprah and Joel promote these positive feelings over dreary doctrine.

While they supposedly operate in separate genres of television, the parallels between Oprah and Joel are strikingly similar. Both claim to be working to improve the lives of their audiences. Oprah's tagline is "Live Your Best Life"; Joel's book is *Your Best Life Now*. Both are on a first-name basis with their audience. Both readily expose themselves to their audiences. Both attract diverse audiences. Both are based on rags-to-riches brand myths. They both preach attainability, which they demonstrate through their personal experiences.

There is something to be said for a more upbeat, entertaining approach to religion. As Joyce Meyer has been quoted as saying, "Who would want to get in on something where you're miserable, poor, broke and ugly and you just have to muddle through until you get to heaven?" (Van Biema and Chu, 2006, p. 52). When you put it that way, who could disagree? But don't we get this same message from everything else in our culture? Every television commercial says you can and should have it all. We have come to believe that we should have what we want and now we believe that God thinks so too. And yet, don't we want something more from our fundamental belief systems? What about being a better person, creating reverence for life, learning to have compassion for your fellow human being, feeding the poor, clothing the naked, caring about the environment? Aren't these more worthy goals than being the best shopper or having the biggest house? The concern of theologians is that God is fast becoming the middle man—the means to a prosperous end instead of the end itself. Moreover, in focusing on the positive, the negative—really, the reality of so many people's lives—is not simply obscured but obliterated altogether.

"Most of us are mediocre at best—average by definition, and being exposed to this nonsense makes us more mediocre," Abt says (Copeland, 2000, p. C1). I agree with her to a point. We are, most of us, mediocre. However, if watching Oprah or Joel makes someone lose weight or leave a bad relationship or decide not to commit suicide, that's a good thing. What is not good is the false belief that Joel or Oprah is your friend or your pastor, who will be there beside you at the hardest times. On one of his tapes, Joel talks about a couple who lost their teenage child in a car accident. Instead of getting down and falling into a "pity party," they thanked the Lord that they had their child for the amount of time that they did. While that is amazing and certainly exceptional on the part of these parents, is it realistic to assume that most people—or even some—will have that response in a time of crisis? Where does prosperity preaching come in during such moments of profound loss? As Joel readily admitted, he doesn't know why God would let that teenager die. But does hoping for abundance make that pain go away? I think not. It will also not be Oprah or Joel who will be there when your parents die or you become seriously ill. It will be the local pastor or rabbi or priest. Which begs the question: how many of those local folks will be around after they have been eschewed for entertainment?

Chapter 7

Kabbalah
Marketing designer spirituality

Kabbalah is significantly different from any of the other faith brands studied here. Because it is a spiritual practice based on Judaism rather than Christianity, it does not have the built-in benefit of a church network. There is no Vatican or Southern Baptist Conference for Jews through which to efficiently disseminate information. Moreover, the promoters of the Kabbalah Centre are not attempting to turn synagogues into "Kabbalah Temples" in the way that Rick Warren is turning churches into Purpose Driven ones. They are trying to spread the wisdom of Kabbalah because they believe it is "a way of creating a better life."

Through classes, products, and a cultivated relationship with Hollywood, the Kabbalah Centre has turned "Kabbalah" into a household name—a brand. The Centre has repackaged and simplified this practice to be sold to the masses, Jew and non-Jew alike. Because the Kabbalah Centre is not a synagogue (though it claims tax-exempt status as a religious institution) and it does not have multitudes of tithing members (though it does have a few very wealthy supporters, like Madonna, who donate generously), practitioners are incessantly required to pay for religious products and services. For that reason, the Kabbalah Centre must continuously market itself just like any other consumer brand.

The long history of Kabbalah

Kabbalah is a Jewish mystical tradition. Historically, to practice it, a person has to be 40, male, and an Orthodox Jew. This last requirement entails, among other things, keeping kosher, keeping the Sabbath, learning and debating Jewish law, and forsaking much of modern-day life. A high level of scholarship is necessary because kabbalistic writings are based on Jewish texts, and a person has to achieve a certain level of Judaic knowledge and discipline before taking on the additional rigors of Kabbalah. As one rabbi said to me, "If you really knew what Kabbalah is, you wouldn't want to do it."

According to Donald Menzi and Zwe Padeh (1999), "The goal of Kabbalah is to penetrate the surface of everyday reality, to explore unseen spiritual worlds through rational inquiry and mystical meditation and thereby to grasp the ultimate meaning and purpose of life" (p. xvii). Mysticism, however, is not a natural aspect of Jewish practice, and in fact did not become part of Jewish faith practice until the nineteenth century. As Joseph Dan explains (2006, p. 9):

> Most traditional definitions of mysticism describe it as the aspiration—and, sometimes, the achievement—of a direct, experiential relationship with God…A unique characteristic of mysticism that is opposed, in most cases, to ordinary religious experience is the denial of language's ability to express religious truth.

Given that Jews are historically known as the "people of the book," it is easy to see how this could be anathema to Jewish teachings. From Torah to Mishnah, Jewish faith and scholarship are based on reading and debating the words—the language—of its scriptural texts. Even so, Kabbalah has withstood this dichotomy for more than 800 years by basing mysticism on book learning.

Scholars agree that Kabbalah has been in existence since the beginning of the thirteenth century. What they do not agree on are the texts that make up kabbalistic thought. The origin of Kabbalah is often pegged to a short book called the *Sefer Yetzirah* (interpreted as Book of Creation or Book of Formation). This work dates from some time between the second and sixth centuries (Scholem, 1987, p. 25), thus predating Kabbalah by several centuries. Whether we call the *Sefer Yetzirah* a kabbalistic text or not, it contains several concepts germane to the study of this mystical practice. It includes an explanation of numerology, demonstrating the importance of certain numbers as they relate to the three layers of existence—cosmic, time, and man. For example, there are seven Hebrew letters that can be pronounced two ways. These letters relate to the seven planets (the cosmic level), the seven days of the week (time), and the seven orifices in the head (man).

This work also introduced the *sefirot*—the ten spheres or emanations—that make up the tree-like structure that is one of the defining elements of Kabbalah (p. 41). The concept of the *sefirot* would not be fleshed out, however, until the *Bahir* was written in the thirteenth century. "While the *Sefirot*, in the *Sefer Yezirah*, were only the ten primary numbers…in the *Bahir* they are divine principles and powers, and supernal lights aiding in the work of creation" (Bloom, 1975, p. 23). These divine powers are described in the shape of an upside down tree with the sphere closest to the material world being feminine, thus introducing gender dualism into the divine (Dan, 2006, p. 22). This female divine power is called the Shekhinah.

[The]...shekhinah (divine residence) is one of the most prominent concepts that distinguishes the Kabbalah from other Jewish worldviews, and it had a significant impact in shaping the kabbalistic theory and practice...[C]oming into spiritual contact with her is a main component of kabbalistic rituals.

(Dan, 2006, p. 45)

The undisputed most important work of Kabbalah is the *Sefer ha-Zohar*, or simply the *Zohar*. The book, or really series of books, was written toward the end of the thirteenth century by Moses de Leon (Bloom, 1974). Written in Aramaic, it was a commentary on the Torah. It tells the story of Rabbi Shimeon bar Yohai and his son, Rabbi Eleazar, and their spiritual adventures. Through these stories, the *Zohar* provides teachings on a wide range of topics from marriage to finances. In addition, the *Zohar* explains the reflection of the material realm into the divine realm and vice versa. Because the *sefirot* are symbolic of man (the material world) and the divine world, what happens in the material world affects what happens at the level of the divine—a key idea to Kabbalah as well as many New Age spiritual practices (Dan, 2006, p. 33).

The final historical kabbalistic text is based on the work of Isaac Luria of Safed (1534–72).[1] Luria's teachings were compiled by a follower into a work called *Etz Chayyim*, which came to be regarded as "the Talmud of the Kabbalists." *Etz Chayyim* is used to aid in deciphering the very complex *Zohar* (Menzi and Padeh, 1999, p. xx). One of the most important contributions of this work is its description of the creation myth. In the beginning there was the Light. When the Light (or the Endless One—*Ein Sof*) created the universe, the Light withdrew, creating empty space. This is known as constriction, or *tzimtzum*. *Ein Sof* created vessels to receive the Light. These vessels, however, were unable to contain the light and they split into pieces. This became known as "the breaking of the vessels."[2] The purpose of our lives, according to Kabbalah, is to mend these broken vessels, to achieve *tikkun*, or mending. This is done through "the observance of the mitzvoth, complete commitment to the norms of ethical behavior, and unselfish pursuit of religious perfection for every person, every community, and for the people as a whole" (Dan, 2006, p. 77). Luria also incorporated and developed the *sefirot*. Building on previous interpretations, he added the dimension of reincarnation to the tree of life, suggesting that the *sefirot* represent various levels of the soul.

In the mid-1920s, Rabbi Yehuda Ashlag, a Lurianic kabbalist, translated the *Zohar* from Aramaic into modern Hebrew and included traditional commentary on the text with this translation. This was an important development toward introducing Kabbalah to a wider audience.

The Kabbalah Centre

The creator of the brand

The Kabbalah Centre is comprised of 27 centers, with the largest institutions in major cities like New York, Los Angeles, Tel Aviv and London, as well as close to 70 satellite offices around the world (Kabbalah Centre, n.d.). There is no definitive information about the establishment of the Centre, but it appears to have been started in the United States in the early 1970s (Ellin, 2004, p. 22).[3] It was founded by Philip S. Berg, an insurance salesman turned rabbi whose given name was Feivel Gruberger (Ellin, 2004, p. 25), and his wife, Karen. Rav Berg, as he is widely known, has a legitimate Kabbalah pedigree having studied with Rabbi Yehudah Brandwein, a student of Rabbi Ashlag (Lappin, 2004). The Rav claims that Brandwein wrote him a letter stating that he should spread the wisdom of Kabbalah to Jews and non-Jews alike. Many dispute this notion (Udovitch, 2005). Whether true or not, the Centre teaches Kabbalah to people of all faiths and by using this strategy, claims to have attracted almost four million people to various Centres around the world for more than 30 years—50 percent of whom were not Jewish. Reportedly there is an additional 20,000 (Ellin, 2004) to 90,000 (Cohen, 2003) people who view the Centre's Web site every month.

The Rav is the spiritual leader of the Kabbalah Centre. His wife, Karen, is credited with being the power behind the throne. Reportedly it was she who came up with the idea of bringing Kabbalah to the masses by playing down its Jewish aspects. She also pushed to bring Kabbalah to the states, opening their first Centre in Los Angeles. There the Bergs became ardent networkers, "making bold phone calls to whatever machers they knew, in order to connect to Hollywood's biggest, wealthiest names" (Peretz, 2005). The Bergs' two sons, Michael and Yehuda, are the co-directors of the Centre in Los Angeles and the authors of numerous books about Kabbalah that are sold through the Centres as well as through mass market outlets.[4]

The first U.S. center opened in 1972 (Ellin, 2004, p. 25), and by 1989 the Kabbalah Centre had become a successful business by selling Kabbalah Water and the *Zohar*, by seeking donations, and by relying on volunteer labor. Volunteer labor continues today and is the backbone to the Kabbalah Centre's structure. At a class I attended, a student mentor mentioned that she had volunteered at the Centre for two years and I wondered how she supported herself, particularly in New York City. I later learned that a number of people are supported by the Centre. These "volunteers" are called chevre, which in Hebrew means gang or friends. These friends are given a place to live that is owned or rented by the Centre and $35 a month in exchange for "volunteering" at the Centre (Peretz, 2005). Kabbalah Centre teachers are also supported in this way. In classes they stress repeatedly that they do not get paid to teach. While this may be technically true, they are compensated in the form of housing and a stipend. While most chevre live in very modest accommodations (Udovitch, 2005), the Bergs and their sons live in side-by-side multimillion dollar Hollywood houses paid for by the Kabbalah Centre. The Bergs explained this in an interview with ABC's Elizabeth Vargas:

KAREN BERG: The house is owned by the Centre. And we're allowed to live in it as any priest would be that belonged to a church or any rabbi would be.

ELIZABETH VARGAS: You said in, in forms that you filed, Karen, that you had taken a vow of poverty, you and your whole family.

KAREN BERG: Right, exactly right.

ELIZABETH VARGAS: But you—some people might argue you don't look like you're living...

KAREN BERG: In poverty.

YEHUDA BERG: I mean, last time I checked, the Vatican looked like a very nice place for people to live, for someone who's taken a vow of poverty. And people around the world that—are in the public work, that don't take for themselves, you know, they still need a place to live.

(ABC News, 2005)

In part, it is the Bergs' lifestyle that has led to critical attention against the Kabbalah Centre. It may also be what drives the need for financial success and growth. That growth began in the 1990s when the connection between the Centre and Hollywood celebrities was established. Through this connection, the Kabbalah Centre soon became a brand name.

The Kabbalah Centre's version of Kabbalah

The Kabbalah Centre loosely bases its teachings on traditional Kabbalah. For example, it teaches the creation story of the Light, the vessels, constriction, and other kabbalistic terms and principles. It teaches classes about the *sefirot* and numerology. However, much of what is taught at the Kabbalah Centre would not be recognizable to a traditional kabbalist.

At the Kabbalah Centre, for example, "The Light" is used to convey two important concepts: God and sharing. The Centre explains that the word "God" has too many negative connotations, and so "Light" is used instead to convey the idea of an all-giving source of energy. This leads to the second concept, which is endless sharing. Sharing in the lexicon of the Kabbalah Centre is equivalent to evangelizing and tithing. Students—and everyone at the Kabbalah Centre, including the teachers, calls themselves a student—are told that the first part of sharing is to tell your friends what you learned in Kabbalah. They even stress that it will be uncomfortable, explaining that if it isn't uncomfortable it is not kabbalistic sharing. Kabbalistic sharing—

sharing that hurts—is proactive sharing, a practice that requires tools to learn. These tools include tithing, which can be contributions in the form of either time or money. Volunteers are primarily directed toward giving their time to Spirituality for Kids, the Centre's community outreach program for children that is heavily supported by Madonna. (They do not recommend giving money or time to places outside of the Centre.) Moreover, students are taught that the sharing is for *their* benefit, not the benefit of the Centre. One long-time student of the L.A. Centre explained it this way:

> I have to look at the participation to my benefit, not as giving my time to the Kabblalah Center. And volunteering two hours is like part of the technology, it's like sharing…the secret is that if something is hard for you to share, if you share it you get more for it. Not even if it is hard for you—if you want love, you share love, if you want money, you share money. It is giving and receiving. And hopefully by giving I will be receiving. So it is an opportunity for me to go and share.
>
> (personal interview, 2006)[5]

The Kabbalah Centre also teaches about the 99 percent world and the 1 percent world (Berg, 2004). The 1 percent world, or physical realm, is the place where people receive "for themselves alone"—a phrase that is used repeatedly in Kabbalah Centre books and coursework. In order to enter the 99 percent realm—the world we cannot see—we have to learn to share. The way to do this is by controlling our minds. Kabbalah Centre teachers explain that the progression of an event starts with thought followed by feeling followed by action. Feelings are part of the 1 percent world, the world of the physical, and therefore cannot be trusted. Emotions keep us from sharing.

When people remain attached to their emotions and are in the state of wanting to receive for themselves alone, they create what the Kabbalah Centre calls "Bread of Shame." This is when someone receives something that they don't deserve or didn't work for. This creates a sense of unworthiness. In order to remove Bread of Shame (and thereby increase fulfillment), a person has to learn to share. Sharing begins by being proactive, that is, consciously deciding to restrict your emotions. This restriction, *tzimtzum*, is what allows the Light to come in.

In striving for the Light, however, you will be met by the Opponent, or Satan. The Opponent exists to provide challenges that help us eliminate the Bread of Shame, and to remind us to ask the Light to enter into the situation. Under this scenario, the Opponent can be viewed as an opportunity, because it is the conduit through which a student can move from being reactive to proactive. If a person learns to be proactive in all situations, then he or she can achieve *tikkun*.

The Kabbalah Centre provides the following as "The Proactive Formula" to fight the Opponent:

1   When a difficult situation arises, acknowledge that it's from the Light.
2   Identify your reaction.
3   Restrict, stop reacting, allow the Light to come in.
4   Now deal with the situation.

As a reminder for students to use this formula, the Centre has printed it on a plastic card that students can keep in their wallets and pull out for easy reference.

In sum, the Centre's teachings are based on: Bread of Shame, restriction (*tzimtzum*), being proactive, the Opponent, and the Light—all leading to *tikkun* (correction). To achieve *tikkun*, we must have tools, or in the Centre's lexicon, technologies for the soul, all of which can be purchased through the Centre. One of these tools is the 72 names of God, which are various combinations of three Hebrew letters. Each name has the ability, when meditated on, to bring clarity about a different aspect of your life— relationships, jealousy, prosperity, even one called dialing God, which is supposed to smooth the way in your connection to the divine (Berg, 2003). These 72 names, usually displayed on a single chart, can be accessed via a one-page sheet handed out in class, on a Web site, in a book, or through myriad products adorned with these symbols including jewelry and key rings. Other Centre tools include books on Kabbalah—particularly the *Zohar*—red strings, candles, and Kabbalah Water, all intended to protect the user against negative energy and bring in the Light. These tools can be supplemented with trips like the Kabbalah Energy Tour, a trip to sacred sites in Israel, and High Holiday services at luxury hotels around the world.

The business of Kabbalah

The Kabbalah Centre is comprised of several business organizations, one of which is for-profit (Kabbalah Enterprises Inc.) while the rest are categorized as religious institutions for tax purposes.[6] Since the Centre has filed for tax-exempt status for most of its businesses, there is only limited financial information available. What we can determine is the following: There are three main Centres in the United States—Los Angeles, New York, and Boca Raton. There are several tax-exempt entities that function through these centers, most notably Spirituality for Kids, the Kabbalah Centre's community outreach program to teach Kabbalah to disadvantaged children.

According to Hoovers (a division of Dun & Bradstreet) the Research Center of Kabbalah, the company's publishing arm, had revenues of $3.6 million, the Los Angeles Centre had $2.4 million in sales, and Light Force Water Source Inc., the marketer of Kabbalah Energy Drink, had sales of $1.5 million. This puts total income at $7.4 million, most of which is tax exempt. Not included are data for centers other than Los Angeles, as these were unavailable. It is unknown if the LA figure includes revenue from other Centres. However, it likely does not account for monies made from classes, a major source of revenue for the Centre, nor does it account for donations, which may be substantial given the Hollywood connection.[7] It has been reported that Madonna alone has donated $6 million to the London center and another $22 million to help build a school in New York (Ellin, 2004, p. 22). As for assets, according to the most recent IRS 990 forms, Spirituality for Kids had assets of more than $15 million (based on a 2005 form), the L.A. Centre $11 million (based on a 2000 form), Florida $3.6 million (2000 form), and the New York Centre $21.5 million (2005 form), putting claimed assets at close to $50 million (see www.guidestar.org).

According to an interview with a Centre member, each of the Kabbalah Centres is run as an individual business; that is, the money generated by the New York Centre stays in New York, while the money generated by the Los Angeles Centre stays in Los Angeles. This sets up a competition among the various offices. The Los Angeles Centre has the obvious advantage of its proximity to Hollywood money. The Los Angeles location also gets monies generated by the Web site and from the telephone teaching services. These are courses sold via an 800 number to students who do not have a Kabbalah Centre near them.

The Centre's organizational structure is difficult to square up against its mission statement to remove chaos and suffering by bringing Kabbalah to the world. For example, the organization closes Centres that cannot generate enough income to be self-supporting—centers in Chicago and Philadelphia were closed for this reason. The Centre claims that a city must be ready to receive the wisdom (personal interview, 2006), but if the goal is to bring peace through the teaching of the *Zohar*, then why not funnel money from other, more successful Centres to those that are in need? Philadelphia has one of the lowest incomes for a major city in the United States—wouldn't this city benefit from Kabbalah?

Not if this brand of Kabbalah is a business. If you take a class, you must pay for it. If you want to be in a small group, you have to pay for it. If you want enlightenment, you have to buy the products to achieve it. And if you want to attend services and parties, you have to pay for them. The Kabbalah Centre justifies these costs by tying them to spiritual significance.

> For example, Rosh Hashanah costs $26, which is the numerical value of one of G-d's names. Sometimes they will charge $151, which is the energy of the *mikvah*. Sometimes they will charge $101, which is the numerical value of the name of our archangel Michael. So there is always significance to the amount that they charge. But why is Purim $72? Why not $26?
>
> (personal interview, 2006)

Further, there is no indication that the money generated is being used for anything other than the expansion of the Centre. That, by definition, is a business.

The products

Kabbalah classes

The entry point for most Kabbalah Centre members is the classes. All students of the Kabbalah Centre must take the Power of Kabbalah I (POK1; also referred to as Kabbalah 101) before they can take any of the other course offerings. This is the most expensive course at $270. The course, however, comes with a money back guarantee and anyone can take the course multiple times, with each subsequent class costing half price.[8] In POK1 students learn the basics of Kabbalah as defined by the Kabbalah Centre. Unlike other courses, this introductory class is targeted in that there is a POK1 class for 20-somethings. POK1 classes tend to be fairly large and can attract 50 to 60 people in a class.[9] It can be taken as a one-day class or over a ten week period.[10]

Students are presented with mentors who sit with them at every class. There is approximately one mentor for every five to six students. Mentors act as an important marketing element in conjunction with the classes. Mentors are current students who have studied Kabbalah for two to five years and are volunteering their time to assist in teaching the course. Some are chevre and some are not. During the first day of class the mentors come to the front of the room and talk about how Kabbalah has helped them and how they hope new students will all have miracles in their lives too—word-of-mouth testimonials that help in supporting students' purchase decision. The mentors also act as personal liaisons between the Centre and the students. At the first class, students provide their e-mail addresses to their mentor; a few days after each class, the mentor is supposed to e-mail his or her charges to check in and see how their experience is going and to see if they have any questions. They also become salespeople as the class progresses. The final two classes become a stronger and stronger sales message for POK2.

Mentors are not the only means of marketing within a Kabbalah class. Throughout POK1, the teacher reads from the *Zohar*, which is prominently displayed at the front of the room. While not expressly stated that students should purchase a set of the *Zohar*, the need for it and other texts becomes increasingly obvious if a student wants to continue with the study of Kabbalah. Starting in the third week, there is another table of books—these written by various Kabbalah Centre teachers, primarily the Berg family. No attention is drawn to the books, but they are there and impossible to avoid because of where they are placed in the room and positioned on the table. While students are not directly told to buy the *Zohar*, they are directed to buy books from the Kabbalah bookstore and CDs of the class they attended.[11] These recommendations are made not only by the teacher, but also by mentors. As students become more immersed in Kabbalah, more products are suggested to further a student's learning.

Marketing postcards—what the Kabbalah Centre calls "invitations"—that promote Kabbalah Centre events are strewn on the classroom tables each week. (Students sit at round tables that are covered with tablecloths and illuminated with candles, giving the feeling of being at a bar or restaurant rather than a classroom.) Elsewhere in the classroom there is always a table of marketing materials, some of which duplicate the invitations. There might be postcards for Rosh Chodesh, an event that occurs monthly in conjunction with the full moon, invitations to upcoming holidays like Purim and Passover, and information for other Kabbalah Centre class offerings. Each class ends with announcements, which again draw students' attention to these events.

One flyer at a class I attended was for something called "Soul Circuit." This program specifically targets 20- and 30-somethings who are currently taking the introductory Kabbalah classes. It was the only invitation I saw that did not have a fee attached to it. According to the "invitation":

> Soul Circuit is the next step to expanding your Kabbalah experience. This dynamic program is exclusively for students in their 20's & 30's giving them an opportunity to make spiritual friends, create a community of like-minded peers and tackle contemporary life issues such as love, career & happiness.

This ties into some fundamental ideas of marketing. It is no accident that marketers are targeting people younger and younger—not 20 but 12 or even younger. The thinking is that brand loyalty, if it even exists anymore, needs to be established at a young age. But for spiritual seekers, those in their 20s and 30s are equivalent to the tween audience for consumer products. They are the age at which people are first seriously entering, or re-entering, the market. This is not to say that the Kabbalah Centre ignores the younger audience. Children can be introduced to Kabbalah through their families and many young families are in evidence at the Centres. There is also the Spirituality for Kids program, which is offered in several cities around the country. Unlike evangelicals, teens are not a prime audience. While Spirituality for Teens does exist, it appears that, as of now, this program is being used as a tool for troubled teens rather than being offered more broadly. In terms of targeting people over 40, the Kabbalah Centre does what most marketers do—it doesn't ignore them, but it doesn't target them either. The assumption here is that older people are set in their ways and are therefore much more difficult to change.

Power of Kabbalah I is followed by Power of Kabbalah II and Power of Kabbalah III. After these basic courses, the classes become more specialized.

Supplemental courses can be taken in kabbalistic meditation, consciousness and healing, kabbalistic astrology, and Kabbalah and business, along with a Shabbat seminar. There are also advanced courses such as Writings of the Zohar, Zohar Consciousness, and Ten Emanations (the *sefirot*).

During POK1, students are told that they get a free meeting with the teacher. When I attended my teacher meeting after having taken the class the first time, it turned out to be a sales pitch during which I was told that I need to buy the *Zohar*, multiple mezuzahs, the red string, and so on. I was asked to give a donation to help build the school in New York and to donate my time. When I took POK1 a second time, the meeting was more of a legitimate teaching aid, which is what the other students I spoke with said as well. It seems that in the last few years, the Centre has started using methods other than this meeting as a sales tool. In fact, they now go out of their way to discourage people from having the meeting, which was not the case a few years ago. Instead, there are phone calls from Centre volunteers, who suggest attending certain events such as Shabbat dinner, which comes at a cost. They also pitch subsequent classes through Kabbalah 101 (POK1), and as students become more immersed, it is suggested that they purchase even more Kabbalah-related items. Finally, students are told that they should attend Saturday services—just about the only thing that does not have a fee attached to it.

Books

There are a slew of products associated with studying at the Kabbalah Centre. The most significant product category is books. As we saw in Chapter 3, books are the largest segment of the spiritual/religious product category, and it is no different for Kabbalah. These books are available both through the Kabbalah Centre and through secular outlets such as Barnes & Noble, Amazon.com, and Target.

For the Kabbalah Centre the most important book, or rather set of books, is the *Zohar*. Originally written in Aramaic, it was translated into modern Hebrew in the 1920s and finally into English in 2000. The Kabbalah Centre claims that the power of the *Zohar* comes from the power of the Hebrew letters, and that it is not necessary for students to know and understand Hebrew; simply scanning the letters will allow them to draw in the positive energy of the letters. They compare it to a barcode at a supermarket.

> YEHUDA BERG: You do what you can do. You do your maximum. You can read, read. You can understand, understand. You can't read, look. You can't see, you touch.
> KAREN BERG: Because your brain, your subconscious, has a way to pick up what is there, almost like a scanner in a supermarket. You know,

it's just a code, and yet they can manage to take the material they need from it.

(ABC News, 2005)

Kabbalah students believe this. One Kabbalah follower said, "That's [the *Zohar*] the telephone line to God. All you have to do is plug it in and you're connected…I have no idea what it says, but that doesn't matter, this is powerful stuff"(ABC News, 2005); and another said, "Basically all of my friends there [at the L.A. Centre] do not read Hebrew, offhand. And they are powerfully connected to the *Zohar*" (personal interview, 2006).

From a marketing perspective this is very interesting. Prior to its English translation, the only people to whom the books would be of value would be those who read Hebrew. Touting the scanning method increases the value of the product to a non-Hebrew speaking audience, obviously a much larger potential consumer group. The Kabbalah Centre also suggests that simply having the books in your home will bring you positive energy. They recommend buying multiple sets so you can have one set at your home and one at your office. The *Zohar* retails for $415 a set.

While the *Zohar* is the basis for kabbalistic study, many other books are sold that present Kabbalah through a more New Age, pop culture lens. *The Power of Kabbalah*, by Yehuda Berg, is an introductory text to Kabbalah that is written in a very simplistic style, as are all the Berg books. This book is given out to Power of Kabbalah I students. It is readily accessible, has few words on each page, and doesn't require a lot of the reader. Another popular book is called *The Way*, written by Michael Berg and published in 2001. It was the first book to get a Madonna endorsement on the cover. The book was also endorsed by Caroline Myss, a best-selling self-help author. This book is the most well-known of the Kabbalah Centre texts and up until recently it was the most widely distributed. In part, this may be due to its having been published by John Wiley rather than the Kabbalah Centre. Another popular text is *The 72 Names of God*, written by Yehuda Berg in 2003. These last two books were highly promoted and distributed in mass market outlets.

In the past few years the Kabbalah Centre has been segmenting its materials to appeal to different target audiences. Two recent much-promoted books were *God Wears Lipstick*, the first book written by Karen Berg, and *True Prosperity*, by Yehuda Berg. *God Wears Lipstick* is an obvious attempt to tap into the women's market for spirituality. The Centre organized a promotional book tour wherein people were invited to hear Karen speak, for which they charged $30, and then attendees were given the book for "free." In this way people felt that they were getting something for nothing when in fact they had paid for the book and heard the lecture for free, which is how most books are launched. *True Prosperity* has been quoted in a Centre internal memo as being aimed at the "Christian, Bible Belt"

(Udovitch, 2005). Given the current popularity of prosperity preaching, this title makes good marketing sense. The Kabbalah Centre has also started translating their books into multiple languages, even putting emphasis on the Hispanic audience, which now has a special section in the New York Centre bookstore.

Just as with the Christian texts discussed in Chapter 3, Kabbalah is having wide crossover appeal as well. Because of the success of some of the Centre's earlier texts (some of which had significant "sales" due to their being given away at book signings or through courses), big box stores were soon open to carrying books coming out the Kabbalah Centre, including Michael Berg's *Becoming Like God*, which launched with a party given by designer, Donna Karan. According to an October 29, 2004, e-mail that Michael Berg sent to people in the Kabbalah Centre's database, "Borders, Costco, Sam's Club, and BJ's, some of the largest book retailers in the United States, have ordered a significant number of books and are currently running various promotions." Like the Christian churches, the Centre exhorted its members to "support the investment that these stores have made in Kabbalah, which is why I am asking you to go to your local stores this week and buy your copy or gift copies of *Becoming Like God*. The holidays are around the corner—what better gift than the gift of Kabbalah."

The red string

The most popular and most publicized of all of the Kabbalah products is the red string. According to its packaging the string has been blessed at the tomb of Rachel, the matriarchal protector of the Jews, and will protect the wearer from the evil eye when worn on the left wrist.

The red string is most commonly packaged with a copy of "Yehuda Berg's best-selling *Red String* book," and sells for $26. After opening the packaging, the string is knotted several times by a member of the Centre (or as the packaging says, "someone who loves you"), who chants a blessing called the Ben Porat Prayer. Simultaneously, the person who is getting the string put on scans one of the 72 names of God (אלד—Daled Lamed Aleph), which is also a symbol of protection. The person is told to "simply focus your eyes on the letters and imagine yourself surrounded by a shield of white light," which is similar to how students are supposed to approach the *Zohar*. The red string package goes on to say, "The complete book, *The 72 Names of God*, by Yehuda Berg, features all the Names and their uses. It promises to be the final antidote to what ails modern man. For more information, visit www.72.com." The last 12 pages of the 95-page *The Red String Book* (Berg 2004b) are filled with promotions for other books, CDs, and student support from the Centre.[12]

It is easy to see the marketing brilliance of the red string. First, it is highly visible. Red is the color that commands attention and therefore is used extensively in consumer product packaging. Second, once Hollywood's A list began wearing the string, it became more visible in the popular culture. Not only has the string been worn by stars like Madonna and Demi Moore, it has also been spotted in television shows like *Queer Eye for the Straight Guy* and *Will & Grace*, product placement that advertisers usually pay top dollar for. Third, because this has become the most popular product of the Centre, it provides the best portal for introducing prospects to other products. *The Red String Book* concludes with 12 pages of advertisements for other Centre products. Even more telling is this line in the main section of the book: "It's important to note that anyone can wear the Red String: they don't necessarily have to be studying Kabbalah" (p. 64). On the one hand, this simple sentence eliminates any barriers to purchase. On the other hand, it could motivate some wearers to study so as to distinguish themselves as sincerely pursing Kabbalah rather than just hooking into a trend.

In 2004 the red string was sold through Target. This sales venue was short-lived, however, because there was consumer protest against the retailer supporting the Kabbalah Centre. While the string itself can no longer be purchased at Target, *The Red String Book* is still available in both English and Spanish through this outlet.

Finally, the Kabbalah Centre attempted to trademark "Kabbalah Red String," the ultimate sign that it is a product to be merchandised. The trademark was denied because "Applicant seeks to register the term KABBALAH RED STRING for items indefinitely identified as 'religious articles'" (U.S. Patent and Trademark Office, 2003).

Kabbalah Energy Drink and Kabbalah Water

Kabbalah Energy Drink is the newest product being promoted by the Centre. According to the company's Web site:

> Kabbalah Energy Drink is a delicious citrus fusion which contains essential vitamins and amino acids that pick you up and keep you going... whether you need to take your dog for a walk, study for finals, bar-hop with friends or just need a second wind at the office, reach for Kabbalah Energy Drink. Also available in a low-carb Sugar Free variety!
>
> (Kabbalah energy drink, n.d.)

The product is produced by Powerbrands and 7-Up and is distributed by Kabbalah Enterprises, the for-profit arm of the Kabbalah Centre.

More than anything else produced by the Centre, Kabbalah Energy Drink crosses a line in terms of full-blown commercialism. The energy drink is a straight-out consumer product that cannot be tied to the study of Kabbalah. It is widely distributed in mass market outlets, from corner bodegas to mass drugstore outlets, and is promoted to both the sports enthusiast and the all-night partyer. Public relations make every effort to associate the product with the celebrities enmeshed with Kabbalah. "The citrus-flavored drink, which beats Red Bull nine out of ten times in taste tests, is infused with Kabbalah water and is the drink of Tinseltown celebrities and Kabbalists such as Ashton Kutcher, Demi Moore, Madonna and Guy Ritchie" (Kabbalah Energy Drink, 2005). Moreover, traditional marketing elements have been used, including posters in store windows and even a shrink wrapped bus that drives up and down the Las Vegas strip (Kabbalah Energy Drink, n.d.).

Unlike the energy drink, Kabbalah Water has been sold through the Centres since the late 1990s and is presented as instrumental to the practice of Kabbalah. It is not uncommon to see people at the Centres walking around with Kabbalah Water in their arms, or for the teachers to have a bottle on a table nearby. Recently the Centre tried to launch a mass market campaign to get wide distribution for the product, much as they did for the energy drink. Madonna was even going to re-launch the water as a mass market product on her 2004 Reinvention tour. According to a series of reports in *Radar* in 2005, Madonna and Alex Bize of Rocawear were going to have an equity stake in the project, but it fell through before it even began. The same article quoted the Rav as stating, "If the damn FDA would just let me put that the water cures cancer on the label, I wouldn't need marketing" (Udovitch, 2005). While the Centre claims that the water has curative powers because it has been blessed by the Rav, in reality it is simple spring water bottled in Canada (Lappin, 2004). It sells for $2 for a one-liter bottle (Ellin, 2004, p. 26).

Marketing Kabbalah

The Internet, the e-mails...and the phone calls

The Kabbalah Centre recently revamped its Web site (kabbalah.com) to be slicker and more streamlined. In the past the site included multiple links to everything from free books to the red string to classes; now the site opens with a 30-minute "television program" that presents the technology of the soul. In this video the Kabbalah Centre shows highly successful people—surgeons, entertainment executives, and the like—who have found spiritual enlightenment and contentment through the Centre. Underneath this video area is information about the Centre's charitable foundation and links to the weekly and monthly e-mail newsletters.

Down the left side of the page is a list of links to information about Kabbalah. On almost every page accessed there are boxes on the right-hand side, under the title of "Related Items," that display products for purchase through the Kabbalah Store. For example, if you click on "What is Kabbalah" on the home page, it takes you to a page where there are a few short paragraphs about Kabbalah; on the right side of this page are pictures and one-line descriptions of the books *The Power of Kabbalah* and *The Way*, which when clicked take you to the site's bookstore. Just below these pictures are more links. One says, "Everything you ever wanted to know about Kabbalah available right here," followed by the questions "Do I have to be Jewish to study Kabbalah?" and "Does studying Kabbalah conflict with my Christian beliefs?" Clicking any of these takes you to the FAQ page.[13]

In addition to links to "Who we are" and the Centre's charitable foundation, there are links to the FAQ, How to study Kabbalah, Student Support, and the Kabbalah store. These are the heart of the site. The "How to study Kabbalah" area lists study groups, books, online courses, CDs, and the Centre's 800 number. The bottom of the page is a presentation of a number of the books written by Kabbalah Centre authors. Student Support directs people to the 800 number where teachers are available "any time" to assist with students who are not near a center or for further teaching.

There are also individual links to the *Zohar*, *72 Names of God*, Red String, Relationships, and Astrology. For these, too, there are one-page explanations of the subject being presented with products for purchase along the right-hand side. There are also links to Yehuda Berg's and Michael Berg's blogs, on which are further links to buy their individual books, a scholarship fund section where students can apply for student aid, and a section where prospective students can find a center near them.

Finally, there are two areas on the Web site that bear special mentioning. First, there are links to the weekly and monthly "connections" or e-mails. These are also highlighted on the bottom of the site. The weekly e-mails present a lesson in Kabbalah, but are also important sales tools as they always end with one of the 72 names of God and a link to www.72. com, yet another Kabbalah Web site. Oftentimes, the e-mails contain links back to the Kabbalah store. Similarly, the monthly connection has links to products for purchase. One link, for example, might take you to Amazon.com where you can purchase "The Wisdom Box," which contains "a veritable Kabbalah starter kit," including the red string and four books by Yehuda Berg. As the site says, "This appealing set is a thoughtful gift for the spiritual seeker."

The other section of note is one that presents information about how to celebrate the current holiday, such as Rosh Hashanah or Pesach (Passover), with the Kabbalah Centre. Let's take a moment here to talk about Pesach, which in 2006 was marketed as "The Great Escape." Most of the time when I went to the Centre in Manhattan in the months leading up to the holiday, there was a widescreen television in the lobby showing a video for this "escape," which included footage from previous years. In the final month before Pesach, there was a sign in the lobby saying, "29 days until Pesach," or whatever the number was in the countdown. The event itself took place at the Westin Diplomat Hotel in Hollywood, Florida. As the Web site readily attested, the hotel has a 5-star 18-hole golf course, luxurious rooms, swimming pools—indoors and out—a spa, and a marina. The cost for two nights with meals included for one adult was more than $1,500. Staying for the full nine nights of the holiday cost close to $5,000. The cost per child was $2,300. Before attending this event, it was recommended that participants purchase the Pesach CD and the Kabbalah Centre matzoh, which cost $36 a case. When you called to register for the trip, the person you reached suggested that you eat as much matzoh as possible over Passover—not a standard Passover ritual (personal interview, 2006).

To put this into perspective, many traditional Jews choose to spend Passover at a hotel or resort because it is more convenient than staying home, which involves a lot of time and effort to eliminate all traces of bread (prohibited during the holiday) and to otherwise make a kitchen kosher for the holiday. The Catskills and several Florida locales have long been popular Passover destinations, with numerous hotels in these areas offering a traditional kosher experience. Even the fact that the Kabbalah Centre was holding the event at a luxury resort is not so out of place. However, comparable resorts in Florida were at the time charging approximately $3,000 for the same nine-day stay. It is this sort of pricing that makes the Kabbalah Centre controversial. Moreover, there is the Centre's traveling marketplace that attends these events as well. The most prominent display is that of an oversized globe with Kabbalah Water being poured over it. At the end of these holiday events, people walk out with cases of the water. Sales are also brisk at booths selling books, CDs, T-shirts, and other Kabbalah paraphernalia.

Finally, the Kabbalah Centre uses telemarketing to supplement its sophisticated Web site and e-mail strategies. Telemarketing is an important tool for the Kabbalah Centre. Once a student has taken a class at the Kabbalah Centre, and particularly after a student has come in for an individual meeting with a teacher, he or she will begin to receive periodic phone calls from Kabbalah Centre volunteers. These calls are to invite students to Shabbat or other Centre events. The volunteers are painfully cheery, and like the one-on-one meetings with the teacher, telemarketing is used less frequently now than it has been in the past.

The advertising

The Kabbalah Centre uses traditional advertising such as print ads in *New York Magazine* that have the headline, "Discover Kabbalah...no strings attached" and billboards in Los Angeles. But like the other faith brands, it relies most heavily on word-of-mouth advertising. A number of people say they came to the Centre because someone they knew suggested they attend.

[A]bout six years ago I actually had a couple of different friends [who] told me about Kabbalah, Kabbalah Center, but they were very vague... like it was Jewish mysticism, Madonna, it was really all they said. So it really wasn't that compelling at the time. And then a few years later I ended a relationship and like many of my patients, you--you're in that mode, there is an opening, you're kind of searching and looking. And then I remembered the Kabbalah Center, and I just wandered in. And, you know, there's constantly free introductory lectures, and it was so compelling, there was so much practicality to the--to the lecture, it just really struck me, you know, there's something deeper.

(*Today*, 2005)

Well, I have been interested in spirituality for many, many years, and I had heard of the Kabbalah Center and I was intrigued, so I thought ok maybe someday I would check it out. And then I ran into a friend that I grew up with in Orlando out here, and it was very funny because we connected and he was into Kabbalah, and I was into Marianne Williamson lectures, so he said you have to come to Kabbalah lectures so we did. And I went to Kabbalah. So this is sort of what happened.

(personal interview, 2006)

Word-of-mouth "advertising" is also perpetuated by the Centres them-selves. Kabbalah classes are a source for significant promotional opportunities that target both the current attendees—either to take more classes or to attend holiday events—as well as attendees' friends and family. Current practitioners are encouraged to invite their friends and families to come to introductory lectures so that they, too, can share in what the student is learning.[14] The following describes one person's experience at an introductory lecture in New York.

I didn't have much time to take in the ambience because I was quickly accosted by a "fellow student" named Jaci. Jaci asked me questions about how I found out about the Kabbalah Centre, what I already knew and what I was there to learn. She continued to tell me about how she never used to believe in Kabbalah, but at her friend's suggestion she gave it a shot, and now her love and work life are so much better....Soon after our instructor walked in. He began his lesson by asking why we wanted to learn about Kabbalah...and then told us about "The Power of Kabbalah" course...He took good care to remind us NOT to call Kabbalah a religion...He went on to explain...the importance of the *Zohar* in studying Kabbalah...he told us we could get a copy from the bookstore downstairs for $415, a small price to pay for the answer to all of life's questions...He guaranteed that after ten weeks of studying Kabbalah, we would be at a place of synchronicity with the world, feel blessed, and understand the reasons and causes behind much of what happens in the universe...[at the end of the lecture] Jaci took her spot at the podium and wrapped up the lecture with a briefing about all the courses the Centre offers.

(personal interview, 2006)

As this anecdote suggests, these introductory lectures are more a sales pitch than a lesson. I suspect that this approach is a turnoff for most people, though not for everyone. A few people I spoke with had signed up for POK1 after having attended a free lecture. However, these were people who attended the lecture because a friend or family member had suggested it. Thus the lecture was not acting as a singular marketing tool but in conjunction with word of mouth. This description also highlights a common practice at the Kabbalah Centre—the use of "plants" in the room. Plants are not only used at free lectures, but also in the classes themselves. Large numbers of people in the classroom help students feel more secure in their decision to be involved with the practice. It is also an opportunity for personal selling—experienced students sell new students on the joys of Kabbalah. The risk is in their giving prospective students a feeling that the Centre is trying to suck them in—certainly a key turnoff. Moreover, when people come in looking for a lecture and instead get a hardcore sales pitch, it is unlikely to have the desired effect of attracting new members. This may be why the Centre reinstituted their annual open house at the beginning of 2007. It is simply more effective to have one big, well-attended event than several little ones that generate minimal turnout and interest.

Madonna and Kabbalah

One of the most important elements of a brand is a humanizing icon. While this is not necessary for all product or service categories, it is imperative for a religious or spiritual organization. For the Kabbalah Centre that icon is Madonna. This, too, makes the Kabbalah Centre different from the other brands we have examined. While Rick Warren is the face of Purpose Driven and Joel Osteen is the Lakewood Church, neither the Rav nor wife Karen nor the brothers Berg are the face of the Kabbalah Centre.

There are a number of reasons for that. For starters, the Bergs are simply not "brandable." We can understand this by first looking at the target audience. The majority of people interested in pursuing Kabbalah are relatively young—in their 20s and 30s—and upscale. The Rav is in his 70s and looks like a traditional Hassidic rabbi. Karen Berg is a middle-aged, Orthodox Jewish woman. She wears an obvious wig (part of the Orthodox tradition), and is likely to remind prospects of their grandmother. As an image—and bear in mind that this has nothing to do with who they are as human beings; we are talking about branding here—the Rav and Karen

Berg are the antithesis of what the target audience wants to be. Moreover, by presenting them as the face of Kabbalah, the Centre risks tipping its hand about what being a member really entails. One of the brilliant tools of Kabbalah is withholding from seekers the expectation that they will take on the more Orthodox aspects of Judaism—keeping kosher and keeping the Sabbath, among other restrictions—in order to fully participate in the wisdom of the Kabbalah.[15] If the Rav or Karen were the spokesperson, that information would be presented too early on in the process.

As for the Berg brothers, they are large men with round faces reminiscent of Charlie Brown. *Vanity Fair* put it succinctly when it described Yehuda as "a bearlike, somewhat insecure-seeming man in a yarmulke" (Peretz, 2005). Nothing about them says to a perspective client, "I want to be like that." Moreover, combine how they look with the glamorous Hollywood lifestyle they lead, and there would more likely be resentment among prospective believers than a wish to be like them.

People buy people or, as discussed in Chapter 4, they buy the story surrounding the people and their product. Prospects have to like, or at least respect, the people that they are buying from. They have to like the story. This helps to explain why the people who run the Kabbalah Centre would use someone other than themselves, specifically celebrities, as their spokespeople. While a number of celebrities have been connected with Kabbalah, including Roseanne Barr and Sandra Bernhard, who is reported to have made the initial connection between the Centre and Hollywood, it is Madonna who has been the face of the Kabbalah Centre for almost a decade.

Madonna's story is one to which a lot of people in the target generation and slightly older can relate. While theologians and rabbis discredit her for her numerous religious changes, it is something that many people who come to the Kabbalah Centre can understand. They, too, have tried multiple belief practices and are looking for one that will stick. Madonna holds out that hope for them. After trying out a number of different religions, she now has something that works for her.

Madonna is an inspiration to these seekers. Messages on the old Kabbalah Web site were full of references to Madonna, people I interviewed talked about Madonna, and one reporter (Hecker, 2004) found that all students she spoke with mentioned Madonna as a factor in getting them to the Centres.

> They'd tell their specific story—an epiphany they had reading in one of Berg's books, a serendipitous glimpse of one of the Centre's ads in the paper—then mention Madonna as an afterthought. Few of them gave her sole credit with bringing them to Kabbalah, but just about everyone mentioned her and most said they had heard about it in the first place because of her.

Madonna promotes Kabbalah in a number of ways. In terms of publicity, she has done numerous television appearances on the major broadcast networks, including a 2003 interview with *Dateline NBC* in which Eitan Yardeni, her teacher and teacher to other celebrities at the Kabbalah Centre, was by her side. Once the queen of scandal, Madonna has transferred that energy to her faith practice. She wrote a song called "Isaac," which is about Isaac Luria, the sixteenth-century kabbalist. In her "Die Another Day" video, Madonna wears tefillin, the leather boxes and straps worn during morning weekday prayers. Both musical events created uproar among traditional Jewish leaders, who were offended by the reference to a much-revered kabbalist in a pop culture context, and by the use of tefillin by a woman (which is considered sacrilege), and worse a gentile. She also got publicity when she took on Esther as her Hebrew name, and more recently when she adopted a boy from Malawi—something that was connected to the Kabbalah Centre but not mentioned in the press.[16]

In addition to promoting Kabbalah through media interviews, Madonna promotes Kabbalah through books and concerts. She has written five children's books about Kabbalah that have been distributed in more than 100 countries. Book proceeds go to support Spirituality for Kids (Udovitch, 2005). Possibly the most effective form of promotion is her concerts. Here, Madonna has a captive audience who are all predisposed to like her. Within this context, Kabbalah merchandise is sold next to Madonna T-shirts, and the 72 names of God flash behind her during the performance. When asked about Madonna's use of the Hebrew letters in her stage show, Karen Berg's response was all positive.

> I think that was good. You know why? Hundreds of thousands of people scanned the names of God, liking it or not...That means that subconsciously there is another energy put into the world, just by having the names of God in front of all of those hundreds of thousands of people.
>
> (ABC News, 2005)

Not all publicity is good

Within the last two years, the Kabbalah Centre has been the focus of several investigative reports in both the United States and London. These reports have roundly criticized the Centre for benign actions like courting Hollywood and giving celebrities special treatment (Peretz, 2005) and more questionable dealings such as promising miracle cures with Kabbalah Water (BBC), being involved in questionable financial transactions (Udovitch, 2005), acting in ways that suggest that the Centre is a cult (Donnelly, 2005; Udovich, 2005), and using people's pain to support the Centre and by extension the Rav and his family.

The most egregious accusation was a story about Leah Zunis, a woman in Israel who was diagnosed with breast cancer in 1995. In 1996 she became involved with the Kabbalah Centre in Tel Aviv. When her cancer spread to her liver in 1999, she turned to the Centre for help because she had by this time heard several lectures about kabbalistic practices that get rid of cancer. According to a report on Ynetnews.com, an Israeli news site in English, her husband, Boris, said that the director of the Centre "told the couple a monetary contribution was needed in order to cure the disease" (Senyor, 2005). Moreover, because of kabbalistic sharing, the contribution had to be "painful," and the Centre suggested $36,000. When Boris said he did not have that kind of money, it was suggested that he quit work and become a volunteer at the Kabbalah Center, which was out of the question because he and Leah have three children. Because he loved his wife and she so believed in these teachings, he gave in and paid the money. "He promised me health and complete recovery if we paid the money. I felt that if I don't pay the money I would be contributing to her death." However, by 2002 the disease progressed and Leah went to the Centre again for guidance. This time there was a new director at the Centre and again she was asked for a contribution, this time for $25,000. Leah had to turn to her mother for the funds because she and Boris could not afford this. Leah died in 2005. While the leader of the Centre was brought in for questioning, the Centre has denied all charges. However, the Centre's leader "admitted receiving the money from the couple, but claims a healthy recovery was never promised in return. He also claimed that the bottled water in question has therapeutic qualities" (Singer, 2005).

While this case is extreme, the tactics are not isolated. There have been reports of the Centre's telling members to give money when their children are sick or to go on a $2,000 High Holiday trip so that their family will not be in danger (Peretz, 2005). The most damning report was a documentary by an undercover BBC reporter. This expose documented workers at the Kabbalah Centre in London using pressure sales tactics to sell people on attending the Kabbalah Energy Tour. Workers are shown saying, "If you think it's a lot of money, then that's a barrier you need to break. Because if you have a doubt what you're actually doing is you're creating a space, this space is where Satan can come in" (ABC News, 2005). The reporter had in fact been a cancer patient and went to the Kabbalah Centre in London posing as a wealthy businessman/cancer patient. When he asked someone at the Centre about whether Kabbalah Water could help his cancer cells, the person at reception said, "It's a very good possibility…We have one girl, who works here, her mother used to have cancer and she doesn't have it any more… Because she drank the water…The water is very, very good because it affects the cells, it cleanses the cells" (Donnelly, 2005, p. 14). However, one of the teachers later stressed that it was not a miracle cure. As the meeting between the reporter and the teacher went on, so did the sales pitch. By the time the reporter left, the Centre was asking for £860 (approximately $1,600) for a case of water, a set of the *Zohar*, and Shabbat dinner that night. After he paid the money several days later, the Centre suggested that he take a trip to Israel with the Rav, which would cost an additional $6,000.

The report by the BBC was followed by ABC's *20/20* investigation, wherein the network had full access to the Centre, including interviews with Karen, Michael, and Yehuda Berg. This report, in addition to including some of the material from the BBC, showed a number of the commercial aspects of the Centre, from selling the *Zohar* to the trips to the promotion of celebrities. It also showed the Centre's fascination with Chernobyl, something that is highlighted in almost every report—the BBC documentary, *Vanity Fair*, and elsewhere—about the Centre. In the course of a group gathering, everyone starts motioning with their hand and chanting "Cher-er-er-er-nobyl" toward a screen with the word Chernobyl on it. Karen Berg explained, "What they're saying is we try to generate energy into that part of the world, so that there will be no more Chernobyls" (ABC News, 2005).

But it is not just the chanting that affects this ravaged part of the world. According to one of the Centre's followers:

> What the Kabbalah Centre did, they took a truckload of this water to Chernobyl. Their scientists have shown that there is approximately 30 to 40 percent, as I understand it, decrease in the radiation in that particular lake after putting the Kabbalah water in it. Now that's pretty cool stuff.
>
> (ABC News, 2005)[17]

The Kabbalah Centre claims that meditating on the water changes its molecular structure, and that the water then has powerful healing abilities. However, they are now careful to say that it is not a miracle cure. "I think that it [Kabbalah Water] can give you a tool to make you more capable of opening yourself to spiritual energy," says Karen Berg (ABC News, 2005).

Throughout the *20/20* report, the Bergs appear very defensive. They say that they have merely brought Kabbalah out of the dark ages and that they are being persecuted:

> KAREN BERG: It was almost like Jesus, that went out and talked on the mount and brought people. And they believed in what he said.
>
> MICHAEL BERG: I mean, you know, my mother mentioned Jesus, I mean, he was certainly persecuted, he was killed. So, many people when they come with a new type of spirituality, and bringing it to the masses, they're persecuted.
>
> KAREN BERG: God forbid, I'm not saying that we're a messiah consciousness. I'm only saying that we built in the same fashion.
>
> (ABC News, 2005)

An interesting analogy, except for one big difference: Jesus did not have an intricate corporate structure, nor did he provide his faith only to those who could pay for it.[18]

These are just some of the negative reports that have appeared about the Kabbalah Centre. In 2005 *Radar*, a now defunct but well-respected pop culture magazine, did an expose about the Centre, covering questionable financial dealings, the celebrity suck up, volunteer exploitation, and even plagiarism cases brought against the Rav. From the *Village Voice* to the *New York Post* to *Vanity Fair*, not one article I found had anything positive to say about the Centre. The overriding theme was documented manipulation by the Centre to get people to spend significant amounts of money.

While not widely publicized in the United States, some of the Centre's worst publicity came with the aid it provided to the tsunami victims in South East Asia. The Kabbalah Centre immediately solicited funds in response to this terrible natural disaster in late December 2005. The monies were used to buy Kabbalah products and send them to the region, including Kabbalah Water instead of far less expensive alternatives that would have arrived more expeditiously (Udovitch, 2005). One reporter wrote of what he saw on the Kabbalah Web site: "a tsunami victim—a little boy with a red string around his wrist and a book in his hand" (Donnelly, 2005, p. 14).

In response to all of this negative publicity, the Kabbalah Centre hired Sitrick and Company, a public relations agency that represents a plethora of clients including Halle Berry and Major League Baseball. It is also a company that has a reputation for being who "you want in your corner if you decide to pay hardball with the media" (Holmesreport.com, n.d.). Unlike Rick Warren or Joel Osteen, however, this consultation is for crisis management, not self-promotion.

Conclusion

At first I believed that the Kabbalah Centre was facing the underlying dilemma that many religious or spiritual groups face—how to balance marketing and merchandising against their stated mission. I realized, however, that the difference between Kabbalah and the other groups studied is its level of blatant consumerism. The Kabbalah Center is a business and its mission —like all marketing-oriented organizations—is growth. Unfortunately, this seems to come at the expense of earnest spiritual seekers.

Some people at the Centre truly believe in the organization's stated mission even while they try to fulfill it within the confines of this commercial environment. The following story is illustrative of the Janus effect going on at the Centre:

Barry[19] is someone who has been at the Centre for thirteen years. He is not Jewish, but he is one of the right-hand men of the main teacher. He knows the inner workings of the Centre, knows a lot of the secrets that they do not reveal in the classes...He is such a guy that walks the walk. He now volunteers at student support, ...which is the 800 number for all around the world—and what it basically is is sales...The head of the student support...told him to write a daily report or a weekly report, whatever it is. Barry writes this report saying that he was 100 percent successful today. So he runs over to Barry and says "wow you sold it to everyone you spoke to?" and he said no, he cared for every person that he spoke to.

(personal interview, 2006)

There are people at the Centre who really do want to do good in the world, and they believe that Kabbalah is the way to do that.

Meanwhile, it seems that the Bergs have gotten caught up in their own talking points, their own PR spin. "The Kabbalah Centre is about getting wisdom out. All of the money from the sales of the t-shirts and the hats goes to support the Kabbalah Centre, its teachings," says Michael Berg (ABC News, 2005). He goes on to say in this interview with *20/20* , "If we wanted to live rich we could from our books and from our tapes...But we don't. I don't have a big bank account. Why? Because I want to make sure that every penny that a person buys a book or one of my tapes [with] goes directly back to support the Kabbalah Centre." By anyone's yardstick, however, homes in Beverly Hills, trips to five-star resorts, a Mercedes and parties with celebrities is living rich. How can that be justified against their stated mission of eliminating chaos in the world?

Also unlike the other organizations researched, the Kabbalah Centre does not have any association with outside charities, nor does it recommend that students volunteer or donate money to any organization other than the Kabbalah Centre. While the Lakewood Church, for instance, collected money and assisted with victims of Katrina, the Bergs sent Kabbalah Water to the victims of South East Asia, promoting their faith at the expense of real relief. Moreover, while the Centre vehemently denies being a religion, it is registered as a religious institution under 501c3 and readily takes the tax breaks offered by this status.

Admittedly some – but certainly not all – of this is a positioning issue. Some of what the Bergs are doing could also be said of Rick Warren. Pastor Rick is not living in poverty. However, Pastor Rick is often quoted as saying that he reverse tithes, that is, he keeps 10 percent of his income for himself and gives 90 percent to Saddleback. When you are making tens of millions of dollars, reverse tithing is scarcely a hardship, but the gesture is usually perceived as admirable. Compare that to what the Bergs say—"we put everything back into the Kabbalah Centre." That's just not credible given the lavish lifestyle they lead.

Because of their missteps, it is not surprising that the Centre has hired a crisis management PR firm. The contradictions in the press by the Bergs are startling. For example, Yehuda Berg has been quoted as saying, "We don't charge for membership; I don't know how many synagogues don't charge... We don't charge for holiday services. We don't hand out envelopes" (Ellin, 2004, p. 26). This is only half true. They don't charge for membership, true, but that is because there is no membership per se. Paying for classes, books, strings, and expensive trips is how you become a member.

From a marketing perspective, they have been very successful up until now. Ultimately, however, the marketing is a losing proposition because the product under-delivers on the promise. While Madonna gets people in the door, the subsequent sales pitches can often be a turnoff to prospective members. Also, as students progress in Kabbalah, they must take on more and more aspects of the Orthodox tradition. Giving up a Friday night is not what a 20-something is thinking about when Madonna promotes the product. I was also very aware of the Israeli-centric aspect of the New York Centre, in the form of a cliquish group of Hebrew speaking insiders that left newcomers wondering how they might break into the club. Certainly learning Hebrew would help in that regard, but that also requires a long-term commitment, which is not something many people ultimately make to the Centre. One person told me, "Most people take Kabbalah 1 and Kabbalah 2 and volunteer for a bit, and then they kind of fizzle out after a year or so." Thus this churning of the client base puts constant pressure on the Centre to bring in new members.

The Kabbalah Centre may have gotten too popular too fast—red strings everywhere, Madonna appearances on prime time, connections to Britney Spears and Paris Hilton—all leading to a lot of sizzle and ultimately media backlash. The Centre seems to be re-grouping in response to the onslaught of negative press. First, they are taking a much lower profile. This was particularly evident during the 2006 Madonna baby fiasco. When Madonna adopted an African boy amid much media frenzy over the legalities of the adoption, the Kabbalah Centre was rarely mentioned. This is surprising given Madonna's connection to the Centre as well as the fact that her trip to this African country was fundamentally tied to the Kabbalah Centre's "Raising Malawi" initiative.[20] Second, the Centre has reinstituted its open houses—one-day events with free Kabbalah lectures—which had not been held for several years. Finally, an essential part of revitalizing the brand will be to determine who will replace the Rav, the organization's leader who never fully recovered after a stroke several years ago. This decision may be the most important marketing decision the Centre has to make because it will likely determine the long-term vitality of the brand.

Chapter 8

The politics of faith brands

What happened in the Senate last week...was about what's gone wrong with Congress, which can't do much of anything anymore. Here is the main reason: Our elected officials have lost the ability to compromise. In order to raise the money needed to get elected, they have to sign off with so many special interest groups before they get to Washington that their positions are set in stone long before they arrive at the Capitol...Don't expect it [Congress] to do much on anything. Our political system is so badly broken there's no longer very much that Congress can do.

Bob Schieffer, *Face the Nation* (CBS News), Sunday, April 9, 2006, on the collapse of the immigration bill in Washington, D.C.

In the Bush administration, the most important—and certainly most visible—special interest group that has contributed to the political gridlock of our democracy is the religious right, or more correctly, the Christian right. These evangelicals—political, if not religious—have set the agenda for politics in America by directing attention to so-called wedge issues like abortion, gay marriage, and stem cell research while obfuscating topics like the civilian death toll in Iraq, the devastation of New Orleans, the lack of adequate health care, the widening gap between rich and poor, and our disintegrating environment. They do it with a smile on their face and a mandate by God, a point of view against which it is difficult to debate.

While the relationship between politics and religion has been historically awkward, today it borderlines on abusive. Because fundamentalist Christians have successfully organized so as to be able to efficiently and effectively deliver the vote, *their* issues have become the *nation's* issues. This is even while polls say that close to 50 percent of Americans have no problem with gay marriage (Pew Forum, 2006, p. 1), nor do they believe that abortions should be made illegal.[1] How did this happen? Why has the Republican Party become so tied to this particular special interest group? Says conservative former Senator Jack Danforth (2006) in his book *Faith and Politics*, it happened quite simply because "it works. It produces electoral victory" (p. 7). However, it works by bludgeon, not compromise, and it has led, as Danforth suggests, to an outright takeover of the Republican Party.

What does all of this have to do with faith brands and marketing religion? A lot. First, electoral victory is tied to getting out "the base," and the base for the Republican Party is the religious right. Megachurches, the oversized conservative churches of 2,000 or more members that serve an ever-growing percentage of U.S. churchgoers, have an exceptional ability to mobilize that base. While megachurches, like all tax-exempt institutions, are not allowed by law to recommend a particular candidate from the pulpit, coded language such as "vote your values" or "vote Christian" allows them to get around regulatory restrictions. Using this language on a single Sunday can reach tens of thousands of voters, incredibly effective compared to the average American congregation, which numbers around 200 people. These churches—which can serve upwards of 40,000 congregants—are growing because of concerted, sophisticated marketing and branding efforts. As these churches have become larger, they have become more profitable and more powerful. Paul Magnusson wrote in a 2005 *BusinessWeek* article, "They Backed Bush—and Expect Him to Deliver," that evangelical churches, particularly white evangelicals, got out the vote for Bush in the 2004 presidential race, and they did it expecting something in return.

Second, and perhaps more importantly, these churches have been able to fly under the radar in terms of their political agenda. Much as these churches do not market the need to take on fundamentalist beliefs in order to become part of the church, they also do not market their political point of view. In fact, many of them denounce politics or claim that they are not politically oriented. A report about megachurches on *Religion & Ethics Newsweekly* claimed that "big congregations tend to be conservative, but most say they are not politically active. Abortion and same-sex marriage are discussed as moral, not political issues. The leaders at New Life [a 15,000 member megachurch in Colorado] say they have no political agenda" (Megachurches, 2006). This is disingenuous at best. Up until his sex and drug scandal in 2006, Ted Haggard was the head pastor of the New Life Church as well as the president of the National Association of Evangelicals (NAE). Prior to the events that led to his embarrassed departure from both organizations his weekly conference calls with the White House had been reported numerous times, most notably on NBC, and he had close ties to ultraconservative James Dobson of Focus on the Family. In fact, it was Haggard's hypocritical hardcore political stance against gay rights that ultimately brought him down (Darman and Murr, 2006, pp. 34–5).[2] These "men of God," while claiming no political ambition, are setting the political agenda. It is an agenda based on the "inerrant word of God," which means that abortion is verboten, as are gay marriage and stem cell research. Moreover, their influence on the White House as well as at the state and local levels suggests continued efforts toward blending church and state, if not the creation of an outright theocracy.

In this chapter we will look at the political economy of religion and spirituality. In the world of faith brands it is the megachurches, and the evangelicals whom they serve, that have the power. Moreover, these large religious institutions are big business, and like all businesses, the people running these institutions do whatever they can to support their continued success. This means being intricately involved in the political process to protect their economic agenda in addition to their conservative social agenda. In exchange for getting out the vote, these groups benefit economically through generous tax exemptions and facilitated access to government grants (something that had been limited prior to the Bush administration). Their social beliefs are supported through the president's appointment of conservative judges and by the subtle instituting of conservative beliefs as part of government policy.

It is important to note here that not all evangelicals are conservative, but it is the white and primarily Southern conservative evangelicals who have particularly strong ties to the Republican party, and who have pressed their agenda on the American public. Before examining these political issues, though, we will first look at the megachurch marketing phenomenon and its success in helping to create a Republican voting machine.

Megachurches

Marketing the oversized church

When marketing is introduced into a product category—any product category, whether it is churches or tchotchkes—the goal of the institution becomes growth. Marketing-oriented institutions measure success by growth indicators—increases in sales, increases in brand awareness, increases in repeat business. The same holds true for churches once they began to track their goals based on a marketing mind-set. It is the culmination of marrying marketing with evangelizing. As discussed in Chapter 4, these are one and the same thing, whether we are talking about God or iPods.

Megachurches have been the focus of much of the discussion to date in regard to religion and marketing, and with good reason: they have to be blatant in their promotion because they target the unchurched—those who do not attend services on a regular basis. More subtle marketing, like billboard advertising or signs in front of a church announcing an upcoming event, can be used to remind people who are already inclined to attend services. But changing someone's thinking and thus converting a prospect into a user (i.e., moving that person through the relationship curve) requires more sophisticated marketing techniques, which is exactly what the megachurches use.

The mythology (remember, storytelling is important to branding) surrounding megachurches and how they started abounds. The most-often cited stories are about pastors going door to door with marketing surveys. The legend of Rick Warren and how he started his Saddleback Church in California is a prime example of this. Here is how Warren describes his marketing research:

> I went door to door, and I knocked on homes for about 12 weeks and just took an opinion poll. I had a survey with me. I just said, "My name is Rick Warren. I'm not here to sell you anything, I'm not here to convert you, I'm not here to witness to you. I just want to ask you three or four questions. Question number one: Are you an active member of a local church—of any kind of religion—synagogue, mosque, whatever?" If they said yes, I said, "Great, God bless you, keep going," and I politely excused myself and went to the next home. When I'd find somebody who'd say, "No, I don't go anywhere," I'd say, "Perfect; you're just the kind of guy I want to talk to. This is great, you don't go anywhere. So let me ask you a question. Why do you think most people don't attend church?" And I just wrote the answers down. I asked, "If you were looking for a church, what kind of things would you look for?" And I'd just list them. "What advice would you give to me as the pastor of a new church? How can I help you?"
>
> (Pew Forum, 2005)

What Warren found in response to these questions is that the nonchurched thought: (1) sermons are boring and have no relevance for their life; (2) members are cliquish and unfriendly; (3) churches are more interested in money than people; and (4) children's programs need to be of a higher quality than what was usually offered. The answers to these questions became the basis for revising church services to attract the unchurched: Get rid of the cross. Update the music. Make church relevant to parishioners' lives. And, if you are denominational (Saddleback is Baptist for example), for God's sake hide it.

Surveys were only the beginning of the marketing push. One-on-one interviews, questionnaires, and focus groups became commonplace. Demographic analyses of neighborhoods were regularly conducted to evaluate church growth opportunities. Many churches even hired consultants from Disney to assist in updating their services to be more entertaining and to design their children's playgrounds. The resultant attention to detail is stunning. The Saddleback Church, for instance, saves the best parking spots for first-time visitors, avoids religious symbolism, including in the church bulletin, keeps the restrooms impeccably clean, and provides a wealth of entry-level ministries to slowly move people toward volunteering their time and money (Lobdell, 2003). Instead of simply being a place of worship, these megachurches have become significant sources of community, creating gathering and networking opportunities through everything from 12-step groups to parenting classes to fast food restaurants to sports teams. They have become what marketers call a "third place"—not home, not work— much like Starbucks and Barnes & Noble. Such congregations are not embarrassed to say that they have created their institutions in the image of the local mall, providing a variety of "shopping experiences" within a single institution—both religious and communal.

Media products are important promotional tools for megachurch growth. Half of megachurch pastors have radio programs, "a third have television programs, and almost all of them have Web sites with streaming video" (Megachurches, 2006). Wanting to avoid the televangelism scandals of the 1980s, Rick Warren and Bill Hybels of Willowcreek made a deliberate decision not to have a television or radio ministry. For others like Joel Osteen and Joyce Meyer, television has been extremely successful. Best-selling books by megachurch pastors also help spread the word as we saw in Chapter 3. These books are promoted on their shows and/or through their churches as are video games, music, and DVDs of either the television program or regular church services. However, these tools are only the beginning of the process. Once the word is out, the most important marketing tool is the congregation itself. Congregants become personal sellers, bringing friends and family into the fold.

Using these marketing tools has been extremely effective when it comes to megachurches and faith brands such as *The Purpose Driven Life* and Joel Osteen. These churches/brands are part of the recent explosion in evangelical Protestantism. Representing 36 percent of all practitioners, evangelicals are now the largest religious group in the United States (Symonds, 2005, p. 81). Much of this expansion can be attributed to the rapid growth of megachurches. According to the Hartford Institute of Religious Research, as of 2005 there were more than 1,200 megachurches in the United States, up from 600 only five years before; weekly attendance at megachurches has reached 4.3 million. While the majority of megachurches (53.8 percent) have memberships between 2,000 and 3,000 people, the 4 percent of megachurches with attendance over 5,000 are the most well-known faith brands fronted by well-known faith brand preachers. A sampling of these churches appears in Table 8.1.

These churches are enormous and still growing. While these statistics put the Lakewood Church at 30,000, for example, just two years later the church claims an additional 10,000 weekly congregants. More recently, the trend among these churches is to add satellite venues or franchises, as is the case with Bill Hybels' Willowcreek and Creflo Dollar's World Changers Church.

To make some sense of all of this, it is helpful to understand what is happening in the religious marketplace overall. According to the 2000

Table 8.1 Largest megachurches in the United States

Church name	Pastor	Average attendance
Lakewood Church	Joel Osteen	30,000
Saddleback Valley Community Church	Rick Warren	22,000
Willow Creek Community Church	Bill Hybels	20,000
Fellowship Church	Ed Young	19,500
Southeast Christian Church	Robert Russell	18,575
The Potter's House	T.D. Jakes	18,500
Calvary Chapel	Robert Coy	18,000
New Birth Missionary Baptist	Eddie Long	18,000
Crenshaw Christian Center	Fred Price	17,000
Calvary Chapel of Costa Mesa	Chuck Smith, Sr.	16,500

Source: Thumma (2005).

Religious Congregations & Membership study by the Glenmary Research Center, conservative churches exploded in the 1990s, growing at double-digit rates (Packaged Facts, 2004, p. 44).[3] At the same time, more liberal denominations did not experience the same increases.

> The Mormon Church grew by 19.3% to 4.2 million members, the Assemblies of God grew by 18.5% to 2.6 million, and Christian Churches and Churches of Christ grew by 18.6% to 1.4 million during the 10-year survey period. The Presbyterian Church's adherents declined by 11.6%, while membership in the nation's second largest Protestant group, United Methodist Church, declined by 6.7%. Membership in the Lutheran Church–Missouri Synod and Episcopal Church also declined across the country. With a roughly 5% increase in its congregation, the growth of the Southern Baptist Convention, the largest Protestant denomination in the United States, fell well below the nation's population growth of 13.2%.

While declines in liberal church attendance can be attributed to any number of sociological changes discussed elsewhere in this book, the rise in evangelicalism can be tied to the effectiveness of megachurch marketing programs and churches' ability to serve an increasingly disenfranchised population. Chris Hedges (2007), journalist and author of *American Fascists: The Christian Right and the War on America*, claims:

> [D]espair crosses economic boundaries, of course, enveloping many in the middle class who live trapped in huge, soulless exurbs where, lacking any form of community rituals or centers, they also feel deeply isolated,

vulnerable and lonely. Those in despair are the most easily manipulated by demagogues, who promise a fantastic utopia, whether it is a worker's paradise, fraternite-egalite-liberte, or the second coming of Jesus Christ. Those in despair search desperately for a solution, the warm embrace of a community to replace the one they lost, a sense of purpose and meaning in life, the assurance they are protected, loved and worthwhile.

These disenfranchised who seek solace in the basketball and food courts of the megachurch are what drive the Christian right. Giving parishioners what they want when they want it and preaching a gospel of prosperity and empowerment, instead of damnation and repentance, appeals to a significantly large segment of the population. And why not? Who doesn't want to think that God would like us to be rich, particularly when our reality is increasingly so poor?

Megachurches, evangelicals, and politics

The growth of conservative evangelicalism did not start with the mega-churches. It has its roots in the 1970s, starting with *Roe v. Wade*, the rise of Jerry Falwell and the Moral Majority as well as Focus on the Family, and the increasing presence of conservative think tanks like the Heritage Foundation. This culminated in the Christian Coalition's being solidly established by the 1980s, with its ability to mobilize at the grassroots level. It was this coalition that put Ronald Reagan in the White House, eschewing Jimmy Carter for being too progressive even though he was a Southern evangelical.

Megachurches, which began to develop in the 1970s as well, are now seen as part of a trend toward a "kinder, gentler" Christian conservative. These churches are all-accepting, with language that allows for inclusiveness. Instead of blaming women for abortions, crisis pregnancy centers are used;[4] instead of gay bashing, they pray for the sinner to become heterosexual and promote conversion therapy and the ex-gay movement. All of it is a repackaging of conservatism, a revision in the marketing strategy, and it has helped megachurches gain more and more congregants, increasing their influence in the political sphere because of their numbers, while at the same time more liberal churches decline.

This consumer-friendly, feel-good, easy-listening type of Christianity conceals the reality that these churches have the same political agenda as the conservatives of the 1970s. They just don't promote it because it is not "on message" and could turn away prospects. Again and again we read that the leaders of these megachurches do not want to take a stand in politics. Rick Warren told ABC News, "I'm a pastor. Not a politician," yet he plies his hand in the background. In one instance, Warren "sent a letter to 150,000 pastors, in effect urging 'those of us who accept the Bible as God's word' to get out the vote for Bush" (Gunther, 2005, p. 110). In another, Warren was quoted as saying, "If I want to rally people, I push a button, and boom!" (Nussbaum, 2006, p. 1). Isn't rallying the people a fundamental part of the political process? Like Haggard, this is an example of promoting what you know will sell and concealing the less appealing aspects of your product.

Warren's true agenda was articulated in an article in *Fortune*:

> Because he would like hard-line churches to play an even bigger role in national and global affairs, he wants to soften the image of evangelical Christianity...*He says he's not interested in politics*, but he stepped into the culture wars to help the President...his ambitions are so vast that they practically invite scorn.
>
> (Gunther, 2005, p. 112, italics added)

Rick Warren is not the only one who claims he is disinterested in politics. Joel Osteen, too, is quoted as being politically standoffish.

> It's not in my heart to be the one who's leading the pack in the political area. What I usually do around election time is encourage people to vote...I feel like the message God's given me is hope and inspiration and how to live life. The moment I go and say I'm a staunch this supporter or that supporter, I divide my audience. I tell people all the time, "We're not for abortion, I don't think that's best, I don't think gay marriage is best, but our doors are open to everybody." We have every kind come in.
>
> (Butler, 2005b)

Rallying people is politics. Telling them to vote is politics. Saying you are against abortion is politics. Whether megachurch leaders and other evangelicals claim they are politically active or not, evangelicals have been inserted into the political arena because of the voting bloc they represent. Though not all evangelicals are conservative—notably, the most conservative tend to be white and Southern[5]—the ones who are represent a large cohesive coalition, one that is more unified than other political groups. Moreover, evangelicals are increasingly educated and affluent (Saddleback and Willowcreek, for instance, are in white, upper middle-class suburbs)—important elements in the political process because they have the ability and the propensity to get out the vote.

And vote religious people do. According to Barna research, while born-again Christians represent 38 percent of the population, they accounted for 53 percent of the vote in the 2004 presidential election. They overwhelmingly supported Bush by 62 percent (Barna Group, 2004). This is in part because over the last ten years, evangelicals have become decidedly more Republican. According to the *Washington Post*, 34 percent of white evangelicals were Republican in 1987, but today that number is 51 percent (Marcus, 2006,

p. A17). Christians were effective in mobilizing the vote in 2000, and they improved on that in 2004. This translated into 3.5 million more evangelicals voting than in the 2000 presidential race, with the bulk of those votes going to George W. Bush (*Dateline* NBC, 2005). Bush's landslide—in the face of an unpopular war and overall populace dissatisfaction—attests to the power of the evangelical political apparatus.

By 2006, even while the Republicans took a beating at the polls, their base remained strong. Sixty percent of religious service attendees who go more than once a week voted Republican in 2006, down only one percentage point from 2002. Most (53 percent) weekly attendees also voted Republican. White evangelicals remained true to the party with 72 percent staying with the GOP in House races across the country (Pew Forum, 2006). These voters put considerable importance on values when making their voting decisions, setting them apart from other voters. For instance, gay marriage and abortion were extremely important issues for 59 percent of these voters, versus only 29 percent for other voters (Pew Forum, 2006).

The power of the evangelical voting bloc is not lost on Democratic politicians. Democrats have been grasping for ways to change their image so that Republicans no longer seem to be the only party with a pipeline to God. Examples of this include House Minority (soon-to-be Majority) leader Nancy Pelosi's attendance at the opening of the new Lakewood Church in 2005; Howard Dean, chair of the National Democratic Committee, appearing on Pat Robertson's *700 Club* (Marcus, 2006); and Barack Obama's appearance at Saddleback even before he announced his bid for the presidency. All of this would suggest that Democrats are fighting for the ears—and the votes— of the evangelicals.

The impact on the broader culture

Pushing the conservative agenda—abortion as case study

Evangelicals claim that they are fighting for the moral values of America, but what they are really doing is pushing their own conservative agenda. This is done in subtle and not-so-subtle ways. For example, while James Dobson of Focus on the Family will trumpet the damnation attached to homosexuality and abortion and a litany of other wedge issues, the faith brands and megachurches will not even though they share similar beliefs.[6] Again, *this is an issue of marketing*—presenting the most pleasant things and hiding what might turn people off. *Fortune* magazine said of Rick Warren that he "believes homosexuality is a sin and Jews will go to hell—but doesn't emphasize them" (Gunther, 2005, p. 110). For Joel Osteen's part, he steers clear of these topics in the press, but as covered in Chapter 5, he is a literal interpreter of the gospel, which means he is fundamentally opposed to abortion, stem cell research, and homosexuality, and he has said as much without broadcasting it. These issues are important because they become the calling card of politics—if a church leader takes a conservative stance on any of them and then tells his congregation to "vote their values," that is all the information they need to make their decision at the polls.

The most contentious and long-running issue when it comes to conservative politics is abortion.[7] It has been a hot-button issue since *Roe v. Wade* was decided in 1973. The fight between pro-choice and pro-life has been historically a national fight. More recently, conservatives have been attacking a woman's right to choose at the local level, targeting local governments to create legislation that will severely restrict abortions so as to make them either impossible or dangerous to obtain. South Dakota, Louisiana, and Missouri are just some of the states that have taken draconian measures against abortion in hopes of pushing the Supreme Court to review *Roe*'s constitutionality. Operation Rescue, an organization once known primarily for harassing abortion clinics, has shifted its strategy to pressuring state capitals to change their legislation—part of the kinder, gentler initiative. By concentrating on the state level, it hopes to systematically ban abortion. Said Troy Newman of Operation Rescue, "We don't want to restrict abortion. We want to eliminate abortion" (Spurlock, 2006).

In addition to attacking abortion regulations directly, conservatives have increased efforts to make abortions more difficult to obtain. Pro-life crisis pregnancy centers, Christian centers where women are talked to/scared out of getting abortions, have sprung up all over the country. There are now upwards of 4,000 such centers around the United States. Meanwhile the number of abortion providers around the country has been declining—just over 1,800 today, down from 3,000 clinics 25 years ago. The biggest declines are seen in hospitals and private doctors' offices that provide abortions. This has been attributed to: "Antichoice harassment and violence, Social stigma/marginalization, Professional isolation/peer pressure, The 'graying of providers,' Inadequate economic/other incentives, and lack of medical training opportunities" (Physicians, 2006). Eighty-seven percent of counties in the United States do not have an abortion provider, and one in four women must travel 50 miles or more to receive this service.

The disappearance of providers has been occurring even while the number of unintended pregnancies has remained stagnant. What has changed, however, is that a disproportionate number of unintended pregnancies occur among poor women—the ones least likely to be able to afford to travel great distances for services and to have access to education and birth control. Moreover, while the percentage of abortions in the United States is lower per capita than in the rest of the world overall (21 abortions per 1,000 women versus 35 abortions per 1,000 women), the percentage of abortions in the United States is *significantly higher than in most industrialized countries.* Only Australia has a higher rate per capita than the United States. What these statistics suggest is not that we lack the ability to reduce the number of abortions, but rather that we lack the political will to do so. Because abortion (and birth control and sex education) is a political issue that generates media attention, attacks on abortion clinics and the picketing of state legislatures remain the norm. It is this lack of political will in service of a Christian agenda that keeps the number of abortions so high.

Significantly, abortion is not a major policy issue for most Americans. According to a 2007 CNN poll, almost two-thirds (62 percent) of Americans believe abortion should be legal in the first trimester, which in essence mirrors the language of *Roe v. Wade*. Close to 83 percent believe that abortion should be legal if the woman's health is in danger and 74 percent are for it if the pregnancy was the result of rape or incest. These last statistics are from a Fox News/Opinion Dynamics poll (Abortion and Birth Control, n.d.).

Because of the religious right's focus on abortion as a political/right-to-life issue based on their beliefs, it obscures the inadequacies of health care for women and access to affordable birth control. There have been discussions of late that Democrats should reframe the abortion issue as an effort to reduce the number of abortions. However recent battles over the morning-after pill suggest this may not be an effective strategy. Here's why: a number of states are enacting conscience clauses for pharmacists. These regulations protect pharmacists from legal action if they refuse to dispense birth control drugs. Anti-abortion groups have helped to push these laws through the state legislatures and the trend has been to pass legislation to protect pharmacists (Morning-After Pill Protest, 2005). If pharmacists can deny women access to a legally prescribed form of birth control, it is likely that more traditional forms of birth control (including condoms) will also be blocked by conservative groups. For conservatives, abstinence before marriage is the only acceptable form of birth control.

Abortion is just one example of how the growth in American evangelicalism has had an impact on agenda politics in the United States. The conservative agenda has wedged its way into more and more areas of Americans' lives, from the selection of judges on the federal bench to who has a right to marry to television censorship. If megachurches continue to grow, and current trends suggest that they will, we should see these conservative issues remain in the political forefront.

God's messenger is running the White House

There is no doubt that faith has played a more significant role in the Bush White House than any other administration. Bush has governed from the right in order to play to his conservative Christian base, which has gained more political power with the rise of the president. As Esther Kaplan states in her book *With God on Their Side*:

Corporate donors may fill GOP coffers, but evangelicals are the party's institutional grass roots, its believers, its get-out-the-vote ground troops, as important to the Republicans as organized labor and African Americans are, combined, to the Democrats. Bush knows, and Christian right leaders know, that he couldn't have been elected without them... The Christian right is not just another special interest group, like the NRA. This is Bush's base.

For the president, maintaining fealty from religious conservatives is a first principle. And to this end he has happily ceded huge swaths of his domestic and international policy to this lobby, from abortion and sex education to gay rights, social services, court appointments, and medical research. He has even used his global AIDS initiative, his foreign aid policy, and his war on terror to please religious radicals....His is not an embrace of spirituality or ethics broadly speaking, or of faith as an important voice among many in the national debate. It is, instead, an embrace of right-wing Christian fundamentalism.

(Kaplan, 2004, pp. 3, 4)

Weekly Bible study in the White House, daily Bible study at the Department of Justice, and lunch hour revival meetings are the norm in this administration (Harris, 2001). There is even an organization, The Presidential Prayer Team, that runs a Web site calling for Americans to pray daily for the president.[8] Susan Jacoby (2004) of the *Los Angeles Times* put it succinctly when she wrote, "There is no precedent in American history for the Bush administration's determination to infuse government with a highly specific set of religious values" (p. B11).

The president's religious beliefs in and of themselves are not the issue. Rather, it is the extent to which they govern his presidency and define the political agenda. As early as the 1999 Iowa debate, Bush let his beliefs be known. During that event, candidates were asked what philosopher or thinker was most influential in their life. Bush responded with: "Christ, because he changed my heart." While this statement was quite blatant and some even thought it political suicide, it did not ultimately hurt him in the polls. Still, he took a more moderate stance throughout the rest of his 2000 campaign. That moderation disappeared, however, once he entered the White House. "On his first day in office Bush reinstated the Reagan-era abortion 'gag rule,' instantaneously withdrawing federal funds from any family planning clinic in the developing world that voices support for abortion or even mentions it as an option to clients" (Kaplan, 2004, p. 6). When Christ changed George Bush's heart, scripture became the basis for American policy decisions.

The relationship between Bush and the Christian right is undeniable. In a 2005 television documentary called *Tom Brokaw Reports: In God They Trust*, the former NBC anchorman analyzed the relationship between the president and the 70 million evangelical Christians in America. Particularly telling is an interview Brokaw had with Ted Haggard, then pastor of the New Life Church and head of the National Association of Evangelicals, an organization made up of 45,000 churches. In the interview, Brokaw asked Haggard how often he talks to the White House; Haggard laughingly looked at his watch and said that he has a conference call in a couple of hours. Not only that, but Haggard admitted that he has regularly scheduled calls with the White House. Haggard told Brokaw:

> It [the evangelical movement] is not political. It is authentically a spiritual renewal, and people are responding to the goodness of the scripture, the goodness of God's love, the assurance of eternal life. And so it's a spiritual renewal that's taking place, and leading to the growth of churches that has political ramifications.
>
> (*Dateline*, NBC, 2005)

That sounds a bit like political doublespeak, particularly when later in the interview Haggard said that part of his job is to "advance God's will through government." Given Haggard's connection to the White House at the time, it is easy to imagine President Bush as the conduit for implementing that will.

The Christian right expected Bush to deliver and he has on numerous fronts—from putting conservative judges on federal benches to allowing religion to encroach into the military to making right-to-life a policy issue and thus the basis for vetoing stem cell research and attacking *Roe*.

Money for nothing

Jesus saves—tax exemptions for religious institutions

Another significant area Bush delivered on was money, which he freed up in record amounts for religious organizations. Consider that since 1989:

> [M]ore than 200 special arrangements, protections or exemptions for religious groups or their adherents were tucked into Congressional legislation, covering topics ranging from pensions to immigration to land use. New breaks have also been provided by a host of pivotal court decisions at the state and federal level, and by numerous rule changes in almost every department and agency of the executive branch.
>
> (Henriques and Lehren, 2006a, p. 1)

Given the timeframe not all of this can be attributed to the Bush administration even while it may be attributable to the Republican-led Congress. But certainly during the Bush years there has been a sense of a gradual eroding of the separation of church and state—more to the benefit of the church than the state—that can in part be traced to the growth in the political influence of religious groups.

Churches influencing government policy is, of course, nothing new. In fact, it was just such intermingling of church and state that led to the creation of the tax code that allowed tax-exempt status for religious institutions. In 1920 Prohibition was enacted under pressure from churches. In response, to stifle political speech in churches, the government amended the tax code— essentially giving tax-exempt status in exchange for churches' relinquishing the right to express political opinions from the pulpit, specifically endorsing one candidate over another.

There are two issues with this tax law: it is difficult to enforce and equally difficult to define. On the one hand, how does the government police thousands of churches? Thus only the most egregious cases of blatant politicking for a specific candidate have led to the repeal of an organization's tax-exempt status. On the other hand, what constitutes political speech? For example, when political candidates speak at a church, is that a violation? Can a pastor preach against abortion but draw the line at endorsing a particular presidential candidate? The lack of scrutiny has led to few attempts to hide a religious organization's political persuasion. In an article about religious broadcasting in the television trade journal *Broadcasting & Cable*, it was reported that "hundreds and probably thousands of ministers gave pro-Bush sermons prior to the election" (Winslow, 2005a, p. 28). It doesn't get much more public or political than that.

Federal tax laws are only one side of the government's largesse. There are other regulatory exemptions. For example, tax-exempt status is not limited to the federal level. Religious institutions do not pay local property taxes, and tax exemptions can go beyond the work of the church itself, being applied even to broadcasting and publishing properties. In addition, newer laws have allowed for religious organizations and their employees to be exempt from "personal-income and payroll taxes, and have made it easier for them to get tax-exempt construction loans for purely religious projects" (Henriques and Lehren, 2006b, p. A1). One of the biggest battles in the war on tax exemption was waged by Rick Warren. Warren fought for the religiously ordained to retain a federal tax exemption on their housing expenses, which according to the *New York Times* is equivalent to one-third of their compensation.

> The deduction, usually called the parsonage exemption, is available to ministers, rabbis and other clergy members of all faiths working at houses of worship. It allows them to live in congregation-owned housing without being taxed on the imputed value of their free housing, as almost all other employees are when they live in company-paid housing.
>
> (Henriques and Lehren, 2006c, p. A1)

This provision also applies to what clergy spend on renting or buying housing with funds designated as housing allowance by their congregation. Warren paid dearly with his own money to win the battle for clergy to have an unlimited parsonage allowance, and he was supported by the Congress and the president. Through this and other exemptions, the government helps religious groups by saving them significant sums of money.

Uncle Sam invests—governmental support for Christian organizations

The other form of governmental largesse is cold, hard cash. Support for religious organizations began with President Clinton's "charitable choice" legislation, which lowered the barriers to religious groups' receiving a limited number of federal grants. Religious group' access to additional funding was furthered through George Bush's White House Office of Faith-Based and Community Initiatives, his first executive order as president. Bush had created a similar program when he was governor of Texas. At the time, an organization called Teen Challenge, a drug rehabilitation program that used faith as the basis for its services, was denied government funding because of its religious component. Under the Texas faith-based initiatives program, Bush removed the roadblocks "for religious organizations participating in charitable work." Specifically, faith-based organizations were exempt from state regulations, thus freeing them to use religion while providing social services. Bush brought this policy with him to the federal level in the expectation of providing federal grants to organizations that had previously been denied these funds on Constitutional grounds. Said Bush, "When it comes to the use of federal money, the days of discriminating against religious institutions simply because they are religious must come to an end" (McGough, 2005, p. B11).

Who are the beneficiaries of this money? That's not an easy question to answer. In contacting the White House Office of Faith-Based and Community Initiatives (OFBCI), I learned that there is no list of funded organizations. We would later learn from David Kuo's (2006) book, *Tempting Faith*, why such a list did not exist. While there was much hoopla surrounding the creation of the OFBCI, there was in reality little to no funding for it. What little money did exist was contained in the Compassion Capital Fund (CCF), a $30 million fund housed in the Department of Health and Human Services (HHS). Legally, funding cannot come directly from the White House (pp. 212–13). This may explain why, in a 2002 executive order, Bush embedded faith-based offices in seven federal agencies, including the Department of Agriculture and the Department of Justice as well as HHS. These offices were ordered to encourage and assist faith-based groups in applying for government funds (Aronson, 2004).

Thus instead of providing direct funds through the CCF (which was expected to be a $1.5 billion program), what the faith-based initiative did instead was open the door for religious groups to receive federal money through existing grants. It may also have contributed to the increased number of earmarks, commonly known as pork, directed toward faith-based groups (Henriques, 2007). This increase in earmarks has also been fueled by the introduction of lobbyists into the process, yet another example of religious marketing.

As previously mentioned, the Christian agenda works in subtle and not-so-subtle ways. While the abortion issue is blatant, the funding of religious organizations is a more surreptitious means of promoting conservative social issues. Let's look at an example of one of the funded organizations that demonstrates this. When I asked OFBCI about how an organization gets its funding, I was told (repeatedly) that the organization has to be "self-identified" as faith-based. Then it has to fulfill one of the goals of the department from which they wish to receive funding. I learned through my research that The Silver Ring Thing, an organization that promotes abstinence before marriage, was receiving funds through the Department of Health and Human Services (HHS).[9] Within HHS is the Administration for Children and Families (ACF). This division currently has four major initiatives: (1) Campaign to Rescue & Restore Victims of Human Trafficking, (2) Faith-Based and Community Initiatives (FBCI), (3) Healthy Marriage Initiative, and (4) Improving Head Start (ACF, 2006). Part of FBCI is the Community-Based Abstinence Education Program, the goal that The Silver Ring Thing fulfills. According to the ACF Web site:

> The Community–Based Abstinence Education program supports communities across the country in delivering the message that abstinence is the surest way to avoid out-of-wedlock pregnancy and STDs…This program provides funding directly to individual organizations to support public and private entities in the development and implementation of abstinence education programs for adolescents, ages 12 through 18, in communities across the country.

This goes on to say that, among other things, the programs should address the health benefits of abstaining from sex, that abstinence is expected outside of marriage for school age children, that this is the only sure way to prevent out-of-wedlock pregnancies and STDs, and "that a mutually faithful monogamous relationship in the context of marriage is the expected standard of human sexual activity" (ACF, 2007).

The Silver Ring Thing tells teens that it is God's plan that they abstain from sex until they are married. If they have engaged in sexual activities, The Silver Ring Thing provides them with an opportunity for a "second virginity." To get teens to sign onto the program, they are entertained with a rock-concert type of event complete with music videos, sketch comedy, and finally an enthusiastic lecture expounding on the benefits of abstinence—a format similar to many megachurch services. The evening ends with teens purchasing silver rings to wear on the middle finger of their left hand to remind them of their commitment to celibacy and as a symbol to others of their commitment.

The relationship among HHS, The Silver Ring Thing, and the Bush administration highlights how the Christian right agenda has become integral to White House policy—and thus by extension American policy. First, HHS's guiding principle is to promote sex within marriage as the societal norm and present abstinence as the most effective means of stemming teen pregnancy and sexually transmitted disease. On the ground, however, numerous studies have demonstrated that abstinence is ineffective as a form of "birth control," and even teens who participate in the Ring ceremony tend to stay with the program for less than two years. Thus the HHS's goals have far more to do with a conservative religious agenda than any governmental concern for the country's long-term health. Second, American tax dollars have been going to support blatant forms of proselytizing—which is the main reason government funds have been traditionally withheld from religious service providers. In the case of The Silver Ring Thing (SRT), proselytizing and evangelizing techniques are used to get teens to make their celibacy commitment. In 2005 the ACLU of Massachusetts sued HHS, claiming that SRT had used federal money for "inherently religious activities." HHS settled with the ACLU by suspending SRT's funding and requiring that all subsequent funding be contingent on a modification to their existing program. In this case, as in most cases in which monies have been misappropriated, there are no penalties beyond a failure to renew subsequent funding. The attitude is "act now and apologize later," since there are no meaningful consequences for using the money to promote Christianity (Henriques, 2006d, p. A1).

Moreover, Christian groups have received grants in disproportionate numbers. Large grants have gone to well-known evangelicals, some with controversial ethics but who are fervent supporters of the Republican agenda (Kaplan, 2004, p. 45). One example is Pat Robertson's Operation Blessing, which received $1.5 million over three years—one of the first grants approved (Benen, 2002; see also ACF Compassion Capital Fund). The monies were provided for Operation Blessing to assist other smaller faith-based organizations in competing for federal dollars. Another is Chuck Colson of Watergate fame, who has an evangelical organization called Prison Fellowship Ministries. This group, with the assistance of the Labor Department's faith-based office, received $22.5 million to assist ex-offenders in reentering the workplace through their Ready4Work program (U.S. Department of Labor, 2003).

In 2005 grants through the seven federal agencies totaled $2.1 billion (White House Office, 2006). Meanwhile opponents of the administration found themselves targets for audits, investigations, and defunding. OMB (Office of Management and Budget) Watch issued a report, *An Attack on Nonprofit Speech*, that said "this administration—and its conservative allies—is stifling free expression and using the heavy hand of government to quash dissent" (Bass *et al.*, 2003).

Instead of leveling the playing field, the scales seem to have tipped in favor of religious organizations. Secular nonprofit agencies that serve the poor do not get local tax exemptions, for example, but their religious counterparts who may or may not provide charitable services automatically do. Moreover, many small communities, and even larger ones, are feeling crushed under the weight of tax-free churches. Megachurches now offer everything from childcare to fitness centers to video arcades, and while there should be benefits allowed for religious institutions that provide social services, does this really need to be applied to a tanning bed? As these churches become larger and more profitable and own more land, they do not contribute to the local tax rolls even as they get the benefits of local services. All the way around—from tax exemptions that save money to government grants that give money—it seems it's good to be Christian.

What marketing has wrought

Megachurches are a political force to be reckoned with, whether their pastors admit participation in this arena or not. Their size alone—driven ever larger by years of sophisticated marketing initiatives—makes them the 900-pound gorilla in the election booth. As suggested throughout this chapter, the means of insinuating the conservative agenda are both blatant and subtle and have been allowed to occur because of an unwritten but well-understood pact between conservative Christian voters and the politicians who serve them. Stated simply: the role of the Christian right in a number of Bush-era policies and initiatives, such as the war in Iraq, the regulatory response to the Janet Jackson equipment malfunction,[10] judicial nominees, political pressure at PBS,[11] attempted censorship of television programming,[12] and others, cannot be understated.

Within a marketing framework, politics is a bothersome attribute to be hidden by pastors who are eager to grow their congregations. Television preachers become entertainers; they are purveyors of the prosperity gospel, the feel-good, "God will make you rich" type of preaching in order to grow, in order to draw a high rating. In a time of war, instead of moral outrage, we get "name it and claim it." Instead of marching in the streets demanding a more equitable distribution of wealth, we get a personalized, market-driven Jesus, with the ultimate goal that God will make you rich. Prosperity preaching and entertainment-based services are commercial America's answer to giving us what we want in the religious marketplace without being asked for anything in return. The focus is on the individual and not the broader social agenda—at least not when selling to religious prospects.

One important method that Christian conservatives use to hide their political agenda from those outside their sphere is direct mail. Evangelical Christian organizations, such as Jerry Falwell's Moral Majority and Pat Robertson's Christian Coalition, developed direct-marketing databases over the last several decades. Karl Rove, at one time the brains behind the Bush White House, has also been amassing these lists of the faithful. Televangelists have been doing this since their programming was created. Using these lists has a two-pronged advantage: it widely disseminates your message and it does not alert the opposition to your position. The Christian right has learned that by avoiding television when presenting controversial points of view, it avoids getting out the opposition vote. Remember, too, that the megachurches and other faith brands are extremely effective in generating databases of their own.

Marketing created the megachurches that now act as the social hub for an increasing number of Americans. These religious institutions fill multiple facets of people's lives, which have been eviscerated by shrinking government programs and an increasing lack of stability in numerous areas of their lives, including an unsure labor market, dire divorce rates, and retirement accounts that have gone up in smoke—never mind the instability of a culture based on planned obsolescence. As "trusted" branded products have become a point of stability in our lives, so, too, have these branded churches become places of reassurance. But as marketers, they show the customer only what he or she wants to see and hide anything that might hinder growth. In this case, what is obscured is a conservative political agenda that threatens to put a stranglehold on our democracy.

Chapter 9

Has religious marketing gone too far?

The increasing commercialization of religion parallels the ascendancy of bean counters at the nightly news broadcasts starting in the 1980s. When Larry Tisch took over CBS, he brought a corporate mentality to an organization that had been mandated by Congress to serve the public interest. Prior to that time, the broadcast television newsroom had been the sacred space of the airwaves, the place of Edward R. Murrow and Walter Cronkite. It was programming with a mission beyond generating revenues or making a profit; theirs was a higher calling—to provide information to the citizenry of a democracy.

The pursuit of profit changed all that. Under corporate ownership news divisions came to serve shareholders, not citizens. Instead of providing information that people need, they give people what they want—all in the interest of larger audiences. Instead of international news, investigative reports, and politics, we see human interest stories, celebrity breakups, and corporate press videos. While the Middle East rages, we see wall-to-wall coverage of mountain climbers in Oregon and Anna Nicole Smith, and in the summer of 2001—before September 11—the nation was obsessed with Chandra Levy and Gary Condit.

In much the same way, the quest for increased audience has changed religion from what people need to what people want. Branding faith solidifies the connection of marketing to evangelizing and further focuses attention on growth as the goal. This has been particularly true in movements that stress prosperity and self-fulfillment over other more altruistic religious goals. When news divisions needed to turn a profit, they changed their programming to attract more viewers; so, too, religions have changed their content to attract more converts. Instead of economics and politics, we get Amber alerts and Hollywood. Instead of Martin Luther King, Jr. and Mahatma Gandhi, we have Joel Osteen and the Rav.

In this concluding chapter we will examine the final cause that is driving religious marketing—the severe decline in participation by the younger generations. We will also look to New Age purveyors—the most successful marketers of religion—to see if they can help us to understand the long-term consequences of marketing religion.

Declines in faith propel the need to increase marketing

Faith brands exist for three reasons: (1) religion must compete against other discretionary leisure activities; (2) religion must compete against the constant barrage of images and information in today's culture; and (3) teens and 20- and 30-somethings are not as attracted to religion as their counterparts in previous generations. While we have looked at the first two issues in previous chapters, here we will examine how declines in audience have increased the pressure on religious institutions to market and brand their product.

The average American born-again Christian is 50 years old. This statistic should not surprise anyone. Those in middle age have traditionally been more enamored of religion than those in younger generations. However, now there is a growing gap between how young people practice their faith versus the previous four generations.

> Mosaics [the psychographic name for the current generation of teens] are substantially less likely than Baby Busters—the next youngest generation, and a group that itself is generally below average on most spiritual indicators—to reflect a commitment to Christianity. For instance, Mosaics are 36% less likely than Busters to say they are absolutely committed to the Christian faith; 18% less likely to describe their religious faith as very important to them; 24% less likely to have made a personal commitment to Christ; 61% less likely to have an "active faith"; 24% less likely to read the Bible and 21% less likely to pray to God during a typical week.
>
> (Barna Group, 2006, p. 52)

This is true not only for Christians. Harris Interactive (2006) confirms that all Americans under 40—not just Christian—are significantly less likely to believe in God than their older counterparts. An American Bible Society study found that "35% of teens surveyed say they never read the Bible and only 9% read it daily. But America's youth is not completely devoid of religion; more than half of teenagers surveyed said they are 'very likely' (22%) or 'somewhat likely' (29%) to attend voluntary prayer meetings at school" (Packaged Facts, 2004, p. 17).

Evangelicals—a group that has to date been successful in targeting younger audiences—are increasingly concerned about where the next generation of believers will come from. To support current young believers and assist them in not feeling isolated, youth ministries like Teen Mania are creating events like the "Christian youth extravaganza and rock concert called Acquire the Fire," making it hip to be a believer amid 3,000 others of your generation (Goodstein, 2006, p. A1). In addition, Teen Mania produces Battlecry (see battlecry.com), which is geared toward senior pastors and youth ministers, to further aid in capturing the teen market. These events have sprung up in response to statistical trends that suggest that the number of current teens who will still be "Bible-believing Christians" as adults is likely to drop to 4 percent. This is in comparison to 35 percent of the baby boom generation and prior to that 65 percent of the World War II generation. Some scholars have noted, however, that evangelicals may not be abandoning religion but the church. As we have seen elsewhere, teens are as likely to find religion in mass-produced rock concerts as they are in a megachurch, which is okay for the seeker but a problem for the churches.

Teens and young adults are a critically important target group for consumer product marketers, including religious institutions. Brand loyalty needs to be established at an early age. If you get people to buy your product when they are young, they are more likely to continue doing so throughout their lifetime. Because of this, the above statistics raise long-term challenges for churches (and marketers), who see in this trend their ultimate demise. This concern leads to employing methods that will draw younger audiences. Thus updated music, video screens, anonymity, and food courts are in a way a measure of the decline in religious participation.

Churches are not alone in this regard. The number of religious Jews has also been falling. According to the National Jewish Population Survey 2000–1, the Jewish population decreased by 300,000 in the decade from 1990 to 2000, putting the current statistic at 5.2 million[1] (NJPS, n.d.). Of more concern for the long term is the rate of intermarriage, which is at 47 percent based on the same study. This number correlates with religious participation. Intermarried couples tend to be unaffiliated with a synagogue. Not only are they unaffiliated before they marry, but they also tend to raise children who do not identify themselves as Jewish, a situation that creates a snowball effect of declining membership.

Synagogues have tried a number of methods to attract Jews, particularly young Jews, back to temple. "Torah cocktail parties," simplified prayer services, coffee houses with poetry readings, lectures on Kabbalah and dating, and even stand-up comedy have been used in conjunction with traditional services as enticements (Luo, 2006).

One of the more ambitious and coordinated attempts to increase attendance is Synaplex, a program begun in 2003 that supports congregations in offering multiple events one Shabbat (Sabbath) per month. Approximately 50 synagogues have tried this program, which turns congregations into religious multiplexes. Tot Shabbat, singles mixers, stand-up comedy, yoga with a Jewish theme, Israeli dancing, and political lectures all become draws to bring Jews to temple on Friday night and Saturday. The expectation is that by offering multiple activities at once, a large audience will be in attendance. Rabbi Hayim Herring, executive director of Synagogues: Transformation and Renewal (STAR), the organization that created Synaplex, said that the goal is "to have the congregation become the place to be, no matter who you are, what you believe" (Netburn, 2005, p. 116). Unlike churches, there is no illusion that people will come to believe in God. The goal of Synaplex is community building, and on that level the program has been very successful. Synagogues that use the program have doubled and tripled attendance at Friday night and Saturday services.

Synaplex is not the only means for increasing attendance. Synagogue 3000, a nonprofit institute that was established to help synagogues become revitalized, offers conferences, curricula, and consulting services to synagogues of all denominations. Shabbat Across America is a heavily advertised project of the National Jewish Outreach Program, an Orthodox organization that promotes this annual event to increase Shabbat participation. More broadly, synagogues have revised services to be more user-friendly; beginner courses in Judaism and Hebrew are made available as are "beginner services" in which knowledge of Hebrew is not required.

These services, similar to their Christian counterparts, tend to put more emphasis on the social and less on scripture so as to attract people to their product. Once in the synagogue, however, the job becomes to entice people to come to beginner worship services and then hopefully over the long term up-sell them to full membership. No one knows how successful this is, because as with megachurches, there are no statistics about how many people actually move from entertainment to enlightenment.

Can we blame religious institutions for using these methods when they see them as a means to their own survival? Aren't they simply doing what other organizations, religious and nonreligious, have done before them— using the culture to sell their product? Perhaps so, though today's marketing is more sophisticated, more saturated, and more blatantly commercial. The question becomes, then, what are the long-term consequences of religious commercialization? To try and answer that question, we will examine one last case study—the New Age. As the most commercialized spiritual product out there, it is a likely bellwether of the fate of faith brands.

Marketing the New Age

History of the New Age

Products, like people, have a life cycle. There are launched (born), and if they are successful, they grow, mature, and inevitably begin to decline. If the company is an innovative marketer, it can resuscitate a product by re-branding or updating it—think Abercrombie & Fitch or Barnes & Noble. The faith brands we have looked at are early along in their product life cycle.

The one exception to this is Oprah, who successfully repositioned her brand in the mid-1990s as a spiritually based product.

There is, however, one segment of the religious market that is in the mature stage of its product life cycle. This is what is commonly known as the New Age. Looked at from a marketing perspective, the New Age, unlike the faith brands, has matured and is looking weatherworn. New Age expos, which used to present established authors like Deepak Chopra, are now selling metal pyramids to wear on your head and any means of herbal health cure. Products have overtaken philosophy. Purchasing has overtaken practice. This is because the New Age has been marketing itself—and doing so aggressively—far longer than any other spiritual or religious product. The New Age used all the tools outlined throughout this book and went from counterculture to mainstream starting in the mid-1980s (Chandler, 1993). Russell Chandler quotes University of Denver Professor Carl A. Raschke as saying, "Until 1986...the New Age was a subculture, a counterculture; but it didn't have the bucks to go public. Somehow...they got the bucks. And they're putting them into celebrities, advertising and testimonies...It got glossy and glitzy overnight...That gets the media interested, and that gets public attention" (p. 22).

The mid-1980s was when the baby boom was reaching middle age. Moving through their 40s and with their children almost grown up, boomers could turn and focus on themselves. Moreover, they had considerable disposable income, more than past generations. Moving through its life cycle with the boomers, the New Age came out of its 1960s counterculture roots and emerged in the 1980s as upscale spirituality, which was a market position that fit the boomer lifestyle.

The New Age made its first major splash in the book industry with the publication of Shirley MacLaine's *Out on a Limb*. The book was turned into a miniseries that aired in January 1987 and has been attributed as giving the segment a huge promotional boost. That same year New Age book sales were over a billion dollars, which was a 30 percent increase over the previous year (Chandler, 1993, p. 124). But books were just the beginning. *Forbes* magazine, quoting the *New England Journal of Medicine*, said that spending on "unconventional therapy" was close to $12 billion, and another $2 billion went annually to "amoratherapists, channelers, macrobiotic-food vendors and assorted massagers of mind and body" (Ferguson, 1996, p. 86). New Age bookstores claimed that as much as half of their revenue came from products other than books, such as candles and scented oil. Service products like lectures, spas, seminars, and private therapy sessions are not so easily measured because of private ownership, but they, too, are likely to have reached into the billions.

New Age purveyors were smart in their use of marketing. Transcendental Meditation (TM), for example, was one of the first to successfully market a movement based on a segmentation strategy in the late 1960s and early

1970s. First, they determined who their target audiences were—students, businessmen, adults with an interest in long-term coursework, and adults with a spiritual interest (Johnston, 1988, p. 168). Then, messages were developed that would attract these different groups based on their needs— spiritual connection for some, relaxation for others. It also didn't hurt that the Beatles were unpaid spokespeople for TM.

Proponents of the New Age are "the reigning champions of religious salesmanship," wrote R. Laurence Moore in the mid-1990s (1994, p. 256). While that may have been true a decade ago, it appears to no longer be the case. Having its roots in the counterrevolution of the 1960s, and even after revising its strategy in the 1980s, the New Age is now hitting middle age and the wrinkles are starting to show, reflecting the aging of its target market.

The New Age defined

Read any work about New Age spirituality and what comes up again and again is that it is virtually impossible to define (Chandler, 1993; Heelas, 1996; Lewis and Melton, 1992).[2] While long-time stalwarts of the category include astrology, tarot cards, channeling, numerology, and meditation, a look at the Barnes & Noble Web site demonstrates how this area of spirituality has expanded.[3] Other ideas and practices include:

- Aliens and UFOs
- Angels
- Atlantis
- Auras and Colors
- Cults
- Demonology and Satanism
- Dreams and Dream Interpretation
- Fortune Telling and Divination
- Fraternal Orders—Freemasonry
- Ghosts and Haunted Places
- Graphology
- Mental and Spiritual Healing
- Mysticism
- Near-Death and Out-of-Body Experiences
- New Thought
- Parapsychology
- Prophecy
- Reincarnation
- Sacred Places
- Spiritualism
- Supernatural
- Witchcraft and Magic

This list shows the breadth that has been identified with the New Age. Moreover, this list is not exhaustive as it does not include Eastern philosophies (like Buddhism) or self-help authors like Wayne Dyer (*The Power of Intention*), Jack Canfield (*Chicken Soup for the Soul*), John Gray (*Men Are from Mars, Women Are from Venus*), Caroline Myss (a "medical intuitive" and author of *Why People Don't Heal and How They Can*), or Deepak Chopra (books too numerous to mention), all of whom are mainstays of this category. Thus we can see the range of philosophies and categories this entails.

These New Age ideas are "a hybrid of spiritual, social, and political forces, and it encompasses sociology, theology, and the physical sciences, medicine, anthropology, history, the human potentials movement, sports and science fiction...There is no organization one must join, no creed one must confess." (Chandler, 1993, p. 17). Practitioners may choose one or multiple belief systems. They can attend a place of worship, but they don't have to.

New Age beliefs seek to raise the consciousness of the individual and by so doing change the world. (It is interesting to note here the parallel to the personalized relationship with Jesus promoted by evangelicals even while they denounce the New Age.) The new consciousness entails a unified worldview—"we are all one"—and a belief in a higher power, though this being need not be clearly defined. It is about healing—healing the earth, healing the workplace, healing the individual psychologically and physically (Heelas, 1996, p. 81). Within the New Age, no one belief system is better than another and all have something to offer, be it Christianity, Buddhism, or Wicca. Being part of the New Age can mean attending seminars, retreats, and expos, or being a bodyworker, shaman, or even just a reader of New Age philosophies. There are no defined boundaries.

The New Age is amorphous. It is difficult to pin down the number of practitioners and therefore to track growth or decline, though a number of people have tried. In the late 1970s, George Gallup estimated that there were six million TM practitioners, five million practitioners of yoga, three million who practiced mysticism, and two million who practiced Eastern religions (quoted in Heelas, p. 17). Barry Kosmin and Seymour Lachman (1993) put the number of New Age practitioners at 20,000 in 1990 (p. 17). When that figure was updated in 2001, the number had reached 68,000. In the more recent study, researchers added separate figures for Buddhist (1,082,000), Hindu (766,000), Native American (103,000), Baha'i (84,000), Taoist (40,000), Eckankar (26,000), Rastafarian (11,000), Sikh (57,000), Wiccan (134,000), Druid (33,000), Santeria (22,000), Pagan (140,000), and Spiritualist (116,00)—most of which would be considered New Age practices. In total, then, this figure is just over two million (Kosmin and Mayer, 2001, p. 13).

But because the New Age is not connected to an institution and because New Agers practice multiple belief systems (JuBus, for instance, is a term for Jewish Buddhists), these figures do not tell us the story. Moreover, there are different levels of participation within the New Age—some people are full-timers who practice New Age professions and some people are "serious part-time[rs]" (Heelas, 1996, p. 118) who seek the New Age for a life crisis or a physical illness. Either way, these participants—particularly part-timers—are unlikely to acknowledge themselves as New Age practitioners on standard surveys.

Adding to definitional difficulties is the declining acceptance of the term "New Age." *New Age* magazine, the former bible of the movement, is now called *Body + Soul* and is part of Martha Stewart Living Omnimedia. The book category as a whole has been renamed Mind/Body/Spirit (Freitas, 2006), and expos are categorized in this way as well. While religion scholars see this negotiating for naming rights as part of a larger power struggle, I see it as simply marketing repositioning—an opportunity for marketers to present this material in a new light to a younger audience without the connotations associated with the baby boom.

No matter how the New Age or the Mind/Body/Spirit movement is defined, and regardless of how people define their relationship to it, the set of practices is ultimately about products. From seminars to spiritual adventure travel to outrageously expensive psychic cruises ($5,000 and up), it is about purchasing spirituality. There are no free churches to go to; there are paid-for lectures. There are no free Bibles to read; there are books to buy. According to Richard Cimino and Don Lattin (1999), this "fee-for-service spirituality of the 1990s reflects deeper changes...Designer religion, the whole search for a personal spirituality, is at its core a very practical approach to faith... [it] is about fixing something—whether it's your sex life, your soul, or your cardiovascular system" (p. 64), much of which quite frankly can't be fixed. New Age consumers end up on a hamster wheel, chasing after the next thing that will help them to improve themselves. Thus while the New Age might have been a deeper search for meaning in the 1960s, today it has become what Jennifer Rindfleish (2005) calls "the commodification of the self." Raising your consciousness to improve the world has devolved for many into straightforward self-care.[4] Within this system, in order to "get better," you must read the latest book or attend the next expo. This need is fed by authors who promise "balance," "enlightenment" or "ultimate consciousness," and when someone cannot attain that state, he or she continually remains on a "quest" because the promise of stability promised by New Agers can never be fulfilled (p. 357).

Paul Rush, a spokesman for the New York Open Center—a leading center for the New Age—has said, "Many [students] sample the practices and teachings, eventually find something that suits them, and develop a regular practice. Others become perpetual students, mixing practices and techniques from a wide range of traditions" (Cimino and Lattin, 1999, p. 63). This demonstrates the very essence of the commercial nature of the New Age—you buy it, you use it, you mix it up with something else, and eventually you throw it away. It is this consumeristic format that has led to the declining fortunes of the New Age. New Age purveyors perpetuate a market mentality toward spirituality because at bottom they are marketers. As marketers, they must continuously have something new to tell the consumer, what marketers call "new news." This new news is what drives new sales. The problem becomes: what happens when you're not new anymore? The following are some examples of how commercialism and the marketing life cycle have affected a sampling of New Age spokespeople and practices. Here I have selected Jack Canfield—arguably the most successful of the New Age writers; the rise and fall of psychics—one of the most popular segments of the New Age; and New Age expos—the product marketplace and "temple" of this spiritual practice.

Examples of the New Age in decline

Jack Canfield

Jack Canfield became a popular New Age writer and motivational speaker after the release of his *Chicken Soup for the Soul* book series. The mythology behind this series is that Jack and his co-author, Mark Victor Hansen, went to more than 100 publishers before they could find someone who would produce the book. The phenomenal success of the series, which has spawned countless brand extensions as well as new product lines like vitamins and a magazine, is now legend in the publishing business.

One day I received an e-mail from Marianne Williamson, another New Age author and motivational speaker, as part of her database through which she contacts her followers. Many of these communications tell of when Marianne will be speaking or of new books that she's written, though now and again they will include information about products and services from other New Agers. One such e-mail was for a teleconference with Jack Canfield. The sales pitch claimed that by signing up and participating in the teleconference, I would receive a $97 gift for free. Leading up to the event, I received several e-mails reminding me of the phone call. When the night finally came, the call began with an exuberant marketing guy reminding me to stay on the line for the entire phone call in order to get my "free gift."

The pre-recorded voice of Jack Canfield came on to talk about how you can't ever give up and to remind me of the *Chicken Soup* publishing mythology. This folksy talk continued for about 50 minutes. At the end came the sales pitch. Canfield was holding a one-week conference at the Ritz-Carlton in Las Vegas that cost $5,000 (this seemed especially pricey for Vegas in August!). But, because I was on the phone call, I could get it discounted to $2,995 including all food and accommodations, plus my spouse could come at half price. I had to be sure to sign up quickly because 25,000 people had signed up for the phone call and only half of the 400 seats for the event were still available.

The call went on to say that if I couldn't find the money, it's because I was blocked. I should borrow from my friends, borrow against my credit cards, and so on. (You may remember from Chapter 7 that this is the same technique that the Kabbalah Centre used in the BBC documentary.) As I continued to listen, there was something not quite right but I couldn't put my finger on it. Throughout the call the price of the event kept dropping. I was also told I would not have to pay all at once. I could put $900 down now, $900 on May 31, and $900 in June. That's when I realized what was wrong. I was listening to this recording in the middle of June—they hadn't hit their numbers! They were making a last-ditch effort with the help of another New Ager, Marianne Williamson, and an outdated sales pitch. It seems that Mr. Canfield is not the draw he used to be. Oh, and the $97 gift—a downloadable pdf file of Canfield's writings.[5]

Since that low point, Jack Canfield has been repositioned as a purveyor of *The Secret*, a book and DVD espousing an amalgam of New Age ideas. In the first few months of 2007, he appeared as a panelist (not a solo guest) on numerous talk shows including *Oprah* and *Montel Williams*. While *The Secret* was popular for several months (and the real secret is how this repackaging of New Age ideas was so popular in the first place), this latest New Age incarnation seems to suffer from a signature phenomenon of consumer culture—it was a short-lived fad. Jack Canfield is likely to have a similar fate—until he reinvents himself again.

Psychics

Many Americans believe that contact with the dead is possible. A 1996 Gallup poll concluded that "20 percent of the respondents believed the dead could contact the living. And another 22 percent admitted it might be possible" (Watt, 2001, p. F01). By 2001, the percentage of Americans who believed communication with the dead is possible had jumped to 28 percent (Barrett, 2001, p. D1). Just as there was increased interest in the *Left Behind* books after September 11, so, too, was there greater fascination with psychic mediums following that event.

Yet even before 2001 many scholars attributed the popularity of psychic mediums—people who profess to talk to the dead—to millennial fever. In the 1990s, as the anxiety and excitement about Y2K approached, more and more psychics began to appear on mainstream television. Once a subject of programming confined to infomercials like *Dionne Warwick's Psychic Network*, or telemarketing scams like *Miss Cleo's Psychic Reader Network*, mediums became regular and respected guests on talk shows throughout the day, appearing on syndicated programs like *Entertainment Tonight* and *The Montel Williams Show*, network news shows like *Today* and *Dateline*, cable outlets like CNN's *Larry King Live*, and even QVC, the all-day shopping network. These television appearances, like those of other talk show guests, were opportunities for them to promote their latest market venture, whether it was a book, a cruise, a television movie based on their life, or even a talk show of their own.

Psychics were some of the best-known faith brands, the most famous being John Edward, Sylvia Browne, and James van Praagh. These media-exposed, medium-savvy mediums are mini-industries whose wide-ranging products include best-selling books, private sessions, large lectures, their own talk shows, T-shirts, coffee mugs, and even a crystal ball. Unlike, say, the *Chicken Soup for the Soul* books, brand extensions cannot be developed from psychic books, so the psychics themselves became the product for promotion. Thus Sylvia Browne graces the cover on most of her books, as does John Edward on his.

Like Joel Osteen, these authors had very elaborate book tours. John Edward held mass events in auditoriums that hold upwards of 2,800 people and charged $41 a ticket (Carr, 2000). Similarly, Sylvia Browne held seminars through the Learning Annex. But unlike Joel, her events were not cheap. If you sat in the first five rows (where you are more likely to be "read"), you paid $199; rows 6 through 13 paid $149, rows 14 through 23 paid $99, rows 24 through 54 paid $69, and the nosebleed seats after row 55 cost $39 (Learning Annex, 2003).[6]

Psychics became the new hot television genre in the early 2000s. Sylvia Browne did not have her own show, but John Edward and James van Praagh did. Van Praagh first gained notice as a regular on a now-defunct show called *The Other Side*, an NBC program about paranormal phenomena (Rosenberg, 1994). His frequent appearances are what led producers to later create a show for him. *Beyond with James van Praagh* (the name of the psychic is fundamental to the promotion of the brand) was launched in syndication in September 2002. The show only lasted half a season, but it may have been the format of the show, rather than the content, that led to its demise. While van Praagh did readings, he also had numerous guests on with whom the audience was unfamiliar, so by not using van Praagh, the brand, to its fullest, the producers did not achieve the success they were looking for.

Crossing Over with John Edward, however, was incredibly successful. The show started as a late night half-hour show in July 2000 on the Sci-Fi Channel, a cable television network devoted to science fiction programming, particularly movies and older syndicated programming like *The Twilight Zone* and *Lost in Space*. The show was such a success that it became the network's signature program and was moved from 11 p.m. to back-to-back episodes in prime time. After two years on Sci-Fi, the show was moved into broadcast syndication in late August 2001 and ran in 180 markets at launch.[7] It was the most successful new daily syndicated show in 2001, drawing audiences of more than three million people (Gilatto and Stoynoff, 2002). At one point the show was so popular that the ticket request line was only open for three hours each month, and the waiting list to see Edward for a $300 half-hour private session was stopped when it became three years long.

But if a product is not updated or re-branded, consumers will move on to the next thing. And they did. John Edward tried to revamp his show by adding celebrity readings with stars like Roma Downey of *Touched by an Angel* and Anne Rice, but this didn't help retain his audience. Unlike Oprah, Edward cannot change the topic of his show on a daily basis. Day in and day out, it was simply Edward talking to dead people. The sameness of the content could not sustain an audience over time, and soon psychics all but disappeared from TV's prime time.

Psychics have not disappeared entirely; they are just no longer in vogue and their brands don't carry the weight they once did. Edward has been downgraded back to nighttime cable with a new show on WE: Women's Entertainment network, a third-tier network and sister station to Lifetime. Sylvia Browne continues to churn out books and has established a relationship with Montel Williams, on whose show she appears as a regular guest. Van Praagh has re-branded himself as a producer and is the creative talent behind *Ghost Whisperer*, a prime-time drama on CBS about a woman who communicates with spirits, but he himself is not in the public eye. Shows about psychic pets and psychic detectives—generic seers of unseeable events—are now just as popular as the real, name brand versions. In early 2007 John Edward made an appearance on *Oprah* with Allison DuBois, the medium on whom the NBC prime-time show *Medium* is based. However, this implied stamp of approval did not return psychics to superstar status.

New Age expos

In the 1990s I attended dozens of New Age expos. What I remember was being able to take workshops with "household names"—at a price of course— where the quality of a brand attached was palpable. Before doing research for this book, I hadn't attended such an expo in more than five years, and it was shocking to see the decline in the level of the talent attracted and the increase in commercialism now at these expos.

Attending a show in New York and one in the Midwest, I began to assess the changes that occurred. The usual smorgasbord of psychics, monks, and channelers were in evidence as were sellers of everything from soap to candles to crystals. The commercialism of it all hit me when, during a break from one of the conferences, I went for a walk at an upscale mall across from the exhibition hall and saw that one of the cart vendors in the mall was selling the exact same products as one of the vendors at the New Age conference.

While any expo is about selling, at a New Age conference there is also the expectation of finding out about the "next big thing" in spirituality. In the Midwest the Akashic records, a cosmic accounting of everything that has ever happened or ever will happen, seemed to be a hot item. In New York there were a lot of products that had to do with using computer technologies, which I thought was fairly odd given most New Agers' tendency to want to slow down their lives—something computers are not particularly known for. But these things were subtle undercurrents. Selling was the focus, and the products were diverse and in some cases suspect. One table was selling meditation DVDs that are supposed to be used to aid in losing weight, quitting smoking, and beating other addictions; but the man who created them looked to be 50 or more pounds overweight. Another booth had monks putting copper pyramids embedded with different-colored stones on people's heads. One of the more interesting booths was for Deep Lake Institute, a New Age condominium retreat in Michigan—clearly a product meant to appeal to the upscale boomer looking for a retirement retreat. But mostly there were booths for vitamins and health cures, products to serve an aging, fix-it minded New Age population.

Some of the obvious marketing techniques were in evidence at the expos. Most tables had a box with a slot cut out of the top and cards on which to fill out your name, address, phone number, and e-mail address. Filling out the card entered you into a drawing to win some type of prize—$250 worth of channeled readings or free health products, for example. For the marketer, of course, the prize was developing a database and being able to inform prospects about future events. Another tool—product sampling—was also widely used at the expos. Free demonstrations—a form of sampling—are very popular, particularly for services related to bodywork, like massages, or divination, like palm reading.

The majority of vendors gave a lecture or talk of some kind. The workshops were very thinly veiled sales pitches—more so in New York than the Midwest. In this way, they were very different from the 1990s, when workshops really were workshops, and you left feeling like you had learned something new, whether it was a new meditation technique or a way to access past lives, if you were inclined to believe in that. In the past, sales pitches were held off until the end of the lecture, but no more. One practitioner spent 45 minutes explaining his new computer technology that enabled him to program his computer to pray for you continuously—a service available for several hundred dollars per year. Another spoke of the many events scheduled at his New Age store. A third talked about all the clients she had "read" and how she had successfully cured their ills. All of the talks ended with the lecturer telling the audience his or her booth number in the exhibition hall.

What was obviously missing from these expos were large-scale producers of New Age products. Major book publishers of highly publicized (branded) authors did not attend, suggesting that they no longer see these expos as an effective marketing tool. I heard anecdotally, but could not confirm, that attendance at the New York event was down significantly from past years. Because the market is no longer there, neither are the big draws. It becomes a self-fulfilling cycle of decline. Thus, instead of Caroline Myss and Deepak Chopra, the shows are populated almost exclusively by product vendors, and most of these are small independents.

Overall, then, the trend at these expos was selling rather than actual service. At one of the expos many of the booths seemed to be pushing pseudo-Amway products. Yes, they were selling vitamins, but more importantly they were selling passersby on becoming their new distributors/salespeople. Compare that to when a New Age expo was the place to be revitalized and inspired, an experience that has all but disappeared. While there is still an aura of spirituality to some of the services being offered, there has been a decided shift away from soothing the spirit to healing the body—and charging good money for whatever form that might take.

The end of the New Age?

The New Age is not the hot topic it used to be. First, there has been a marked decline in the book category. Sylvia Browne, for example, continues to write books that appear on the New Age recommended lists, but these works are no longer a staple of the best-seller lists. Whereas in the 1980s the specialized Advice and How-to best-seller lists were essentially created for this category, now these books are in little evidence. Rachel Ray cookbooks and Dr. Oz diets, both of whom have been heavily promoted by Oprah, have replaced Oprah's guests from just a few years ago.

Second, the New Age moniker has fallen out of favor. *Body + Soul* has replaced *New Age* magazine, reflecting a more health-oriented spirituality. Moreover, we have seen the renaming of the book category and the expos to Mind/Body/Spirit. This is a repositioning of the New Age, which has connotations of being out of date and is overly associated with the aging baby boom generation. It is also an opportunity for marketers to expand their product lines to include a younger target audience, while at the same time not alienating their current boomer base.

While the name is less in evidence, the products are not; it's just that their emphasis is now on health and feeling good. Aromatherapy has become a product line for multiple mainstream corporations, from the Body Shop to Bath & Body Works (Lau, 2000). The spiritual aspect of aromatherapy has been stripped from these products, and it's now about smelling and feeling good rather than achieving spiritual change. Similarly, yoga is available at most health clubs throughout the country, but this has become more about toning your body than connecting with the divine. As for meditation, it has become so commonplace for stress relief, anger management, and enhanced personal productivity that its once-spiritual origins are almost unworthy of mention.

For some Mind/Body/Spirit seekers, products themselves become the conduit for expressing their spiritual beliefs. This market segment—and it is a *market* segment and not a spiritual practice per se—which embodies both the more traditional "save the earth" philosophies and the market orientation of the New Age, is the Lifestyles of Health and Sustainability (LOHAS) movement. LOHAS is defined as "a market segment focused on health and fitness, the environment, personal development, sustainable living, and social justice" (LOHAS, n.d.). This movement is a defining example of the marriage between belief system and the market. Called Cultural Creatives or Lohasians, consumers of LOHAS products claim that it is through their product choices—responsible investing, organic products, eco-tourism, green products, and so on—that they can change the world and themselves. Building on the work and spirituality movement of the 1990s, the purveyors of LOHAS products believe that business and spirituality can work in tandem, that being socially and environmentally responsible is not mutually excusive from business practices. The appeal of these products is evident in that they represent a market of almost $230 billion made up of close to 50 million U.S. adults. Currently LOHAS has more recognition in the business-to-business segment than in the consumer arena. We will have to wait to see if this becomes integrated more fully into the re-branding of the New Age for the consumer market.

Because of market segments like LOHAS and the renaming of the movement, it is unlikely that the New Age will completely disappear or die off anytime soon. There is way too much money to be made. Middle-aged boomers are the major purchasers of these products and services, and as long as these folks find value in them—and every indication is that they do—they will continue to be produced.[8] As we saw in Chapter 3, movies with New Age themes have been increasing in appeal. Another way that New Age product purveyors have been growing is through creating inventive ways to combine their products and services with other faiths to expand their appeal. One of the latest examples of syncretism to reach the market is Christian yoga. Instead of Eastern mantras, reciting "Yahwey" is suggested (Cullen, 2005). Again, this is clever marketing because it taps into the fastest growing segment in the religious marketplace.

Even as these products and services may endure, what is happening to the spirituality they are meant to nurture? Much of the spending on the New Age is for products that are no longer connected to their spiritual roots. An average yoga center is estimated to generate $30,000 a week (Lau, 2000, p. 1) and aromatherapy products rake in $300 to $500 million per year with an annual growth rate of 30 percent (p. 34). But these are produced by Bath & Body Works, not a Buddhist meditation center. As Jeremy Carrette and Richard King (2005) say in their book *Selling Spirituality*, the spiritual has been overtaken by the market. Spiritual practice is increasingly being "fundamentally shaped by economic ideology" with the consequence being that "spirituality is appropriated for the market instead of offering a countervailing social force to the ethos and values of the business world" (p. 126). This is most evident in the New Age, where the spirit has been taken out of spirituality. Where in the New Age is there a place for the healing of the soul beyond the healing of body and mind?

Is there a lesson in the New Age for the more established religious institutions? Yes and no. The downfall of the New Age is that much of it was based on the prediction of the Harmonic Convergence—the Age of Aquarius—that was supposed to materialize in the late 1980s. When that didn't occur, many adherents lost faith in the movement even while products and services around the New Age continued to thrive and do well. As people became increasingly disappointed, they moved on to other things. It is likely that as other religious brands become more market driven, they will follow in the footsteps of the New Age movement. Just as New Agers were disappointed that there was no Age of Aquarius, so, too, the congregant who waits for prosperity to manifest is going to seek out pastimes that are more in line with his reality if he finds, after years of praying, that he is still driving a beat-up Chevy and not the Beemer that the pastor is driving. Marketing doesn't work if you don't deliver on your product promise. So yes, it is very possible that we will see declines in Christianity, Kabbalah, and other faith brands that preach prosperity (and take your money in return) as people become disillusioned.

Where these traditional institutions differ from the New Age, however, is through the stability and relationships they engender. The New Age doesn't have a church. It doesn't have a place where people can make connections. Because it is exclusively a marketed product, it is driven to continually produce the next big thing. If traditional faiths can maintain their product, even while promoting their new packaging, they can use the best of marketing to remain relevant within the culture.

Conclusion

Marketing is a necessary evil—even for religion. In an article in *USA Today*, G. Jeffrey MacDonald describes the growth of religious marketing service companies and the many products they use to entice people back to church. One church in Virginia, for example, uses an ice cream truck. Other churches use traditional advertising on television and billboards, or they use marketing premiums like Frisbees and water bottles with the church's contact information and logo on them. Newer offerings are free coffee and free computer access. These marketing ideas may sound silly on the surface, but the reality is that they work. Tens of thousands of congregations are using packaged marketing programs to increase awareness. In 2005 just one religious marketing company, Outreach, "helped churches send out 60 million invitations to worship services or special events, up from 1 million in 1996" (MacDonald, 2005, p. D4).

Marketing in and of itself is not the issue. Evangelizing *is* marketing. People are lured to religion, or any other product or service, with the promise of something in return.

> While religious ideologies often provide non-material rationales for conversion in their various promotions of brotherhood, equality, and salvation, material incentives have frequently proven essential in order to motivate converts and adherents to their missions and messages. Even while they ostensibly deplore extreme wealth, material greed, and the love of things rather than people, missionaries have nevertheless found it necessary to appeal to the same "base" materialist motives as other marketers in order to mobilize masses of followers.
>
> (Belk, 2000, p. 337)

It is the bounties of the material world that get people in the door to explore a world unknown. Evangelicals promise abundance as the product of exchange for giving your life to Jesus. Oprah promises that you'll live your best life. Alpha offers a good meal and fellowship.

Ultimately the marketer must deliver on its promise, which is something that most religion providers have been unable to do, so they do a little tap dance instead. They can't deliver bonuses—all they can really do is encourage people to ask for them. They can't deliver peace—but they give people a feel-good moment while rhapsodizing about it. In doing this, religious marketers have made their products ones that consumers want, not necessarily what they need. Some may justify this by saying that they are adapting to the culture in which religion exists. This is true when the goal is just to get people through the door. It's when you need to get them to stay that the issue occurs. It is easy to lure people in with music and happy faces. The problem is, life isn't like that all the time. Eventually people are going to feel disappointed and betrayed—but that doesn't mean marketing is the problem.

Throughout this book I have suggested that religion and marketing have a symbiotic relationship, with each side having something to teach the other. Religion can use marketing to perpetuate itself within a commercial culture. Commodity goods can harness the power of evangelizing. There is a point, however, where the marriage becomes incestuous. In a May 2004 issue of *Time* magazine there was an article called, "Yo, Where's My Bible?" It looked at an assortment of religious objects and icons within the popular culture, including *Refuel*, which is one of the glossy teen Bibles we looked at in Chapter 3. The article quotes the brand manager for its publisher, Thomas Nelson, as saying, "The main criticism we get is that we have trivialized scripture by putting images of girls on the same page...But if Jesus was here today, he'd be hanging out at the Clinique booth with teen girls. He went where the people were, and that's the message of the Bible—it's about understanding the connection between the Bible and the world we live in" (Novack, 2004, p. 85). Okay, but where do you draw the line? More precisely, where would Jesus draw the line? At a disco? At a strip club? People go to these places, too. There's a reason why Jesus flipped over the tables when the Pharisees tried to turn his church into a marketplace—he was furious at the commercialism and the idolatry of the market. Religion cannot become so of the market that it loses its unique selling proposition: its ability to raise us *above* the market. The importance of this is best understood when we evaluate how material culture cannot make us happy, no matter what marketers tell us. In studies done around the world, researchers have found that:

> [P]eople with predominantly materialistic values—those who believe happiness rests in the next car, CD, toy, or pair of shoes are actually less happy than their neighbors...[and] researchers have found no difference in the (collective) happiness of people in wealthy countries and of people in less wealthy countries whose basic needs are being met.
>
> (Linn, 2004, p. 184)

This research has important ramifications for religion. If it no longer offers what it does best, it will be to its own (and to people's) detriment.

That doesn't mean we should walk away from this discussion feeling cynical about religion. There are plenty of churches that are doing good works and continuing the social gospel. Jim Wallis, author of *God's Politics* (2005), is a well-known example of that and there are thousands of lesser-known and lesser-honored pastors, rabbis, and imams who are looking beyond their personal interests to serve the broader community. Nor is it the intent of this book to convey the idea that religious seekers are spiritual dupes. They are not. When people make decisions about their truth systems, they are not flippant about their choices.

> While much in consumer culture may well be transient, ephemeral, inconsequential, this does not necessarily mean that those qualities feature prominently, let alone exclusively, in the religious decisions confronted in the course of accomplishing individual self-identities... "switchers" who move from one denomination to another do so on the basis of spiritual and moral choice rather than for more cynical reasons; it is religious change, sometimes conversion, that prompts such moves.
>
> (Lyon, 2000, p. 77)

However, we also know that many of these decisions are made at a point of trial in someone's life. At the time of a death or the dissolution of a marriage, a person is not likely to be thinking clearly and may be more vulnerable to marketing suggestions.

But no matter what a person believes about religion, it is impossible to miss the spiritual crisis in America—even if the evangelicals say it does not exist. How can we be bombarded day after day with messages about the importance of money, material goods, and individuality and not believe it's true? It is a simple fact of marketing that you will never hear, "You are fabulous just the way you are." If marketers told you that, you would never need to go out and buy their product. On top of this, we are constantly told—particularly Americans—that if we do not reach a certain level of achievement, it is our own fault. These messages get replayed to us over and over again. But these messages have it all wrong. As Mother Theresa said, "We are not here to be successful. We are here to be faithful." That faithfulness—whether your belief system is spiritual or not—has traditionally been the means for us to step out of our culture.

We are less able to do this because all products—religious and otherwise—are presented to us as quick and easy fixes. The reality is that most things—that is, most valuable things—are not quickly and easily achieved. Moreover, religion isn't supposed to be comfortable, and it is through discomfort that we find new parts of ourselves. "Consumers want everything now, and they want it as inexpensively as possible," says sociologist Robert Wuthnow. "This is the *passivity* problem. People who watch television programs about angels can sit back and somehow 'feel spiritual' without having to do anything. The same is true of people who 'get saved' at a revival meeting: after saying a short prayer, they are home free" (2003, p. 44). As with most things in life, though, you get out of it what you put into it. Faith is built on consistency over the long term and lots of hard work.

The truth of this was brought home for me during the writing of this book, when five girls were wounded and another five were shot to death by a deranged killer while they were sitting in a one-room schoolhouse in a small Amish community in Pennsylvania. While the event itself was beyond awful, the response of the community was awe-inspiring. The Amish rallied together to grieve; within days, they forgave the man who perpetrated this terrible act and they leveled the school building so as to turn it into a pasture and to create closure for the community. That such forgiveness and caring could come out of such a horrible event confirms that faith is not easy, but it is valuable—perhaps priceless.

Life becomes about the myths we tell ourselves. Ultimately the decision must be made about who you believe to be the better storyteller—religion or the market. Or, you may decide that it can be both. Brand cults suggested that products could be religion; so now faith brands present the idea that religions can be products. We have yet to see what this means to our perception of and engagement with our various faiths. One scholar has gone so far as to say that "consumerism has become a predominant characteristic of American religion" (Sargeant, 2000, p. 1). However, it doesn't have to be the *defining* characteristic. It can be a characteristic means for bringing people to faith, without becoming the faith itself.

Notes

1 Introduction

1 Even after the film opened publicity ran for months, which is an unusual course of events for a Hollywood film. Stories subsequent to the film's release focused on audiences' response to the film. In particular, news stories centered around the idea that people viewed the film not so much as entertainment but as a religious experience. There were several reports of audience members having heart attacks; one man confessed to a murder he had committed years ago; still others were moved to affirm or reaffirm their faith.

2 A DVD called *Church Resource* is still being sold today so that churches can continue to use the film as a teaching tool.

3 The need to compete is credited by many scholars for keeping secularization at bay in the United States. The prevailing wisdom until recently was that industrialized societies would become less religious with the advent of science and technology, and while that has been true in most countries around the world, it has not been the case in the United States. This is known as supply-side religion. Based in economics, this theory posits that the simple fact that there are so many religious options competing for membership makes Americans more religious. While more than 90 percent of Americans claim at least a belief in a higher power, statistics put religious belief in other industrialized countries below 50 percent and regular church attendance at approximately 20 percent. Supply-side religion and rational choice theory will be discussed more fully in Chapter 2.

4 I am limiting my discussion to the purchase of products and services and will not include contributions to churches or tithing, which Giving USA Foundation estimated to be $88 billion in 2004 (www.findarticles.com/p/articles/mi_m1058/is_14_122/ai_n14839665), though this number suggests an enthusiastic willingness to pay for, or at least support, religion.

5 The exception to this is Islam, which has increased significantly over the last several decades.

6 Young children, who have traditionally been off limits to marketers for ethical reasons, have now become fair game and are widely pursued by packaged goods marketers, particularly the makers of snack foods and sugar-laden cereals. See Schor (2004).

2 The changing religious marketplace

1 Latin America is an important growth area for the Catholic Church, though this is changing due to the booming growth in evangelical and neo-Pentecostal movements there.

2 The "old paradigm" contains additional elements beyond the idea that religion will inevitably disappear. These include: (1) religion is fake and detrimental; (2) religion is an "epiphenomenon…[religion] was but a reflection of more fundamental social phenomena"; (3) religion is psychological; and (4) monopoly religion is preferred over religious pluralism (Stark and Finke, 2000). While all of these are important, I am limiting my discussion to those that have the greatest impact on marketing religion.

3 Since the FCC could not decide who among many to give the airtime to, they left that in the hands of the Federal Council of Churches, who favored their member churches, "respectable" Protestant denominations. Televangelism grew out of a need to produce programs that listeners would pay for, which will be discussed further in Chapter 6.

4 This particular regulation is noted by a number of scholars as having had a considerable impact on religious practice (Berthrong, 1999; Porterfield, 2001; Roof, 1993b).

5 Supply-side theory and rational choice theory are often bandied about as one and the same thing. Warner (1997) says while they are not the same thing, there is an affinity between the two. "Religious producers and consumers act rationally, and, given the inefficiency of monopoly, religion flourishes the more choice is available…as I understand the new paradigm, rational choice theories contribute to it but do not define or constitute it" (p. 196).

6 Hotelling's Law, an economic theory, explains how increasing competition can, however, lead to a decrease in diversity. As more and more churches compete for the same audience, it is likely that there will be an increasing similarity in the product that they offer. Competitors vying for the same customers without easy access to alternatives will produce similar products. The more fierce the competition, the more excessive sameness of product which is why this is also know as Hotelling's Law of Excessive Sameness.

7 Others have argued against this theory saying that a combination of supply side and demand side—an ecological approach—would be more encompassing (Montgomery, 2003).

8 See Wuthnow (1998) *After Heaven: Spirituality in America Since the 1950s* for an in-depth look into the new ways that Americans search for the sacred.

9 Marler and Hadaway (2002) stated that while they could not conclude that Americans were more spiritual and less religious, they could argue that religion and spirituality were not mutually exclusive. However, given the lack of church attendance, it's logical to wonder how Americans are defining religion.

10 Ted Haggart of course had his own encounter with salvation in 2006, including reported drug use and homosexual activities. This is discussed in Chapter 8.

11 The importance of small groups was not lost on the pastors of the megachurches, who readily use these gatherings to solidify commitment.

12 In Chapter 4, I will discuss brand communities, groups that arise from individual's affinity with a particular product. Much of the same fulfillment garnished from support groups exist within these communities.

13 Movies, books, and music will be discussed in the next chapter when I address how the structure of the religious products industry is changing. Televangelism is covered in Chapter 6.

14 A limited number of channels had been developed in the 1970s, like HBO and CNN, but the vast majority of programming did not become available until the 1980s.

15 Terri Schiavo was a Florida woman who had been diagnosed as being in a persistent vegetative state and had been institutionalized for 15 years. She was being kept alive through the use of a feeding tube. Her husband, Michael, wanted to remove the tube and allow her to die. Her family, devout Catholics, fought Mr. Schiavo with the support of the Christian Right, the governor of Florida (President Bush's brother), the Congress, and the president. The fight over the removal of Ms. Schiavo's feeding tube became a media circus with right-to-life supporters holding vigil outside the nursing home where Terri was living. The affair reached its peak when Congress wrote a bill whose sole purpose was to prevent the removal of Terri's feeding tube. Dramatically, President Bush flew back from vacation at his Texas ranch to sign the bill. But after much legal maneuvering, Michael Schiavo was given the right to remove his wife's feeding tube against the objections of well-funded Christian conservatives and the government of the United States (Eisenberg, 2005).

16 A note here, on what religious conservatives are watching versus what is available to them. Like any consumer group they are not all alike and they do not all have the same tastes. Simmons Research estimates that religious conservatives make up 21 percent of the population, which makes them a sizable audience. There is no reason to assume that they would all watch Fox News and only listen to right-wing radio, and they don't. According to Simmons research, while Pax (now Ion) was unsurprisingly the number one network watched by this group, CBS was third on the list and that was because of the heavy viewership of soap operas. "Religious conservatives may preach God-fearing, churchgoing conservative values as their core, fundamental beliefs, but they are just as likely to watch violent and sexually provocative programming as the average viewer" (Mandese, 2002, p. 10).

3 The business of religion

1 Producing multiple products from a single branded line is what publishers today call a platform, and it is the holy grail of publishing. Another good example of this is the *Chicken Soup for the Soul* series, which was one overriding idea that turned into multiple products to be sold to multiple target audiences.

2 Major publishers are described in the following section.

3 A number of booksellers I spoke with said that the show had very low attendance in comparison to previous years. In fairness, they attributed it to the fact that most retailers are in the south and east, making the show's Denver location (for the second year in a row) less than optimum.

4 HarperCollins also cashed in by releasing 150 new *Narnia* and/or C. S. Lewis titles in the wake of the film's success (Steinmetz, 2006).

5 Big Idea now produces *3-2-1 Penguins* and *Larry Boy: The Cartoon Adventures* in addition to *Veggie Tales*. These shows are part of Qubo, which is NBC's Saturday morning children's lineup of shows (www.qubo.com). Big Idea also has a new *Veggie Tales* movie planned for 2008.

6 Max Lucado's books have appeared on numerous best-seller lists, including those of the *New York Times* Book Review. According to the Tyndale Web site, "Aside from hardcover books, Lucado's writings have also been published as children's books, videos, CD-ROMs, DVDs, music CDs, mass paperback booklets, apparel, giftware, bookmarks, calendars, study Bibles, workbooks, curricula, and plush

products. In spring 2003, Hallmark/Dayspring Cards launched a new gift card line featuring excerpts from Lucado's writings—and has already sold more than one million cards" (http://www.tyndale.com/authors/bio.asp?code=388).

7 Hybels and Warren are likely distancing themselves from Schuller because he is considered too loose in his doctrine.

8 As mentioned there are thousands of consulting companies, big and small, and it would be impossible to cover them all here. However, it is worth noting one of the largest, best-known, and therefore most influential consultancies in the Christian arena is the Barna Group. As its Web site states, the company's mission is "to provide leadership and unique, strategic information and resources that help facilitate spiritual transformation in America" (www.barna. org). The company started as a marketing research firm for primarily Christian ministries and nonprofit organizations in the mid-1980s. In 2004 the company reorganized to provide more strategic direction to clients; in other words, they became consultants. The resources of the Barna Group are vast, with a plethora of audio, film, and resource materials available to its clients and others. George Barna, the company's founder, is a popular speaker at conferences and conventions, including large events like the CBA. Even while this organization is religiously focused, it is very corporate in it presentation. This company is similar to Gallup in that it produces extensive empirical research and by and large takes a balanced view of the statistics, even while having a religious agenda.

4 Branding faith

1 The amount of time that teenagers in the United States spend working versus their international counterparts is significant. "Today, 55 percent of American high school seniors labor more than three hours a day, while only 27 percent of foreign students report that they work at all" (p. 16). This raises two important concerns: (1) students have less time to do their homework, which studies have shown can lead to depression (never mind what it is doing to Americans' ability to compete in the world market), and (2) Americans get caught younger and younger in the cycle of needing to work to get the "right brand," perpetuating the sense of never having enough and reinforcing their judgments of themselves and others based on brands rather than on personal character.

2 An example of this is explained in detail in Chapter 6 on the new televangelists, wherein the secular aspects of Joel Osteen and the sacred aspects of Oprah Winfrey are described.

3 External factors such as personal crisis may be involved here. However, the decision is far more personal than what is involved for most consumer product decisions.

4 There is dispute as to whether it was Atkin or Ragas and Bueno who were the first to develop this idea. Based on Atkin's work appearing in *Forbes* before the Ragas and Bueno book, I am crediting the concept to Atkin.

5 Here, do not confuse religion's going to war with other products as religion and marketing being at war. What is meant here is marketplace competition, not the culture war.

5 The course to God

1 For more information about megachurches, see Chapter 8. See also Hartford Institute for Religion Research (http://hirr.hartsem.edu/).

2 Warren stresses that the book is not about church growth but church health. In *Rick Warren and the Purpose That Drives Him*, an overly effusive book written by a Saddleback member, Warren is quoted as saying, "[Purpose Driven] has *nothing* to do with the size of your church. There are little, tiny purpose-driven churches, medium-sized churches, large churches and megachurches...The vast majority of purpose-driven churches have 100 people" (Abanes, 2005, p. 26).

3 "Corporate mission statements...are the operational, ethical, and financial guiding lights of companies. They are not simply mottoes or slogans; they articulate the goals, dreams, behavior, culture, and strategies of companies" (Jones and Kahaner, 1995, p. ix).

4 These groups are similar to the Alpha Course described in this chapter. Like Alpha, Purpose Driven Ministries provides materials including DVDs of Warren teaching the lessons. Small Group series include: "What on Earth Am I Here For?" "You Were Planned for God's Pleasure," and "You were Formed for God's Family," among others.

5 The teachings from these seminars became the basis for *The Purpose Driven Church*.

6 I was unable to find separate verification for this quote.

7 Interestingly, in a recent Barna poll (Barna Group, 2006) 72 percent of Americans say they have never heard of Rick Warren and 63 percent of born-again Christians hadn't heard of him either. Barna did not ask if they knew of Purpose Driven, which I suspect would have generated higher numbers.

8 Willow Creek also generates revenue from its bookstore ($3.2 million), coffee shop and restaurants ($2.5 million), auto repair service ($1 million), and summer camp ($300,000)—all of this beyond church contributions that exceed $23 million annually (*BusinessWeek*, 2005, p. 84).

9 The exact date seems to be in dispute. Some sources say 1973, some say 1977.

10 I asked Kimberly Reeve (personal interview, 2006), the director of marketing for Alpha, about the number of people who do their own lectures as opposed to using the tapes. "There are not that many people who do their own lectures because it is so time consuming," she said. "But obviously they can be very effective; [in] the course that I went through the person did their own lectures and because they are using their own life experiences it can obviously be very powerful. What a lot of churches do is they have a senior pastor do one or two lectures, but that's about it." This happened in one of the courses I attended. In the other I attended, they used the DVD. In addition to the DVDs being less time-consuming, presenting the material in this way allows for a consistent message.

11 Denominations include: United Methodist, Episcopal, Lutheran, Presbyterian, Assemblies of God, Vineyard, Roman Catholic, American Baptist, Evangelical Covenant, Baptist, Foursquare Gospel, Christian Reformed, United Church of Christ, Evangelical Free, Southern Baptist, Anglican, Disciples of Christ, Salvation Army, Nazarene, Mennonite, Independent, Congregational, Pentecostal.

12 These e-mails are opt-in only and consist primarily of people who have ordered Alpha materials.

13 For more information, see www.alphaforschools.org.

14 The materials cost does not cover the work that Alpha does, according to Reeve.

15 The people I spoke with at one of the courses I attended did not have such training before they ran the course.

16 All names are changed.

17 Many people take the course multiple times and at multiple locales. Because the information is presented via taped lecture, the Alpha course is consistent. It becomes a brand that seekers can trust, or as one Alpha host put it, "It's kind of like McDonald's...You know what you're going to get" (McCabe, 2002, p. 8).

6 The new televangelists

1 Lakewood has successfully sued to protect "Joel Osteen" as a trademark, demonstrating both the legal acceptance and value of the name as a brand.

2 Lakewood does have a Web site (www.lakewood.cc) that has recently been redesigned to essentially mirror the Joel Osteen site.

3 *Joel Osteen* (the television program) is now widely distributed, the extent of which will be discussed in this chapter.

4 Some reports put the number of congregants at 15,000 but the most consistent figure is 6,000.

5 While Joel has been accused of not mentioning Satan, this is not true. He calls the evil force in the world "the Enemy," which no one could mistake for being anything other than Satan. Alternatively, while he says that he does not preach about money, that's not true either. In an interview with *Time* magazine, Joel said, "I don't think I've ever preached a sermon about money...Does God want us to be rich?" he asks. "When I hear that word rich, I think people say, 'Well, he's preaching that everybody's going to be a millionaire.' I don't think that's it." Rather, he explains, "I preach that anybody can improve their lives. I think God wants us to be prosperous. I think he wants us to be happy. To me, you need to have money to pay your bills. I think God wants us to send our kids to college. I think he wants us to be a blessing to other people. But I don't think I'd say God wants us to be rich. It's all relative, isn't it?" (Van Biema and Chu, 2006, p. 53). However, Joel prays that people will have wealth and favor in their jobs which is preaching about finances, so it seems to be a matter of semantics.

6 The station was sold in November 2006 (Hall, 2006).

7 Note here again the emphasis on prosperity though that word is not used.

8 Their first date was at the Compaq Center—the new home of Lakewood—and Victoria got beer spilled all over her.

9 Lakewood made a video of the Madison Square Garden event. The presentation from Time Warner was edited out of the video as was the passing of the buckets.

10 Media people gauge the health of a publication by its newsstand sales. Whereas a yearly subscription of a publication might be $12 for 12 issues, a single copy can cost $3 to $5. At that price, people are more committed to actually reading the publication.

11 A version of this show has been developed for a prime-time reality series, Oprah's first venture into regular prime-time programming (Wyatt, 2006, p. B9).

12 These ideas relate to how Americans perceive spirituality. In a 2006 *Time* poll, "61% [of Americans] believed that God wants people to be prosperous. And 31%...agreed that if you give your money to God, God will bless you with more money" (Van Biema and Chu, 2006, p. 50).

13 Dr. Robin Smith has joined Oprah's group of "friends" who periodically appear on the show. Oprah's friends are also part of her new radio lineup, *Oprah & Friends*, on XM, which includes regulars from her TV show including Smith, Dr. Mehmet Oz, Marianne Williamson, Bob Greene (formerly Oprah's personal trainer), and her best friend Gayle King, among others.

14 Spiritual content is not limited to the television show. It is also included in *O, The Oprah Magazine* and on Oprah.com. Each issue has a theme such as faith, transformation, happiness, or love: the real thing. Based on these themes, the magazine has a page of inspirational quotes, a mission calendar of how to implement the theme, and a work page where readers can answer questions about their lives based on the theme. Oprah.com has Oprah's Angel Network, a community area with bulletin boards, and chat rooms dedicated to "self and spirit."

15 Oprah has had more than one mishap in her selection of authors. The first was when she chose *The Corrections* by Jonathan Franzen as a book club selection. Franzen refused to appear on the show, in part because he was upset about the Oprah book club logo being placed on his book. The second, and more frenzied, snafu occurred when James Frey's addiction memoir, *A Million Little Pieces*, was exposed to be fiction. Oprah had chosen this work to be a book club selection and dedicated an entire show to discussing it with the author because she and her staff had been so moved by it. After the show, The Smoking Gun Web site began investigating Mr. Frey and found numerous inconsistencies in the work. Oprah brought Mr. Frey back on the show, along with his editor, so that he could explain why he lied (he blamed it on his addictive personality) and she could chastise him—and, to a certain extent, the publishing industry—in no uncertain terms.

7 Kabbalah: marketing designer spirituality

1 Moses Cordovero was another popular kabbalist in Safed, but it is Luria's teachings that were most widely practiced.

2 The Kabbalah Centre compares this to the big bang theory of creation; it is one of many concepts they compare to modern-day science.

3 Kabbalah.com claims that the Kabbalah Centre was founded in 1922 by Rabbi Ashlag in Jerusalem, though this ancestry seems to be in dispute (Beam, 2002, p. C1). (Berg did teach Kabbalah in Israel in the late 1960s.) The Kabbalah Centres in the United States were reportedly not founded until the early 1970s (Ellin, 2004; Udovitch, 2005).

4 It has been reported that the Kabbalah Centre uses ghostwriters for some of its books. While there is no way to confirm this, it seems quite possible given how prolific the Berg brothers are (Udovitch, 2005).

What may support this is something Yehuda Berg said. "We go directly to the source, directly to the Zohar. We don't claim to be teachers, we don't even—we don't care if anyone respects us or not. Our job is to bring content to people. Content that wasn't—that wasn't there before. Nothing we do comes from our brain" (ABC News, 2005). This sounds very similar to Rick Warren's description of *The Purpose Driven Life*.

5 While this view of sharing is not part of traditional Judaism, sharing itself is. Charity, or *tzedakah*, is intended as a means of spreading the wealth to those less fortunate. Proselytizing, on the other hand, is verboten in the Jewish tradition. Jews believe that you are born whatever religion you are born, because that is what you need to be in order to achieve your *tikkun*, or correction. The Kabbalah Centre gets around this by claiming that they are not a religion and so are not trying to convert anyone.

6 According to the 2005 IRS 990 form, the tax information that 501c3 tax exempt institutions must file, the Kabbalah Centre's related nonprofit entities are: Kabbalah Centre International, Inc., Kabbalah Centres of United States,

Inc., Kabbalah Centres of Florida, Inc., Kabbalah Centres of New York, Inc., Research Center of Kabbalah (also in NY), and Spirituality for Kids.

7 Reportedly a number of Hollywood elite, including Britney Spears and Jerry Hall, left the Centre due to repeated requests to tithe and to ask others to do the same.

8 I have not heard of anyone getting their money back, but the Centre did readily honor the half-price repeat cost. This is in part due to the Centre's strong suggestion that students take this class once a year.

9 It is hard to determine exact numbers as the Kabbalah Centre would not release this information. Also, the Kabbalah Centre is known for "papering" the room with current students to make the place look crowded. Therefore, when attending classes, it was impossible to know who is a real student and who is a volunteer. What I do know is that by the third week, there were about half the number of people in the room as there was on the first night.

10 The 10-week course turned out to contain less information than the one-day class. In the one-day class I had been given course materials in a loose-leaf notebook, a card with the red string, and a tape of the Ana Be Koach, a daily prayer used for cleansing the body. None of this was given out in the 10-week course, which I took two years after the first. I can only guess that the Centre decided to stop giving things away for free.

11 If you miss the class, you get the CD for free. If you are at the class, you are charged $5 for the CD.

12 The red string is in no way tied (forgive the pun) to traditional Kabbalah. There are some limited mentions of tying objects around the wrist in the Talmud to ward off the evil eye, but this is not connected to Rachel or a red string. The one place where participating in this practice is mentioned actually prohibits the practice, calling it superstitious and idol worship (Lopiansky, 2004).

13 Interestingly, these last two questions appear on almost every page of the Web site. This would suggest that these issues are the biggest stumbling block to potential prospects pursuing Kabbalah. If the Centre can alleviate that fear from the beginning, it opens up the product to the wider audience they want to attract.

14 In years past, the centers held open houses, but these were replaced with hour-long free introductory classes once a month. While the free introductory classes are fairly bare bones, the open houses are quite elaborate events. (See the preface of this book for a description of an open house.) The open houses began again in early 2007.

15 Whiles students weren't forced to do this, what I saw was that those who spoke Hebrew and/or kept the Sabbath were part of the "inner circle."

16 Much like Rick Warren has adopted Rwanda, the Kabbalah Centre has "adopted" Malawi (see www.Kabbalah.com and raisingmalawi.org).

17 The first time I took a class at the Centre, they showed a video explaining the powers of the Kabbalah Water. I was not shown the video on subsequent visits.

18 The Centre has begun to provide scholarships and they promote this on their Web site and in their classes. They are limited in number and until recently have not been heavily promoted.

19 Name is changed to protect identity.

20 See raisingmalawi.org.

8 The politics of faith brands

1 Most Americans do not want to see *Roe v. Wade* overturned. However the majority of Americans (73 percent) would like some restrictions, such as parental consent for women under 18 (Pew Forum on Relgion and Public Life, n.d.).

2 In the same article an unnamed White House source claims that the president is not on a first-name basis with Haggard. However, it is hard to see this as anything but spin. As reported in *Harper's Magazine* in 2005, "Pastor Ted [Haggard]...talks to President George W. Bush or his advisors every Monday" (Sharlet and Hedges, 2005, p. 42). Weekly phone calls were also noted in Kuo's book (2006, p. 171).

3 The Catholic church is also growing, but this is due to a change in demographics rather than any marketing initiative. The significant growth in the Hispanic population in primarily southern and western regions of the United States has contributed to a 16.2 percent increase in this denomination.

4 Crisis pregnancy centers are pro-life centers that dissuade women from getting abortions.

5 This type of conservative also voted to put Bush into the Texas governor's mansion.

6 James Dobson continues to be an important political figure, even with the recent changes in Congress. He controls a substantial mailing list, reportedly with a million names, and has a huge following from his radio show. Dick Armey, the former House majority leader, was quoted as saying, "It's painful to have him angry at you...He responds in a manner that's damaging. You know, he'll say, 'I'm leaving, and I promise you, I'm taking a lot of people with me.' Well, elected officials know what that means...I think we call it a Dobson's choice" (Miller, 2006, p. 37).

7 While there are multiple issues that constitute the Christian right agenda, I have opted to focus here on abortion as it has consistently been a topic of debate. This is in no way meant to minimize the issues of gay marriage, stem cell research, right to life, and the other issues that continue to divide the electorate.

8 There was initially some confusion when this Web site was launched in 2001 as to whether it was actually being run by the White House. It is not. The organization claims that three million people come to its site on a daily basis to pray for the president.

9 The Silver Ring Thing (SRT) received funding through an HHS earmark contained in the 2003 omnibus appropriations bill, not through the CCF. SRT received $700,000 in 2003 (SIECUS, 2003), with additional funding of more than $200,000 over the next few years (see www.whitehouse.gov/omb).

10 In the wake of the exposure of Janet Jackson's bare breast during the prime-time broadcast of the 2004 Super Bowl, the FCC significantly increased its indecency fines against broadcasters.

11 Conservative Republicans were inserted into top ranking positions at PBS and the Corporation for Public Broadcasting in order the change the tone of the Public Broadcasting System. Several liberal voices, notably Bill Moyers, quickly disappeared after these administrative changes. In early 2007 Moyers came out of "retirement" and returned to PBS after some of the more conservative administrators had left CPB.

12 Notable here was Viacom's decision to air the CBS miniseries *The Reagans* on Showtime, their sister pay cable channel. This was done in response to reported pressure from Republicans who did not like the miniseries's portrayal of the former president and first lady.

9 Has religious marketing gone too far?

1 According to the Pluralism Project at Harvard, a site that aggregates multiple data sources, there are somewhere between 5.6 and 6.2 million Jews in America (Statistics by Tradition, http://www.pluralism.org/resources/statistics/tradition.php#Judaism).

2 In this section, "New Age" is used to describe this group of spiritual practices because of this term's acceptance over the last several decades. That name is in flux, however, which will be discussed shortly.

3 Since we know from Chapter 3 that books are the largest area of spiritual commerce, this is an appropriate source for evaluating the elements of the New Age.

4 A growing movement within Mind/Body/Spirit is the LOHAS movement, which believes that through conscious product purchases you can change yourself and the world. This will be discussed more fully later in this chapter.

5 While some scholars (Albanese, 1992; Mears and Ellison, 2000) have asserted that it is the less affluent and younger (Gen X, Gen Y) groups that are purchasing New Age products, this may be true when it comes to attending expos and buying books and paraphernalia, but seminars such as these are far beyond the means of these cohorts.

6 John Edward and Sylvia Browne are still touring (and James van Praagh is still going on cruises). A recent viewing of their sites showed that John Edward is now charging $175 a ticket and Sylvia Browne is charging $50 or $75 for a ticket. Even at these prices, John Edward (I couldn't verify Sylvia Browne's sales) is selling out. However, it seems that psychics now appeal to a more narrow niche audience, and no longer enjoy the wider popularity that followed immediately after the start of the new millennium.

7 The show continued to run on cable as well, but was eventually moved back to its 11 p.m. time slot on the Sci-Fi Channel.

8 I suspect they are the drivers behind LOHAS, though I have no hard data on that.

References

Abanes, R. (2005). *Rick Warren and the purpose that drives him*. Eugene, OR: Harvest House Publishers.

ABC News (2005). Kabbalah [Television series episode]. In *20/20* (June 17). New York: ABC.

ABC Statement (2006). Paid and verified magazine publisher's statement— O Magazine (June). Retrieved December 2, 2006, from www.omediakit. com/hotdata/publishers/oprahmaga3395825/advertiser/3744995/278094/ ABCStatementJune06.pdf.

Abortion and Birth Control (n.d.). Retrieved January 22, 2007, from www. pollingreport.com/abortion.htm.

Adamy, J. (2005). Bare essentials: To find growth, no-frills grocer goes where other chains won't. *Wall Street Journal* (August 30), A1.

Administration for Children and Families (ACF) (n.d.). ACF Capital Compassion Fund (CCF). Retrieved May 18, 2007, from www.act.hhs.gov/programs/ddf/ about_ccf/fundings_demonstration_prg.html.

Administration for Children and Families (ACF) (2006). Office of public affairs fact sheet (December). Retrieved January 22, 2007, from www.acf.hhs.gov/opa/fact_ sheets/acf_factsheet.html.

Administration for Children and Families (ACF) (2007). Community-based abstinence education program (January 5). Retrieved January 22, 2007, from www.acf.hhs. gov/programs/fbci/progs/fbci_cbaep.html.

Adweek (1998). Mixed blessings: Professions of faith, death-row humor, etc. *Adweek* (March 2), 16.

Albanese, C. L. (1992). The magical staff: Quantum healing in the new age. In J. R. Lewis and J. G. Melton (eds), *Perspectives on the New Age* (pp. 68–84). Albany: State University of New York Press.

Alpha (n.d.). The Alpha Course. Retrieved August 30, 2006, from alphacourse.org.

Alpha (2006a). Alpha endorsements: What church leaders are saying about Alpha. *Alpha News*, 17. Available at www.journeygroup.com/clientcontent/alpha/ AlphaNews_Fall06.pdf.

Alpha (2006b). Building better Alpha courses. *Alpha News*, 1, 3. Retrieved October 30, 2006, from www.journeygroup.com/clientcontent/alpha/AlphaNews_Fall06. pdf.

Alpha (2006c). New names, enlarged vision. *Alpha News*, 9. Available at www. journeygroup.com/clientcontent/alpha/AlphaNews_Fall06.pdf.

Aronson, R. (2004). The Jesus factor [Televison series episode]. *Frontline*. Boston: WGBH.

Atkin, D. (2004). *The culting of brands: When customers become true believers*. New York: Portfolio.

Aucoin, D. (2005). We want to know it all, but please, keep it brief. *Boston Globe* (November 19), D1, D5.

Baker, S. (2000). Consumer buyer behaviour. In Cranfield School of Management (ed.), *Marketing management: A relationship marketing perspective*. New York: St. Martin's Press.

Barna Group (2001). More Americans are seeking net-based faith experiences (May 21). Retrieved January 22, 2006, from www.barna.org/FlexPage.aspx?Page =BarnaUpdate&BarnaUpdateID=90.

Barna Group (2004). Born again Christians were a significant factor in President Bush's re-election. Retrieved January 22, 2007, from www.barna.org/FlexPage. aspx?Page=BarnaUpdate&BarnaUpdateID=174.

Barna Group (2005). Technology use is growing rapidly in churches. Retrieved November 10, 2006, from www.barna.org/FlexPage.aspx?Page=BarnaUpdate& BarnaUpdateID=199.

Barna Group (2006). State of the church 2006: A report from George Barna (April). Retrieved May 1, 2006, from www.barna.org/FlexPage.aspx?Page=Resource&R esourceID=221.

Barrett, G. (2001). Can the living talk to the dead? Psychics say they connect with the spirit world, but skeptics respond: "Prove it." *USA Today* (June 20), D1.

Bass, G. G., Guinane, K., and Turner, R. (2003). *An attack on nonprofit speech: Death by a thousand cuts*. OMB Watch (July 28). Retrieved January 22, 2007, from www.ombwatch.org/article/articleview/1706/1/41.

Beam, A. (2002). LA-style Kabbalah opens locally. *Boston Globe* (January 31), C1.

Beaudoin, T. (2003). *Consuming faith: Integrating who we are with what we buy*. Chicago, IL: Sheed and Ward.

Becker, A. (2005). TV's religious revival: A slew of new channels clamor for carriage. *Broadcasting & Cable* (April 25), 26, 28.

Bednarski, P. J. (2005). All about Oprah, Inc. *Broadcasting & Cable* (January 24), 46–54.

Belk, R. W. (2000). Pimps for paradise: Missionaries, monetary funds, and marketers. *Marketing Intelligence & Planning*, 18, 6/7, 337–44.

Belk, R. W., Wallendorf, M., and Sherry, J. F. (1989). The sacred and the profane in consumer behavior: Theodicy on the odyssey. *Journal of Consumer Research*, 16(1), 1–38.

Bellah, R., Madsen, R., Sullivan, W. M., Swidler, A., and Tipton, S. (1985). *Habits of the heart: Individualism and commitment in American life*. Berkeley, CA: University of California Press.

Bendis, D. (2004). The ABCs of faith: Beginning with Alpha. *Christian Century* (March 9). Retrieved October 28, 2004, from www.findarticles.com/p/articles/ mi_m1058/is_5_121/ai_114243181/.

Benen, S. (2002). Pat gets paid: TV preacher Robertson gets "faith-based" grant from Bush administration. *Church & State* (November), 4–6.

Berg, Y. (2003). *The 72 names of God: Technology for the soul*. New York: Kabbalah Publishing.

Berg, Y. (2004a). *The power of Kabbalah: Technology for the soul.* New York: Kabbalah Publishing.

Berg, Y. (2004b). *The red string book: The power of protection.* New York: Kabbalah Publishing.

Bergner, D. (2006). The call. *New York Times Magazine* (January 29), 40–6, 72, 74–5.

Berkowitz, B. (2006). Purpose-driven preacher eschews religious right. *Global Information Network* (March 9), 1.

Berthrong, J. H. (1999). *The divine deli: Religious identity in the North American cultural mosaic.* Maryknoll, NY: Orbis Books.

Bloom, H. (1975). *Kabbalah and criticism.* New York: The Seabury Press.

Boorstin, D. J. (1974). *The Americans: The democratic experience.* New York: Vintage.

Boorstin, J. (2003). For God's sake. *Fortune* (November 24), 62.

Borden, A. L. (2007). Making money, saving souls: Christian bookstores and the commodification of Christianity. In L. S. Clark (ed.), *Religion, media, and the marketplace* (pp. 67–89). New Brunswick, NJ: Rutgers University Press.

Brachear, M. A. (2006). Rev. Bill Hybels, the father of Willow Creek. His South Barrington ministry inspired the megachurch movement. Now he seeks to widen its reach—both at home and abroad. *Chicago Tribune* (August 6), 1.

Brand Strategy (2003). Case Study—Religion: A is for Alpha, C is for Christ. *Brand Strategy* (October 10), 23.

Broadcasting & Cable (2006). A TV industry guide to religious and faith-based programming. *Broadcasting & Cable*, Advertising Supplement (August).

Brown, L. L. (2006). Fans flock to NLR to see Osteen preach his theme: Develop habit of happiness. *Arkansas Democrat-Gazette* (June 10).

BRS (n.d.). "Mission Statement." Business Resource Software. Retrieved September 1, 2006, from www.businessplans.org/Mission.html.

Bruce, S. (1990). *Pray TV: Televangelism in America.* London: Routledge.

BusinessWeek (2005). One church's way. *BusinessWeek* (May 23), 84.

Butler, C. K. (2005a). Sermon with a smile. *U.S. News & World Report* (October 3), 57–8.

Butler, C. K. (2005b). Religion in America: What makes a televangelist tick? *U.S. News & World Report* (September 13). Retrieved January 3, 2006, from www. usnews.com/usnews/culture/articles/050913/13religion.htm.

Carr, M. (2000). Psychic feels vibes of the spirit world: Medium says he is a musical instrument for energy. *Times-Picayune* (November 13), 1.

Carrette, J., and King, R. (2005). *Selling spirituality: The silent takeover of religion.* London: Routledge.

Carroll, C. (2002). *The new faithful: Why young adults are embracing Christian orthodoxy.* Chicago, IL: Loyola Press.

Casabona, L. (2004). Sam's Club markets "Passion" to churches. *Supermarket News* (June 28), 26.

CBA. Christian retail channel embraces increasing cooperation at international Christian retail show. [Press release]. Retrieved August 7, 2006, from www.ctaintl. com/CBAICRSnewsrelease.pdf.

CBS News' *Face the Nation* [Television series episode]. (2006). Washington DC: CBS News (April 9).

Chandler, R. (1993). *Understanding the New Age: Revised—updated—The most powerful and revealing analysis of the New Age.* Grand Rapids, MI: Zondervan Publishing House (HarperCollins division).

Chang, J. (2005). Decade of divinity: Creator feels vindicated that family drama endures. *Variety* (September 19), A1, A6.

Charles, R. (2004). Religious book sales show a miraculous rise. *The Christian Science Monitor* (April 9), 11.

Children's Business (1999). Landmark study identifies Generation Y preferences. *Children's Business*, 32(1), (March 1).

Cho, D. (2005). The business of filling pews: Congregations employ marketing consultants to step up appeal. *Washington Post* (March 6), C1.

Cimino, R., and Lattin, D. (1998). *Shopping for faith: American religion in the new millennium.* San Francisco, CA: Jossey-Bass.

Cimino, R., and Lattin, D. (1999). Choosing my religion. *American Demographics* (April), 60–65.

Clifton, R., and Maughan, E. (eds) (2000). *The future of brands: Twenty-five visions.* New York: New York University Press.

Cohen, D. N. (2003). Jewish mysticism surges on a tide of red strings. *New York Times* (December 13), A15.

Cole, W. (2005). Faith in downloads. *Time* (March 21), 19.

Colyer, E. (2005). Churches put their faith in branding (March 14). Retrieved June 24, 2006, from www.brandchannel.com/features_effect.asp?pf_id=254.

Coolidge, C. (2003). David vs. goliath. Retrieved April 29, 2007, from www.forbes.com/2003/09/15/cz_cc_0915wmt.html.

Copeland, L. (2000). Our lady of perpetual help: In the church of feel-good pop psychology, spiritual rebirth means starting at O. *Washington Post* (June 26), C1.

Cullen, L. T. (2005). Stretching for Jesus: Christian yoga is gaining a devout following—upsetting purists, Hindus and some Christians. *Time* (September 5), 75.

Dan, J. (2006). *Kabbalah: A very short introduction.* Oxford: Oxford University Press.

Danforth, J. (2006). *Faith and politics: How the "moral values" debate divides America and how to move forward together.* New York: Viking.

Darman, J., and Murr, A. (2006). A pastor's fall from grace. *Newsweek* (November 13), 34–35.

Dart, J. (2002). Schuller's glass act. *The Christian Century* (April 10–April 17), 24.

Dateline (2005). Tom Brokaw reports: In God they trust [Television news special] (October 26). New York: NBC News.

deChant, D. (2002). *The sacred Santa: Religious dimensions of consumer culture.* Cleveland, OH: The Pilgrim Press.

Divine Profits (2004). *NewsHour with Jim Lehrer* (August 26). Retrieved October 16, 2006, from www.pbs.org/newshour/bb/entertainment/july-dec04/christian_8-26.html.

Dodds, D. (Producer), and Swearingen, J. (Director). (2004). *An evening with Joel Osteen at Madison Square Garden* [Video]. Houston, TX: Joel Osteen Ministries.

Donnelly, T. (2005). The great Kabbalah con exposed. *The Daily Telegraph* [London] (January 10), 14.

Dooley, T. (2004). Lakewood trips target TV viewers. *Houston Chronicle* (July 3), 1.

Dooley, T., Karkabi, B., and Vara, R. (2006). Returning the favor/best life redux/ Osteen's megadeal is one more layer of religious crossover. *Houston Chronicle* (March 18), 1.

Downey, K. (2006). Jesus is my homeboy. *Broadcasting & Cable* (July 31), 18, 20.

Economist (1998). Britain: Alpha plus. *Economist* (November 7), 61.

Eisenberg, J. B. (2005). *Using Terri: The religious right's conspiracy to take away our rights*. San Francisco, CA: HarperSanFrancisco.

Ellin, A. (2004). The string that binds. *Village Voice* (August 11–17), 22–26.

Ferguson, T. W. (1996). Coin of the new age. *Forbes* (September 9), 86–88.

Finke, R., and Iannaccone, L. R. (1993). Supply-side explanations for religious change. *The Annals of the American Academy*, AAPSS, 527, 27–39.

Fish, S. (1980). *Is there a text in this class?* Cambridge, MA: Harvard University Press.

Fleming, M. (2006). Rice will trace faith. *Variety* (June 28), 1, 13.

Freitas, D. (2006). A new age for mind/body/spirit? *Publishers Weekly* (September 4), 25.

Galen, M., and West, K. (1995). Companies hit the road less traveled. *BusinessWeek* (June 5), 82.

Gallagher, W. (1996). God is alive, in spirit. Retrieved December 11, 1996, from MSNBC Web site: www.msnbc.comnews/45735.asp.

Garrett, L. and Tickle, P. (1999). Christian booksellers optimistic in Orlando. *Publishers Weekly* (July 26), 12, 19.

Gibbs, N. (2002). Apocalypse now: The biggest book of the summer is about the end of the world. It's also a sign of our troubled times. *Time* (July 1), 40–53.

Gilatto, T., and Stoynoff, N. (2002). Medium rare. *People* (May 6).

Gilbreath, E. (1994). The birth of a megachurch. *Christianity Today* (July 18), 23.

Goff, P. K. (2006). Houses of worship: TV's healing powers. *Wall Street Journal* (September 15), W11.

Gold, S. (2000). Speaking from a digital dais; Religion: Megachurch leader's Web site offers pastors everything from sermons and songs to fund-raising plans. He talks of providing "R&D for Christianity" but others fear commercialism. *Los Angeles Times* (February 4), B1.

Goldman, R., and Papson, S. (1998). *Nike culture: The sign of the swoosh*. Thousand Oaks, CA: Sage Publications.

Goodstein, L. (2006). Fearing the loss of teenagers, evangelicals turn up the fire. *New York Times* (October 6), A1.

Gooren, H. (2006a). Towards a new model of religious conversion careers: The impact of social and institutional factors. In W. J. van Bekkum, J. N. Bremmer, and A. Molendijk (eds), *Paradigms, poetics and politics of conversion* (pp. 25–40). Leuven: Peeters.

Gooren, H. (2006b) Religious market theory and conversion: Towards an alternative approach. *Exchange*, 35, 1, pp. 39–60.

Gopez-Sindac, R. (2005). Fast facts on the church consulting profession (October). Retrieved August 10, 2006, from *Church Executive Magazine* Web site: www. churchexecutive.com/2005/10/Fast_facts_on_the_church_consulting_profession. asp.

Gorski, E. (2003). "40 Days" formula inspires churches; Best-seller resonates among Christians. *Denver Post* (November 2), A1.

Grabois, A. (2005). U.S. book production. Retrieved August 6, 2006, from www. bookwire.com/bookwire/decadebookproduction.html.

Granatstein, L. (2004). Editors of the year. *Adweek* (March 1), SR13–SR14, SR30.

Grossman, C. L. (2005). Starbucks stirs things up with a God quote on cups. *USA Today* (October 19), D8.

Gunther, M. (2005). Will success spoil Rick Warren? *Fortune* (October 31), 108–20.

Gusfield, J. (1978). *Community: A critical response*. New York: Harper & Row.

Hall, C. (2006). Channel 55 purchased by USFR Media Group (November 10). Retrieved November 17, 2006, from *Houston Business Journal* Web site: houston. bizjournals.com/houston/stories/2006/11/06/daily73.html.

Hangen, T. (2002). *Redeeming the dial: Radio, religion and popular culture in America*. Chapel Hill, NC: The University of North Carolina Press.

Harris, H. R. (2001). Putting worship into their workday: More federal employees participating in prayer services at the office. *Washington Post* (November 19), A19.

Harris, S. (2005). *The end of faith: Religion, terror and the future of reason*. New York: W.W. Norton.

Harris Interactive (2003). While most Americans believe in God, only 36% attend a religious service once a month or more often (October 15). Retrieved August 16, 2006, from www.harrisinteractive.com/harris_poll/index.asp?PID=408.

Harris Interactive (2006). While most U.S. adults believe in God, only 58 percent are "absolutely certain" (October 31). Retrieved January 23, 2007, from www. harrisinteractive.com/harris_poll/index.asp?PID=707.

Harrison, J. (1997). Advertising joins the journey of the soul. *American Demographics* (June), 22, 24–25, 28.

Hecker, R. (2004). Give me back my old Madonna. *The Observer* (October 31), 22.

Hedges, C. (2007). The radical Christian right is built on suburban despair. *AlterNet* (January 19). Retrieved January 20, 2007, from www.alternet.org/ stories/46908/.

Heelas, P. (1996). *The New Age movement: The celebration of the self and the sacralization of modernity*. Oxford: Blackwell Publishers.

Heeter, C. (1985). Program selection with abundance of choice: A process model. *Human Communication Research, 12*, 125–52.

Hendershot, H. (2004). *Shaking the world for Jesus: Media and conservative evangelical culture*. Chicago, IL: University of Chicago Press.

Henriques, D. B., and Lehren, A. (2006a). Religion trumps regulation as legal exemptions grow; In God's name: Favors for the faithful. *New York Times* (October 8), 1.

Henriques, D. B., and Lehren, A. (2006b). As religion programs expand, disputes rise over tax breaks; In God's name: Giving exemptions. *New York Times* (October 10), 1.

Henriques, D. B., and Lehren, A. (2006c). Religion-based tax breaks: Housing to paychecks to books. *New York Times* (October 11), 1.

Henriques, D. B. and Lehren, A. (2006d). Religion for captive audiences, with taxpayers footing the bill. *New York Times* (December 10), A1.

Henriques, D. B. and Lehren, A. (2007). Religious groups reap federal aid for pet projects. *New York Times* (May 13), A1.

Hettrick, S. (2004). "Christ" rises to 4.1 mil sold. *Variety* (September 2), 3.

Hewitt, B., Bowers, P., Morrissey, S., Rozsa, L., Helling, S., and Truesdell, J. (2005). Seven hours of terror. *People* (March 28), 54–9.

Higgins, B. (2005). New Age aud in the "know": Quirky "Bleep" banks $10 million in B.O. *Variety* (January 31–February 6), 6.

Hilliard, J. C. (2005). Mega tactics for mega-hits. *Publishers Weekly* (May 23), S12.

Holmesreport.com (n.d.). Retrieved October 16, 2006, from www.sitrick.com/pdfs/Blog%2004-07-06.pdf.

Holt, K. (2003). Catholic publisher seeks to up trade sales. *Publishers Weekly* (August 25), 10.

Hoover, S. M. (1996). The George Gerbner Lecture: The Annenberg School for Communication. Retrieved November 15, 2006, from www.colorado.edu/journalism/mcm/word_papers/hoover-gerbner-lecture.doc.

Hoover, S. M. (2006). *Religion in the media age*. London: Routledge.

Hoover, S. M., Clark, L. S., and Rainie, L. (2004). *Faith online*. Retrieved February 17, 2005, from Pew Internet and Public Life Project Web site: www.pewinternet.org/pdfs/PIP_Faith_Online_2004.pdf.

Howard, T. (2004). Promoting "The Passion"; Film's creators look to believers to help sell the show. *USA Today* (February 24), B3.

Howell, D. (2004). Christian retailing ascending to new heights. *DSN Retailing Today* (April 19), 4–5, 28.

Hunter, A. J., and Suttles G. D. (1972). The expanding community of limited liability. In G. D. Suttles (ed.), *The social construction of communities* (pp. 44–80). Chicago, IL: University of Chicago Press.

Hunter, G. G., III (1992). The legacy of Donald A. McGavran. *International Bulletin of Missionary Research* (October), 158–61.

Iannaccone, L. R. (1990). Religious practice: A human capital approach. *Journal for the Scientific Study of Religion*, 29(3), 297–314.

Italie, H. (2004). Specialty books hit mainstream success; But Christian stores struggle to benefit. *Washington Post* (May 30), A16.

Jacoby, S. (2004). A new meaning for "bully pulpit". *Los Angeles Times* (April 12), B11.

Jannowitz, M. (1952). *The community press in an urban setting*. Glencoe, IL: Free Press.

Johnston, H. (1988). The marketed social movement: A case study of the rapid growth of TM. In J. T. Richardson (ed.), *Money and powering in the new religions* (pp. 163–80). Lewiston, NY: The Edwin Mellen Press.

Jones, P., and Kahaner, L. (1995). *Say it and live it: The 50 corporate mission statements that hit the mark*. New York: Doubleday.

Just walk across the room (n.d.). Retrieved September 15, 2006, from www.justwalkacrosstheroom.com/.

The Kabbalah Centre (n.d.). Locations. Retrieved October 16, 2006, from www.kabbalah.com/16.php.

Kabbalah Energy Drink. (n.d.). Current Events. Retrieved October 16, 2006, from Kabbalah Energy Drink Web site: www.kabbalahenergydrink.com/current_events/.

Kabbalah energy drink hits beverage market shelves (2005) (May 31). Retrieved October 16, 2006, from www.nutritionhorizon.com/newsmaker_article.asp?idNewsMaker=8301&fSite=AO545&category=24&page=44.

Kaminer, W. (2005). Rick Warren, "America's pastor." *The Nation* (September 12), 28–30.

Kang, C. (2003). Next stop, the pearly gates; Nearly two-thirds think they're going to heaven, while few believe they're hell-bound, poll finds. *Los Angeles Times* (October 24), A18.

Kaplan, E. (2004). *With God on their side: How Christian fundamentalists trampled science, policy, and democracy in George W. Bush's White House*. New York: New Press.

Karlgaard, R. (2004). Digital rules. *Forbes* (February 16), 39.

Kiesling, A. J. (2003). God, sex and rock 'n' roll. *Publishers Weekly* (August 11), 130.

Kiesling, A. J. (2004). Religion publishing's black hole. *Publishers Weekly* (March 22), S10.

Kilbourne, J. (1999). *Deadly persuasion: Why women and girls must fight the addictive power of advertising*. New York: Free Press.

Klein, N. (2000). *No Logo*. New York: Picador.

Kogan, L. (2005). The Oprah Show turns 20! *O, The Oprah Magazine* (October), 278–9.

Kosmin, B. A., and Lachman, S. P. (1993). *One nation under God: Religion in contemporary American society*. New York: Crown Trade Paperbacks.

Kosmin, B. A., and Mayer, E. (2001). American Religious Identification Survey (December 19). Retrieved on December 29, 2006, from www.gc.cuny.edu/faculty/research_studies/aris.pdf.

Kuo, D. (2006). *Tempting faith: An inside story of political seduction*. New York: Free Press.

LaPorte, N. (2006). Sony showing faith. *Variety* (April 19), 4, 11.

Lappin, E. (2004). The thin red line. *The Guardian* (December 11). Retrieved October 16, 2004, from www.guardian.co.uk/weekend/story/0,3605,1369895,00.html.

Larsen, E. (2004). Cyberfaith: How Americans pursue religion online. In L. L. Dawson, and D. E. Cowan (eds), *Religion online: Finding faith on the Internet* (pp. 17–20). New York: Routledge.

Larson, M. (1998). A new station sets it debut. *Mediaweek* (June 29), 16.

Lau, K. (2000). *New age capitalism: Making money east of Eden*. Philadelphia, PA: University of Pennsylvania Press.

Learning Annex (2003) (February 7). Retrieved November 10, 2003, from www.learningannex.com/default.taf?newcity=OT.

The "Left Behind" phenomenon (2001). *Religion & Ethics Newsweekly* (February 2), 423. Retrieved February 2, 2001, from www.pbs.org/wnet/religionandethics/week423/feature.html.

Leland, J. (2005). A church that packs them in 16,000 at a time. *New York Times* (July 18), A1.

Lewis, D., and Bridger, D. (2001). *The soul of the new consumer: Authenticity--what we buy and why in the new economy*. London: Nicholas Brealey Publishing.

Lewis, J. R., and Melton, J. G. (eds) (1992). *Perspectives on the New Age*. Albany, NY: State University of New York Press.

Lewis, M. (1996). God is in the packaging. *New York Times Magazine* (July 21), 14, 16.

Leydon, J. (2004). The best two years. *Variety* (September), 13.

Linn, S. (2004). *Consuming kids: The hostile takeover of childhood.* New York: New Press.

Lisotta, C. (2005). Jesus Christ, TV star. *TelevisionWeek* (August 15), 2.

Lobdell, W. (2002). Pastor of megachurch making equally big splash with book; Media: Rick Warren of Saddleback Church in Lake Forest began "The Purpose-Driven Life" as a series of sermons; The launch is a kind of virtual Sunday school. *Los Angeles Times* (October 12), B8.

Lobdell, W. (2003). A how-to kit for the ministry; From his Lake Forest mega-church, Rick Warren offers seminars, stats and items on the Internet to help pastors boost attendance. *Los Angeles Times* (September 19), A1.

Lockwood, F. E. (2006). A church like none other: Megapastor fills former stadium and spans the globe. *Knight Ridder Tribune Business News* (July 29), 1.

Lofton, K. (2006, August). Practicing Oprah; or, the prescriptive compulsion of a spiritual capitalism. *Journal of Popular Culture, 39*(4), 599–622.

LOHAS (n.d.). Retrieved February 15, 2007, from www.lohas.com/.

Lopiansky, Rabbi A. (2004). Threadbare: Is there any substance behind the latest fad; kabbalistic red strings? (August 29). Retrieved October 16, 2006, from www.aish.com/spirituality/kabbala101/Threadbare.asp?s=g&k=redstrings.

Luecke, D. S. (1997). Is Willow Creek the way of the future? *The Christian Century* (May 14), 479, 481–3, 485.

Luo, M. (2006, April 4). With yoga, comedy and parties, synagogues entice newcomers. *New York Times*, A1.

Lyon, D. (2000). *Jesus in Disneyland: Religion in postmodern times.* Cambridge: Polity Press.

Magnusson, P. (2005). They backed Bush--and expect him to deliver. *BusinessWeek* (May 23), 86–7.

Mandese, J. (2004). How to target religious conservatives. *Broadcasting & Cable* (December 20), 10.

Marcus, R. (2006). The new temptation of Democrats. *Washington Post* (May 23), A17.

Maresco, P. A. (2004). Mel Gibson's *The Passion of the Christ*: Market segmentation, mass marketing and promotion, and the Internet. *The Journal of Religion and Popular Culture, VIII* (Fall). Retrieved August 10, 2006, from www.usask.ca/relst/jrpc/art8-melgibsonmarketing.html.

Marler, P. L., and Hadaway, C. K. (2002). "Being religious" or "being spiritual" in America: A zero-sum proposition? *Journal for the Scientific Study of Religion* (June), 41(2), 289–300.

Martin, W. (2005). Prime minister; Joel Osteen's Houston gigachurch has a congregation of more than 30,000. His television show is the highest-rated religious broadcast in the country. His first book has already sold nearly three million copies. How did the former TV producer become the world's most talked about "pastorpreneur"? He is who he says he is. He has what he says he has. He can do what he says he can do. *Texas Monthly* (August), 106–13,167–75.

Maryles, D. (2003). Behind the bestsellers. *Publishers Weekly* (February 10), 60.

Mathieu, J. (2002). Power house: What do Lakewood Church and its pastor Joel Osteen have that most mainline Protestant don't? People. Lots of them. And in an assortment of colors (April 4). Retrieved January 27, 2006, from www.houstonpress.com/Issues/2002-04-04/news/feature.html.

McAlexander, J. H., Schouten, J. W., and Koening, H. F. (2002). Building brand community. *Journal of Marketing*, 66(January), 38–54.

McCabe, C. (2002). Alpha movement gathers converts. *Boston Globe* (October 6), 8.

McDannell, C. (1995). *Material Christianity: Religion and popular culture in America*. New Haven, CT: Yale University Press.

MacDonald, G. J. (2005). The message: God is cool; Ice cream, Frisbees and marketing get the word out. *USA Today* (August 21), D4.

McGough, M. (2005). Church and state: Blurring the line. *Los Angeles Times* (August 29), B11.

Mears, D. P., and Ellison, C. G. (2000). Who buys New Age materials? Exploring sociodemographic, religious, network and contextual correlates of New Age consumption. *Sociology of Religion*, 61(3), 289–313.

Meet the Press (2006). Sister Joan Chittister, Rabbi Michael Lerner, Pastor Joel Osteen, Reverend Richard John Neuhaus, Professor Seyyed Hossein Nasr and Jon Meacham of *Newsweek* discuss the state of religion in America [Television series episode] (April 16). Washington, DC: NBC News.

Megachurches (2006). *Religion & Ethics Newsweekly* (July 28). Web site: Retrieved July 31, 2006, from www.pbs.org/wnet/religionandethics/week948/cover.html.

Menzi, D. W., and Padeh, Z. (1999). *The tree of life: Chayyim Vital's introduction to the Kabbalah of Isaac Luria*. Northvale, NJ: Jason Aronson.

Miller, J., and Muir, D. (2004). *The business of brands*. Hoboken, NJ: John Wiley & Sons.

Miller, L. (2006). An evangelical identity crisis. *Newsweek*, 30–7.

Miller, V. J. (2004). *Consuming religion: Christian faith and practice in a consumer culture*. New York: Continuum.

Milliot, J. (2002). Baker book house to buy Bethany House. *Publishers Weekly* (December 23), 10.

Milliot, J. (2003). Nelson adds more Bibles. *Publishers Weekly* (October 6), 12.

Montgomery, J. D. (2003). A formalization and test of the religious economies model. *American Sociological Review* (October), 782–809.

Moore, R. L. (1994). *Selling God: American religion in the marketplace of culture*. New York: Oxford University Press.

Morgan, C. M., and Levy, D. J. (2002). *Marketing to the mindset of boomers and their elders*. Saint Paul, MN: Attitudebase.

Morning-After Pill Protest. (2005). *Newshour with Jim Lehrer* (June 30). Retrieved January 29, 2007 from www.pbs.org/newshour/bb/health/jan-june05/pill_6-30.html.

Muniz, A. M., and O'Guinn, T. C. (2001). Brand community. *Journal of Consumer Research* (March), 27(4), 412–32.

Muniz, A. M., and Schau, H. J. (2005). Religiosity in the abandoned Apple Newton brand community. *Journal of Consumer Research* (March), 31(4), 737–47.

Nawotka, E. (2006). Faith in religious publishing deepens among largest firms/ Multnomah for sale; Random House among potential buyers. *Houston Chronicle* (July 29), 2.

NCTA (2006a). Industry statistics. Retrieved August 27, 2006, from www.ncta.com/ Docs/PageContent.cfm?pageID=304.

NCTA (2006b). *National Cable & Telecommunications Association 2006 Industry Overview.* Retrieved August 28, 2006, from http://i.ncta.com/ncta_com/PDFs/ NCTAAnnual%20Report4-06FINAL.pdf.

Nelson, M. Z., and Garrett, L. (2004). Gimme that old-time spirituality. *Publishers Weekly* (March 22), S2, S4–S7.

Netburn, D. (2005). Shabbat; Synagogues across the country are selling Sabbath services with a new brand name: Synaplex. To some, it sounds like Judaism lite. *Los Angeles Times* (October 23), I16.

NJPS Executive Summary (n.d.). Retrieved January 10, 2007, from www.ujc.org/ content_display.html?ArticleID=83623).

Novack, K. (2004). Yo, where's my Bible? *Time* (May 17), 85.

Nussbaum, P. (2006). The purpose-driven pastor. *Knight Ridder Tribune Business News* (January 8), 1.

O Philanthropy (2007). Retrieved April 21, 2007, from www2.oprah.com/uyl/angel/ uyl_angel_about.jhtml.

Ostwalt, C. (2003). *Secular steeples: Popular culture and the religious imagination.* Harrisburg, PA: Trinity Press International.

Packaged Facts (2004). *The U.S. market for religious publishing and products* (August). New York: Packaged Facts (a division of Marketresearch.com).

Papper, R. A., Holmes, M. E., and Popovich, M. N. (2004). Middletown media studies: media multitasking…and how much people really use the media. *The International Digital Media and Arts Association Journal*, 7–56.

Payne, A. (2000). Customer retention. In Cranfield School of Management (ed.), *Marketing management: A relationship marketing perspective* (pp. 110–22). New York: St. Martin's Press.

Peretz, E. (2005). The garden of Kabbalah. *Vanity Fair* (March), 296.

Pew Forum on Religion and Public Life (n.d.). Abortion seen as most important issue for Supreme Court. Most favor legal abortion, but with more limits. Retrieved on January 22, 2007, from pewforum.org/docs/index.php?DocID=127.

Pew Forum on Religion and Public Life (2005). Myths of the modern mega-church (May 23). Retrieved August 30, 2006, from pewforum.org/events/index. php?EventID=R80.

Pew Forum on Religion and Public Life (2006). Religion and the 2006 elections. Retrieved January 10, 2007, from pewforum.org/docs/index.php?DocID=174.

Pew Global Attitudes Project (2002). U.S. stands alone in its embrace of religion. Retrieved July 27, 2006, from pewglobal.org/reports/display. php?ReportID=167.

Pew Internet and American Life Project (2006). Home broadband goes mainstream: Fast Internet connections are going mainstream with user-generated content now coming from all sorts of subscribers. Retrieved August 10, 2006, from pewresearch.org/reports/?ReportID=25.

Pew Research Center for People and the Press (2006). Less opposition to gay marriage, adoption and military service. Only 34% favor South Dakota abortion ban. Retrieved January 10, 2007, from people-press.org/reports/display. php3?ReportID=273.

Peyser, M. (2001). God, Mammon, and "Bibleman." *Newsweek* (July 16), 45–8.

Physicians for Reproductive Choice and Health (PRCH) and the Guttmacher Institute (2006). An overview of abortion in the United States. Retrieved January 19, 2007, from www.guttmacher.org/presentations/abort_slides.pdf.

The Pluralism Project at Harvard University (n.d.). Statistics by tradition. Retrieved January 24, 2007, from www.pluralism.org/resources/statistics/tradition.php#Judaism.

Poniewozik, J. (2003). Losing God's religion: *Joan of Arcadia* ducks some divisive issues of faith, but its miracle is finding the drama in ordinary life. *Time* (November 3), 74.

Porter, E. (2004). Where *Playboy* and "Will and Grace" reign. *New York Times* (November 21), D14.

Porterfield, A. (2001). *The transformation of American religion: The story of a late-twentieth-century awakening.* Oxford: Oxford University Press.

Purpose Driven Life Web site (n.d.a). Rick Warren. Retrieved September 27, 2006, from www.purposedrivenlife.com/rickwarren.aspx.

Purpose Driven Web site (n.d.b). What is the Peace Plan? Retrieved September 27, 2006, from www.purposedriven.com/en-US/PEACE/PEACE_Plan.htm.

Purpose Driven Web site (n.d.c). 40 days of purpose. Retrieved August 21, 2006, from www.purposedriven.com/en-US/40DayCampaigns/40DaysOfPurpose/preparation andtraining.htm.

Quart, A. (2003). *Branded: The buying and selling of teenagers.* Cambridge, MA: Perseus Publishing.

Ragas, M. W., and Bueno, B. J. (2002). *The power of cult branding: How 9 magnetic brands turned customers into loyal followers (and yours can, too).* New York: Crown Business.

Raugust, K. (2003). Licensing gets religion. *Publishers Weekly* (May 19), 38.

Religion surges in pop culture (2004). *Chicago Tribune* (April 19), 9.

Rheingold, H. (2000). *The virtual community: Homesteading on the electronic frontier.* Cambridge, MA: MIT Press.

Rindfleish, J. (2005). Consuming the self: New Age spirituality as "social product" in consumer society. *Consumption, Markets and Culture,* 8(4), 343–60.

Romanowski, W. D. (2000). Evangelicals and popular music: The contemporary Christian music industry. In D. A. Stout and J. M. Buddenbaum (eds), *Religion and popular culture: Studies on the interaction of worldviews* (pp. 105–24). Ames, IA: Iowa State Press.

Roof, W. C. (1993a). *A generation of seekers: The spiritual journey of the baby boom generation.* New York: HarperCollins.

Roof, W. C. (1993b). Toward the year 2000: Reconstructions of religious space. *The Annals of the American Academy, AAPSS,* 527, 155–70.

Roof, W. C. (1999). *Spiritual marketplace: Baby boomers and the remaking of American religion.* Princeton, NJ: Princeton University Press.

Roof, W. C., and McKinney, W. (1987). *American mainline religion: Its changing shape and future.* New Brunswick, NJ: Rutgers University Press.

Rosenberg, H. (1994). Talking to the dead, Part two: The skeptics. *Los Angeles Times* (November 23), 1.

Russell, C. (1993). *The master trend: How the baby boom generation is remaking America.* New York: Perseus.

Salamon, J. (2003). Marketing strategy splits the sacred and the secular. *New York Times* (December 27), A1.

Sargeant, K. H. (2000). *Seeker churches: Promoting traditional religion in a nontraditional way.* New Brunswick, NJ: Rutgers University Press.

Saroyan, S. (2006). Christianity, the brand. *New York Times Magazine* (April 16), 46–51.

Schmelzer, R. (2006a). Faith groups offset film with PR crusade. *PR Week* (March 6), 8.

Schmelzer, R. (2006b). Licensing impact players: George Leon. *Variety* (June 20), A15.

Schmidt, L. E. (1995). *Consumer rites: The buying and selling of American holidays.* Princeton, NJ: Princeton University Press.

Scholem, G. (1987). *Origins of the Kabbalah.* Ed. R. J. Zwi Werblowsky. Trans. Allan Arkush. Princeton, NJ: Princeton University Press.

Schor, J. B. (1998). *The overspent American: Why we want what we don't need.* New York: HarperPerennial.

Schor, J. B. (2004). *Born to buy: The commercialized child and the new consumer culture.* New York: Scribner.

Schouten, J. W., and McAlexander, J. H. (1995). Subcultures of consumption: An ethnography of the new bikers. *Journal of Consumer Research,* 22(June), 43–61.

Schudson, M., (1984). *Advertising, the uneasy persuasion: Its dubious impact on American society.* New York: Basic Books.

Schultz, D. E., and Schultz, H. (2004). *Brand babble: sense and nonsense about branding.* Mason, OH: Thomson/South-Western.

Scott, L. M. (1994). The bridge from text to mind: Adapting reader response theory to consumer research. *Journal of Consumer Research,* 21 (December), 461–86.

Senyor, E. (2005). Kabbalah victim: I couldn't keep quiet. *Ynetnews.com* (November 3). Retrieved October 14, 2006, from www.ynetnews.com/articles/0,7340,L-3163763,00.html.

Seybert, J. (2004). *EPM's guide to the Christian marketplace: Selling books, music, gifts and videos to America's 218 million Christians.* New York: EPM Communications.

Shaffer, E. H. (1993). TV evangelism, public goods, and imperfect competition. *Journal of Economic Issues,* 27(2) (June), 639–46.

Sharlet, J., and Hedges, C. (2005). Soldiers of Christ. *Harper's Magazine* (May), 41–61.

Sheahen, L. (2004a). Fanning the passion (January 27). Retrieved February 13, 2004, from www.beliefnet.com/story/139/story_13915_1.html.

Sheahen, L. (2004b). Expect God's favor: Interview with Joel Osteen (December). Retrieved December 12, 2004, from www.beliefnet.com/story/157/story_15735_1.html.

SIECUS (2003). Abstinence-only earmarks signify new federal funding agenda. Policy Update (April). Retrieved May 18, 2007, from www.siecus.org/policy/PUpdates/arch03/acrh030054.html.

Singer, R. (2005). Kabbalah Center head charged with defrauding cancer patient. *Haaretz Daily* (October 30). Retrieved October 14, 2006, from www.religionnewsblog.com/12648/kabbalah-center-head-charged-with-defrauding-cancer-patient.

Spiegler, M. (1996). Scouting for souls. *American Demographics* (March), 42–9.

Spurlock, M. (2006). Abortion [Television series episode]. In Spurlock, M. (Executive Producer) *30 Days* (August 23). FX Network.

Stafford, T. (2002). A regular purpose-driven guy: Rick Warren's genius is in helping pastors see the obvious. *Christianity Today*, 42–8.

Stark, R., and Finke, R. (1992). *The churching of America 1776–1990: Winners and losers in our religious economy*. New Brunswick, NJ: Rutgers University Press.

Stark, R., and Finke, R. (2000). *Acts of faith: Explaining the human side of religion*. Berkley, CA: University of California Press.

Steinmetz, M. (2006). Narnia mania: Cashing in on a major movie launch. *Book Business* (April), 12–13.

Steptoe, S. (2004). The man with the purpose: Rick Warren's plan for spiritual fulfillment is making him one of America's most influential ministers. *Time* (March 21), 54–6.

Stewart, T. A. (1989). Turning around the Lord's business. *Fortune* (September 25), 116–28.

Symonds, W. C. (2005). Earthly empires: How evangelical churches are borrowing from the business playbook. *BusinessWeek* (May 23), 78–88.

Tapia, A., and Stream, C. (1995). Engaging the marketplace. *Christianity Today* (October 2), 103.

Taylor, L. (2001). Adaptable Alpha course draws praise and worry. *Christianity Today* (November 12), 27–9.

Taylor, L. (2002). The church of O: With a congregation of 22 million viewers, Oprah Winfrey has become one of the most influential spiritual leaders in America. *Christianity Today* (March 3), 38–45.

Thumma, S. (2005). Hartford Institute for Religious Research, database of megachurches in the U.S. Retrieved December 21, 2006, from hirr.hartsem.edu/cgi-bin/mega/db.pl?db=default&uid=default&view_records=1&ID=*&sb=3&so=descend.

Tickle, P. (n.d.). It's the book, seeker! Retrieved July 10, 1994, from www.beliefnet.com/story/97/story_9779_3.html.

Today (2005). Mysterious faiths: Secrets of Kabbalah [Television series episode] (November 2). New York: NBC News.

Trappey, R. J., III, and Woodside, A. G. (2005). *Brand choice: Revealing customers' unconscious-automatic and strategic thinking processes*. New York: Palgrave Macmillan.

Turow, J. (1997). *Breaking up America: Advertisers and the new media world*. Chicago, IL: University of Chicago Press.

Twitchell, J. B. (2004). *Branded nation: The marketing of megachurch, college inc., and museumworld*. New York: Simon & Schuster.

Udovitch, M. (2005). The Kabbalah chronicles: Inside Hollywood's hottest cult (October 16). Retrieved February 17, 2006, from *Radar* Web site: www.radaronline.com/web-only/the-kabbalah-chronicles/2005/06/inside-hollywoods-hottest-cult-ii.php.

U.S. Department of Labor (2003). President Bush is joined by Labor Secretary Elaine L. Chao and Attorney General John Ashcroft for discussion on job training programs for ex-offenders [Press release] (June 18). Retrieved January 22, 2007, from www.dol.gov/opa/media/press/opa/OPA2003321.htm.

U.S. Patent and Trademark Office (2003). Kabbalah red string application (August 11). Retrieved October 14, 2006, from www.thesmokinggun.com/archive/kabbalah1.html.

Van Biema, D. (2005). The 25 most influential evangelicals in America. *Time* (February 7), 34–45.

Van Biema, D., and Chu, T. (2006). Does God want you to be rich? *Time* (September 18), 48–56.

Walker, R. (2005). Cross selling. *New York Times Magazine* (March 6), 28.

Wallis, J. (2005). *God's politics: Why the right gets it wrong and the left doesn't get it*. San Francisco, CA: HarperCollins.

Warner, R. S. (1993). Work in progress toward a new paradigm for the sociological study of religion in the United States. *American Journal of Sociology*, 98(5), 1044–93.

Warner, R. S. (1997). A paradigm is not a theory: Reply to Lechner. *American Journal of Sociology*, 103(1) (July), 192–8.

Warren, H. (2005). *There's never been a show like "Veggie Tales:" Sacred messages in a secular market*. Lanham, MD: Altamira Press.

Warren, R. (1995). *The purpose-driven church: Growth without compromising your message and your mission*. Grand Rapids, MI: Zondervan.

Warren, R. (2002). *The purpose-driven life*. Grand Rapids, MI: Zondervan.

Waterbrook Press (n.d.). Retrieved August 9, 2006, from www.randomhouse.com/waterbrook/waterbrook/distinctives.html.

Watt, L. (2001). Contacting spirits right up there: Communication with "other side" gains followers. *Denver Post* (January 7), F1.

White House Office of Faith-Based and Community Initiatives (2006). Grants to faith-based organizations fiscal year 2005. Based on a review of 130 competitive programs and 28 program areas at seven federal agencies (March 9). Retrieved January 22, 2007, from www.whitehouse.gov/government/fbci/final_report_2005.pdf.

Why I hate myself: Mothers confess [Television series episode] (2006). *The Oprah Winfrey Show* (May 11). Chicago, IL: Harpo Productions.

Willow Creek Association (2007). Membership matters: Member benefits. Retrieved January 27, 2007, from www.willowcreek.com/wca_info/member_benefits.asp.

Winslow, G. (2005a). More clout, more problems. *Broadcasting & Cable* (February 14), 28.

Winslow, G. (2005b). Go with the flow: Hispanic religious channels grow. *Broadcasting & Cable* (February 21), 32.

Winston, K. (1999). Give me that name-brand religion. *Publishers Weekly* (March 8), 36–8.

Wolfe, A. (2003). *The transformation of American religion: How we actually live our faith*. New York: Free Press.

The woman without a face [Television series episode] (2005). *The Oprah Winfrey Show* (May 26). Chicago, IL: Harpo Productions.

Wuthnow, R. (1994). *Sharing the journey: Support groups and America's new quest for community*. New York: Free Press.

Wuthnow, R. (1998). *After heaven: Spirituality in America since the 1950s*. Berkeley, CA: University of California Press.

Wuthnow, R. (2003). *All in sync: How music and art are revitalizing American religion*. Berkeley, CA: University of California Press.

Wyatt, E. (2006). Next project for Oprah: Feel-good reality TV. *New York Times* (December 16), B9.

Index